Women's Incomes over the Lifetime

Editor: Katherine Rake

Contributing authors: Hugh Davies
Heather Joshi
Katherine Rake
Randa Alami

BETTER FOR
WOMEN
BETTER FOR
ALL

London: The Stationery Office

NOTE ON AUTHORSHIP

This report was edited by Dr. Katherine Rake (Department of Social Policy, London School of Economics) who was seconded to the Women's Unit to direct the research project. She also contributed to the literature review.

The bulk of the report is based on research carried under contract to the Women's Unit by a team based at Birkbeck College and the Institute of Education. The model of lifetime incomes which underlies the simulations reported here was constructed and analysed by Dr. Hugh Davies (Department of Economics, Birkbeck College) and Professor Heather Joshi (Centre for Longitudinal Studies, Institute of Education). Randa Alami was employed in the Department of Economics, Birkbeck College to assist Davies and Joshi.

The contractors commented on the whole report, but the sections for which they are primarily responsible are identified in the Table of Contents by an asterisk.

ACKNOWLEDGEMENTS

The authors would like to acknowledge the help that a number people extended in preparing this document. At the Women's Unit, Claire Callender, Sian Owen and Fiona Reynolds provided useful comments on early drafts of the report, Sian also took on the unenviable task of seeing the document through its final stages; Carys Thomas helped to collate data from a range of Government sources; Richard Harris and Felicity Moore provided valuable administrative support; the input of Juliet Mountford, now at the Family Policy Studies Centre, into the early stages of the project are also much appreciated. At the Office for National Statistics, the labour market team, particularly Tim Thair and Darren Stillwell, conducted additional analysis and provided a number of tables for the report. At the Department of Social Security, special thanks go to Di Lewis for her work on the 'Women's Individual Incomes' series and also to the HBAI team for their additional analysis. We are grateful to Dr. Alan Marsh of the Policy Studies Institute for making available unpublished tabulations from the DSS/PSI Lone Parent Cohort dataset and to staff at the Centre for Longitudinal Studies, Institute of Education, for preparing tabulations from the BCS70 dataset. The project's steering group gave guidance throughout the life of the project.

Published with the permission of the Cabinet Office on behalf of the Controller of Her Majesty's Stationery Office.

© Crown Copyright 2000

All rights reserved.

Copyright in the typographical arrangement and design is vested in the Crown. Applications for reproduction should be made in writing to the Copyright Unit, Her Majesty's Stationery Office, St Clements House, 2-16 Colegate, Norwich NR3 1BQ.

First Published 2000

ISBN 0 11 430162 X

Produced for Cabinet Office
by Central Office of Information.
J00-5377/0002/D8

TABLE OF CONTENTS

OVERVIEW AND SUMMARY   1

1. INTRODUCTION   11

     1.1 Why a report on women's incomes?   12
     1.2 Why look at incomes over the lifetime?   15
     1.3 Outline of the report   16

2. GENDER DIFFERENTIALS IN PAID WORK   17

     2.1 Education, training and skills   18
         2.1.1 Gender differences in basic skills   19
         2.1.2 Educational attainment   19
         2.1.3 Educational choice   22
         2.1.4 Educational attainment and participation in the labour market   24
         2.1.5 Training   25

     2.2 Employment, unemployment and underemployment   26
         2.2.1 The changing labour market   26
         2.2.2 Labour market activity   27
         2.2.3 Types of paid work   30
         2.2.4 Employment and ethnic minority women   36
         2.2.5 Employment status and income   39

     2.3 Job segregation   40
         2.3.1 Men's jobs, women's jobs   40
         2.3.2 Glass ceilings and sticky floors   42

     2.4 The changing pay gap*   45
         2.4.1 The pay gap over time   45
         2.4.2 Pay by ethnicity   47
         2.4.3 Pay differentials in England, Scotland and Wales   48

2.5	The causes of the pay gap*		49
	2.5.1	Differences in characteristics or differences in rewards?	49
	2.5.2	Motherhood as a source of low pay	52
2.6	Changing earnings and changing incomes*		54
2.7	Conclusions and key findings		56

3. WOMEN'S INCOMES OVER THE LIFETIME*   59

3.1	Simulating lifetime incomes – methods and assumptions		60
	3.1.1	Why use a hypothetical model of lifetime incomes?	60
	3.1.2	The development of the simulation model	61
	3.1.3	The components of the model	62
	3.1.4	The hypothetical individuals	64
	3.1.5	Marriage and fertility patterns of the hypothetical individuals	66
	3.1.6	Labour market behaviour of the hypothetical individuals	70
	3.1.7	The tax-benefit environment	72
3.2	Women's lifetime labour market participation and earnings		73
	3.2.1	Projected participation probabilities	73
	3.2.2	Women's lifetime earnings	76
3.3	From earnings to income – the impact of the tax-benefit system		78
3.4	The impact of the pay gap over the lifetime		81
	3.4.1	The gender gap in lifetime earnings	81
	3.4.2	Women's share in family earnings	84
3.5	Conclusions and key findings		85

4. PARTNERSHIP AND PARTNERSHIP BREAKDOWN*   87

4.1 Partnership and economic status   88
4.1.1 Changing patterns of family formation and dissolution   88
4.1.2 Partnership and economic status   90

4.2 Sharing within partnerships   92
4.2.1 Assumptions about income sharing   92
4.2.2 Income sharing among the hypothetical couples   93

4.3 Sources of income across the lifecycle   94
4.3.1 Sources of income over the whole lifetime   94
4.3.2 Sources of income at four different stages of the lifecycle   96

4.4 The impact of divorce on lifetime income   99
4.4.1 The timing of divorce   99
4.4.2 The impact of divorce on labour market participation   100
4.4.3 Divorce and lifetime earnings   102
4.4.4 Divorce: from earnings to income   106

4.5 Conclusions and key findings   110

5. PARENTING AND CARING FOR OTHERS   113

5.1 The earnings and income cost of children*   114
5.1.1 The impact of children on earnings   115
5.1.2 The timing of motherhood   116
5.1.3 The income costs of children   121
5.1.4 How do the earnings and income costs of children compare?   124
5.1.5 How are the costs of children divided?   125

5.2 Motherhood, parenthood and the pay gap*   126

5.3	The lifetime incomes of teenage mothers*	129
	5.3.1 A profile of teenage mothers	129
	5.3.2 Modelling teenage motherhood	131
	5.3.3 Projected participation probabilities of teenage mothers	133
	5.3.4 The lifetime earnings of teenage mothers	136
	5.3.5 Sources of income of teenage mothers	139
	5.3.6 How do teenage mothers fare in retirement?	143
5.4	Women's incomes and childhood poverty	144
5.5	Caring for others, income and employment	147
5.6	Conclusions and key findings	151

6. LATER LIFE — 155

6.1	Economic resources in later life	156
	6.1.1 Income in later life	156
	6.1.2 Women and pensions	159
	6.1.3 Wealth, savings and financial planning	161
6.2	Simulated income in later life*	163
	6.2.1 Individual income in retirement	163
	6.2.2 The family as a source of income in retirement	164
	6.2.3 Sources of income in retirement	165
6.3	Life events and income in later life*	167
	6.3.1 The pension consequences of children	167
	6.3.2 The pension consequences of divorce	168
6.4	Interruptions to employment in later life*	171
	6.4.1 Unemployment and lifetime incomes	171
	6.4.2 Unemployment and the earnings cost of children	174
	6.4.3 Unemployment and retirement income	174
	6.4.4 Early retirement and lifetime incomes	176
	6.4.5 Early retirement and the earnings cost of children	177
	6.4.6 Early retirement and retirement income	178
6.5	Conclusions and key findings	179

APPENDICES

    I   Gender wage differentials*   183

    II   The simulated tax-benefit system*   187

    III   Econometric equations in the simulation model*   193

BIBLIOGRAPHY

TABLE OF TABLES

Table 2.1:	Percent of employed in specific education groups (1974/6–1993/5)	21
Table 2.2:	Changes in the gender gap in entry to different subjects at GCSE (1984–1994)	22
Table 2.3:	Changes in the gender gap in entry to different subjects at A-Level (1984–1994)	23
Table 2.4:	Percent of the employed with degrees by degree type (1980/2–1993/5)	24
Table 2.5:	Incidence of training among full- and part-time employees by sex (1999)	26
Table 2.6:	Labour market change (1983–1997)	27
Table 2.7:	Employees who work part-time by age (1999)	32
Table 2.8:	Usual weekly hours of work of employees (1997–98)	33
Table 2.9:	Unemployment and duration of unemployment (1999)	35
Table 2.10:	Economic status by sex and ethnic origin (1998–99)	37
Table 2.11:	Average hourly earnings of full-time employeess in highest/lowest paid occupations (1998)	42
Table 2.12:	Pay by ethnicity (1998–99)	48
Table 2.13:	Average pay of full-time employees: England, Scotland and Wales (1999)	49
Table 2.14:	The sex composition of employment and earnings (1968–90)	55
Table 3.1:	The educational levels of women and men in couples (1994)	65
Table 3.2:	Hypothetical individuals: assumed ages at key family events	70

Table 3.3:	Women's gross lifetime earnings	78
Table 3.4:	The impact of the tax-benefit system on the lifetime income of women by skill level and family characteristics	81
Table 3.5:	The gender gap in lifetime earnings	82
Table 3.6:	Percentage contribution of wife's earnings to couple's joint lifetime earnings	84
Table 4.1:	Sources of women's income over the lifetime	95
Table 4.2:	Sources of women's income by stages of working life	97
Table 4.3:	Age at which hypothetical individuals experience divorce	99
Table 4.4:	Women's total years in employment and divorce	101
Table 4.5:	Women's lifetime labour market income and divorce	103
Table 4.6:	The incomes of divorced women compared to those with unbroken marriages	108
Table 5.1:	Forgone earnings costs of motherhood	116
Table 5.2:	Gross earnings and net income costs of children to women and couples	123
Table 5.3:	Who pays the cost of children?	126
Table 5.4:	Gender, mother and parent gaps in lifetime earnings	128
Table 5.5:	Hypothetical teenage mothers: assumed ages at key family events	133
Table 5.6:	Lifetime gross earnings of teenage mothers and others	137
Table 5.7:	Teenage mothers vs. others: components of lifetime income	140
Table 5.8:	Percentage distribution of income for children by the economic status of the family	146

Table 5.9:	Couples of working age at three censuses (1971, 1981 and 1991) by number of earners	147
Table 5.10:	Percentage of adults who were carers: by age (1995–96)	148
Table 5.11:	Dependant's relationship to carer by gender of carer (1995–96)	148
Table 5.12:	Hours spent caring per week by carers (1985–95/96)	149
Table 6.1:	Distribution of income of single male and female pensioners by age (1996–98)	158
Table 6.2:	Employees who are members of pension schemes: by socio-economic group (1994–96)	160
Table 6.3:	Sources of women's retirement income by stages of lifecycle	166
Table 6.4:	Pension consequences of children	168
Table 6.5:	Retirement income: consequences of divorce	169
Table 6.6:	Unemployment: lifetime incomes of married women	173
Table 6.7:	Unemployed: forgone earnings cost of children	174
Table 6.8:	Women experiencing unemployment: retirement income as percent of that of fully employed counterpart	176
Table 6.9:	Early retirement: earnings cost of children	177
Table A1:	Summary of recent empirical results on decomposing gender wage differentials in Britain	186
Table A2:	Working Family Tax Credit – lifetime totals paid in standard cases 189	
Table A3:	Male wages	197
Table A4:	Female wages	198
Table A5:	Multinomial logit female participation estimates	199

TABLE OF FIGURES

Figure 1.1:	Median gross individual income by age, all women and all men (1996/97)	13
Figure 2.1:	Percentage of men and women with higher and no educational qualifications (1974/5 and 1995)	20
Figure 2.2:	Women's labour market activity by age of youngest dependent child and level of highest qualification held (1998)	25
Figure 2.3:	Women and men's labour market activity rates (1971–2006)	28
Figure 2.4:	Women and men's full and part-time employment (1987–99)	31
Figure 2.5:	Length of time in current employment (1998)	34
Figure 2.6:	Employment and unemployment rates for women by ethnic group (1984 to 1999)	38
Figure 2.7:	Employment status and median gross individual income by sex (1996–97)	39
Figure 2.8:	Women's hourly pay relative to men's full-time hourly pay (1972–99)	46
Figure 2.9	Women's hourly pay relative to men's by age (1976–99)	47
Figure 2.10	Decomposition of gender pay gaps	51
Figure 3.1:	The lifetime income simulation model (individuals)	63
Figure 3.2:	Distribution of completed family sizes by birth cohort of mothers	67
Figure 3.3:	Age of mother at first birth by highest educational qualification (1986 and 1996)	69
Figure 3.4:	Probabilities of participation in any or full-time employment for childless women and mothers of two by skill level	74
Figure 3.5:	Women's earnings profile over the lifetime by skill level and number of children	77
Figure 3.6:	Lifetime income profile: high-skilled unmarried woman	79
Figure 3.7:	Lifetime income profile: low-skilled mother of two	80
Figure 3.8:	Hourly wages of men and childless women by age	83
Figure 4.1:	Marriages and divorces (1961–98)	89
Figure 4.2:	Individual gross income by marital status and source of income, women and men without dependent children (1996–97)	91

Figure 4.3:	Income sharing in partnership: mid-skilled married couple with children	94
Figure 4.4:	Sources of income by stages of lifecycle: mothers of two	98
Figure 4.5:	Participation probabilities of the mid-skilled mother: divorce with and without remarriage	102
Figure 4.6:	Earnings with and without divorce: low-skilled women	104
Figure 4.7:	Earnings with and without divorce: mid-skilled women	105
Figure 4.8:	Earnings for divorced mid-skilled mother – with and without remarriage	106
Figure 5.1:	Total gross lifetime earnings	115
Figure 5.2:	The earnings cost of two children: total and composition	117
Figure 5.3:	Participation probabilities by age at first birth: mid-skilled women	119
Figure 5.4:	Decomposition of forgone earnings cost of two children by age of mother at first birth: mid-skilled woman	121
Figure 5.5:	Probabilities of participation of teenage mothers and a teen bride: low-skilled women	134
Figure 5.6:	Probabilities of participation of teenage mothers and a teen bride: mid-skilled women	135
Figure 5.7:	Earning profiles of teenage mothers and a teen bride	138
Figure 5.8:	Teenage mothers and others: components of lifetime income	142
Figure 5.9:	Woman's portion in retirement for teenage bride and teenage mothers	143
Figure 6.1:	Women and men pensioners: percentage distribution of weekly individual income in £100 bands, 1996/97	157
Figure 6.2:	Women's own net income in retirement by skill level and number of children	164
Figure 6.3:	Retirement income by skill level and number of children	165
Figure 6.4:	Pensions and divorce: share of ex-spouse's pension as a fraction of lost family transfer by number of children and length of marriage	170
Figure 6.5:	Woman's portion in retirement with experience of unemployment	175
Figure 6.6:	Early retirement: woman's portion	177
Figure 6.7:	'Woman's portion' in retirement with experience of early retirement	178

OVERVIEW

OVERVIEW

In spring 1999, the Women's Unit, Cabinet Office commissioned the research into Women's Incomes over the Lifetime that forms the core of this report. Its purpose was to document and explore the causes and consequences of differences between women's and men's incomes across their lifetimes. Enormous social, and economic and demographic changes have transformed women's and men's lives in the latter half of the 20th century, but have not eliminated differences between them. The research shows how the remaining differences in income vary over the life cycle and by educational level.

The report has two objectives:

1. To gather together empirical evidence on the factors affecting women's lifetime incomes from diverse publications in order to review the economic position of women and men at the end of the 20th century.

2. To build a simulation model of women's and men's *lifetime* incomes. This evaluates the lifetime income consequences of life events such as childbirth and divorce, as well as the lifetime 'costs' of the gender pay gap.

The model specifies characteristics of the hypothetical individuals – such as levels of education, the age at which they marry, the education of their spouses and the ages at which they bear children. Statistical relationships estimated from 1994 BHPS data are used to predict labour market participation and wages. These determine gross earnings for the hypothetical people in each year of their lives. Modules for tax, benefits and pensions enable the computation of net income, whose transfer between spouses can also be modelled. The results are best thought of as illustrations of how much women with a range of simplified biographies would earn over a lifetime. They are neither averages nor forecasts. The hypothetical lifetime takes place in a time warp, where current relationships between the family, the labour market, taxes and benefits all apply in perpetuity.

The model of lifetime incomes was constructed and analysed by Dr Hugh Davies (Department of Economics, Birkbeck College) and Professor Heather Joshi (Centre for Longitudinal Studies, Institute of Education). Dr Katherine Rake (Department of Social Policy, London School of Economics) was seconded to the Women's Unit to direct the research project. She edited this volume and contributed to the literature review. Randa Alami was employed in the Department of Economics, Birkbeck College to assist Davies and Joshi.

SUMMARY

SUMMARY

The following key findings emerge:

1. The gap between men's and women's pay in full-time jobs has narrowed, partly due to more equal education and experience, and partly due to a falling gender penalty – more equal rates of remuneration for a given characteristic. In 1980 the pure gender penalty lowered married women's pay in full-time work by 16%, in 1994 by 8%.

2. The penalty to part-time employment lowered the average hourly pay of all married part-timers by another 16% compared to women working full-time in 1980. By 1994, this had increased to 35%.

3. The model produces striking differences in women's lifetime earnings by qualification level. Childless women are estimated to earn £518,000 over the entire lifetime if they have no qualifications, £650,000 if mid-skilled and nearly double, £1,190,000, if graduates.

4. The lifetime gender earnings gap (the gap between men's and women's earnings above and beyond any penalties attached to motherhood) is estimated to be worth just under a quarter of a million pounds for the mid-skilled woman over her lifetime. Her lifetime earnings are 37% below those of an equivalently skilled man – 16% is due to fewer hours spent in the labour market while 18% is due to differences in hourly pay.

5. Divorce can have major consequences for women's lifetime incomes. These vary by the woman's educational level, length of marriage, number of children and whether remarriage occurs. The research shows that increases in women's labour supply, the tax-benefit system, pension sharing and child support payments may all play an important part in offsetting the initial cost of divorce.

6. The amount of earnings forgone by mothers varies by number of children, and most importantly, skill level of the woman. The low-skilled mother of two is calculated to forgo earnings of over a quarter of a million pounds (almost 60% of her potential earnings after childbirth), compared to £140,000 for the mid-skilled and under £20,000 for the high-skilled mother of two (just 2% of her potential earnings after childbirth). The latter two cases are likely to involve extensive use of daycare while the children are young.

7. The timing of motherhood has an important impact on lost earnings – the mid-skilled mother of two who starts her family at 24 forgoes more than double the sum of the mother whose first birth is at age 30.

8. Teenage mothers forgo more earnings than those who postpone their first birth – the low-skilled never-married teenage mother of two children, for example, forgoes £300,000 in gross earnings (just under 60% of the lifetime earnings of the low-skilled childless woman).

Gender differentials in paid work (Chapter 2) explores continuing differentials between women and men in the type of paid work they undertake and examines the changing profile of the pay gap. On a number of levels, while gender differentials are narrowing they remain a persistent feature of the British labour market:

- There is considerable differentiation *among* women in their experience of paid employment. Educational attainment has a strong influence on labour market activity. For example, in 1998, 76% of mothers with a child under five and qualifications of at least A level were active in the labour market compared to just 27% of mothers without qualifications.

- Part-time jobs tend to be low-paid and low-skilled. This is a reflection both of the quality of these jobs and of the fact that there are limited opportunities available to work part-time in higher grade occupations.

- Since the Equal Pay Act, the gap between the hourly wages of men and women working full-time has narrowed (although change in recent years has been slow). The pay of women working part-time relative to men working full-time has however remained unchanged since the early 1980s, and the pay gap is now wider than it was in the mid 1970s. Younger cohorts of women appear to be experiencing a narrower full-time gender pay gap.

- The gap between men's and women's pay in full-time jobs has narrowed, partly due to less unequal education and experience, and partly due to a falling gender penalty – less unequal rates of remuneration for a given characteristic. In 1980 the pure gender penalty lowered married women's pay in full-time work by 16%, in 1994 by 8%.

- The fact that women spend fewer hours in the labour market, in combination with their lower wages, means that women's share of employment is not matched by their the share of earnings. For example, the proportion of employees who were female grew from 37% in 1968 to 48% in 1990, while the proportion of all earnings earned by women rose from 20% to 31%.

Chapter 3 considers **Women's Incomes over the Lifetime.** A model of women's and men's lifetime incomes is used to illustrate a variety of family and labour market experiences. The model mainly simulates the tax-benefit policies as they stood in 1999, but allows for a number of important policies in process or not yet fully implemented including the Working Families Tax Credit, the Children's Tax Credit, the new rules for child support and pension sharing on divorce.

The model simulates the biographies of women with three different skill levels – no qualifications (Mrs Low); mid-level qualifications of up to GCSE level (Mrs Mid); and graduate level qualifications (Mrs High). Striking features are:

- The differences in women's earnings by qualification level. The married, childless woman is estimated to earn £518,000 over the entire lifetime if she has no qualifications, £650,000 if mid-skilled and £1,190,000 if a graduate.

- The effect of children on employment patterns varies enormously by qualification level. Unlike low- and mid-skilled mothers, women with high qualification levels have their probability of employment barely affected by having children. Thus, a high-skilled mother of two is estimated to remain continuously employed, with only a year of part-time work following the birth of her second child.

- The mid-skilled mother of two contributes about 35% of the couple's joint lifetime earnings. This figure rises to 42% if she remains childless. Again, the contribution varies across educational levels, from 24% for the low-skilled mother of two to 47% for the high-skilled. These figures suggest that for many women, especially those of lower skills, financial dependence on a man's wage is still a reality.

- The simulated benefits paid to the low- and mid-skilled mothers outweigh the lifetime taxes paid. These benefits include Child Benefit, Child Tax Credit and Working Families' Tax Credit and the Basic Pension.

The report examines the impact of **Partnership and Partnership Breakdown** (Chapter 4) on women's lifetime incomes. Here, the potential contribution of a partner to a woman's income, and, conversely, the economic consequences of divorce are examined:

- Though families might not actually share income equally, the analysis shows how important a transfer of income from husband to wife *might* be to a women's lifetime incomes, if a wife earns less than her husband and income is pooled. If there is equal sharing, the family transfer accounts for over 30% of the lifetime incomes (from date of marriage) of the low- and mid-skilled mothers of two.

- The financial impact of divorce varies according to the timing of the divorce, subsequent changes in paid work, whether remarriage occurs and the woman's educational level. It is greatest where there is most financial dependence within marriage. The impact of divorce would also be modified by the payments of child support and pension splitting.

The consequences of **Parenting and Caring for Others** (Chapter 5) on lifetime incomes are then considered. The report examines the link between income and children in two directions: the impact of having and raising children on women's lifetime incomes is examined before looking at the connection between women's incomes and the risk that their children will be in poverty. The timing of motherhood can be of critical importance and in light of this, a scenario of teenage lone parenthood is explored. The following key findings emerge:

- Comparisons between this simulation (based on data from the mid 1990s) and a previous model (modelled on data from 1980) show a dramatic drop in the earnings cost of motherhood for the mid-skilled mother. Her forgone earnings have fallen from £230,000 to £140,000, as a result of increased participation rates.

- The amount of earnings forgone by mothers varies by number of children, and most importantly, skill level of the mother. The low-skilled mother of two is calculated to forgo earnings of over a quarter of a million pounds (almost 60% of her potential earnings after childbirth). The high-skilled mother of two forgoes under £20,000 (just 2% of her potential earnings after childbirth), although her pattern of labour market activity may result in high childcare costs.

- The timing of motherhood has an important impact on lost earnings – the mid-skilled mother of two who starts her family at 24 forgoes more than twice the amount of earnings than the mother whose first birth is at age 30.

- For the mid-skilled woman the lifetime earnings penalty of motherhood is smaller in absolute, and relative terms, than the penalty of being a woman. This is not the case for women of all skill levels – the mother gap is £285,000 for the low-skilled mother (114% of the mother of two's lifetime earnings) compared to a gender earnings gap of £197,000.

- Teenage motherhood is estimated to have a negative impact on lifetime incomes both because of reduced employment in her twenties and, if unpartnered, loss of shared income.

- Turning to contemporary cross-sectional data, 56% of children from households with one earner are in the bottom two-fifths of the income distribution compared to 21% of children from households with two earners. In light of this, and the growth in two-earner families over the past 30 years, women's incomes are an important factor in protecting children from poverty. The percentage of poor children living in lone parent families has grown faster than the percentage of all children living in lone parent families, suggesting that lone parent households have become increasingly vulnerable to poverty over the past 20 years.

Lastly, the report focuses on **Later life** (Chapter 6) where differentials in the level and sources of income in later life are explored alongside an examination of the consequences of children and of divorce on income in retirement. The authors also examine the impact of a spell of unemployment in later life and of early retirement on lifetime income. The key findings are:

- All pensioner households are disproportionately represented at the bottom of the income distribution, but the risk of being at the bottom of the income distribution is higher for single female households (in 1997/8, 60% fell within the bottom 40% of the income distribution). In common with lone parents, single female pensioners experience high levels of persistently low incomes.

- The retirement incomes estimated by the model show a large variation among women according to their skill level and type of pension scheme membership. The graduate mother of two receives a total income in retirement of £289,000, over four times as much as the £69,000 received by the low-skilled mother. In widowhood, especially, low-skilled mothers are heavily reliant on the Basic Pension.

- The model calculates the pension consequences of children. For the high-skilled cases these are zero. By contrast, the low-skilled mothers of two lose 42% of their earnings-related pension (rising to 84% for mothers of four), while the mid-skilled lose 21% if they have two children and 69% if they have four.

- The income costs of divorce extend into retirement – the net loss in retirement incurred by the mid-skilled mother of two who divorces after seven years is £49,000, even after we take into account the value of the pension shared on divorce (worth £35,000 in this case). For longer marriages, the value of the shared pension is higher – in the same case, a woman with a marriage of 17 years is estimated to derive £57,000 from the pension split on divorce.

- These biographies illustrate how a specialisation between husband and wife which keeps the woman out of paid work as a young woman implies a lifelong reduction in earnings and pension. Provided the marriage is also lifelong, sharing the husband's income and inheriting a survivor's pension might compensate for some of this shortfall.

1. INTRODUCTION

1. INTRODUCTION

1.1　Why a report on women's incomes?

In the latter half of the 20th century, social, economic and demographic trends have all affected and, indeed, transformed women's and men's lives, in Britain, as elsewhere. To illustrate, compared to 1971, an additional three million women are now active in the labour force. In spring 1999 72.5% of working age women were active in the labour market (ONS 1997, Table 1; Labour Market Trends, December, 1999, Table D1). Projections suggest that 1.7 million new jobs will come into existence before 2011 of which an estimated 1.4 million will be taken by women (ONS 1998a). Women's contribution to the economic success of Britain is, therefore, critical and set to sincrease. At the same time as this economic change, a revolution has been taking place in family size and living arrangements. Since the early 1970s, the average number of children born to a woman fell from 2.4 to 1.7 and the average age at first birth has risen by over two years. The total number of divorces has doubled, the proportion of families headed by lone parents has almost tripled and the percentage of all births occurring outside marriage has grown from 8.2% to 37.6% (ONS 1999 Table 2.2; General Household Survey).

Existing research tells us there continue to be gender-based differences in access to economic resources. For example, women working full-time earned 63 pence for every pound earned by a man working full-time in 1971; by 1999 this stood at 84 pence. For women working part-time, the increase was from 51 pence in the pound to just 58 pence.[1] Figure 1.1 illustrates how differences in women's and men's gross individual income[2] exist at every age. As the figure shows, the gap between women's and men's incomes is relatively small for those in their early 20s but increases for later age cohorts and is most marked for those aged 30-50. For men, the hump-backed profile of income by age reflects the premium attached to men's skills and experience in the labour market, with incomes tailing off into retirement. The pattern is different for women as the incomes of women currently in their 40s are higher than those of women in their 30s, when many women have young children.

---

[1] All figures calculated from the New Earnings Survey on the basis of median hourly earnings of women compared to median hourly earnings of men working full-time. 1971 part-timers may not be comparable because of changed NES sampling frame.

[2] Gross weekly personal income of women and men which includes earnings income from self-employment, investments and occupational pensions/annuities, benefit income and income from other miscellaneous sources.

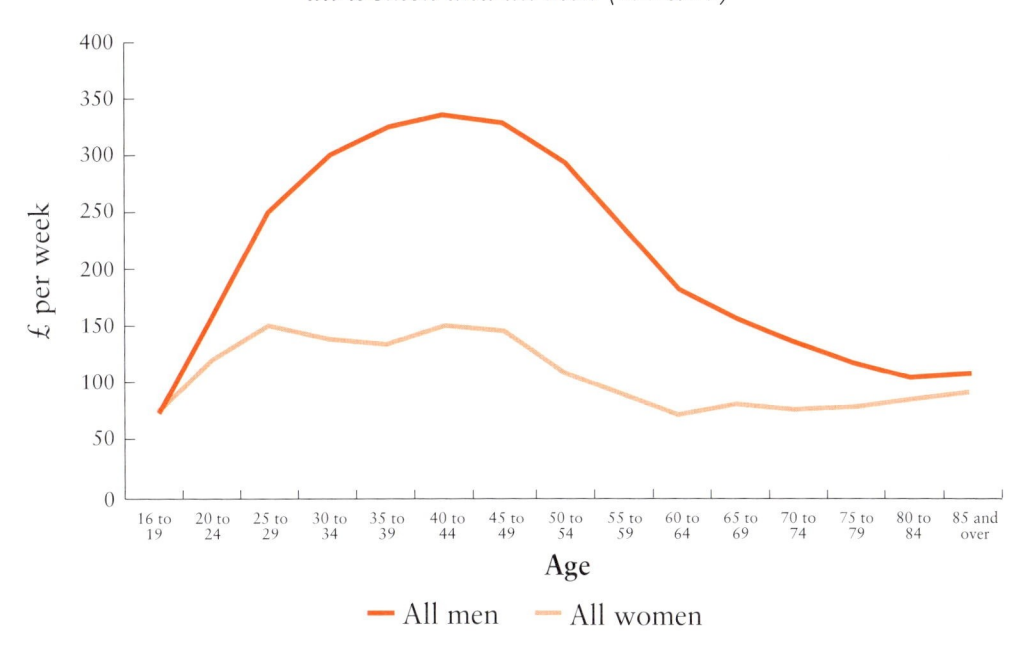

Figure 1.1: Median gross individual income by age, all women and all men (1996/97)

[Chart: Median gross individual income (£ per week) by age group for All men and All women]

Source: Women's Unit 1999: Figure 3.1.

Currently, over 45% of women have gross individual income of less than £100 per week compared to just over 20% of men. 10% of men had gross individual income of more than £500 compared to only 2% of women. Thus, women are over-represented at the bottom of the income distribution and under-represented at the top. Twice the proportion of women (53%) as men (27%) fall in the bottom two-fifths of the income distribution, while 30% of men and only 10% of women find themselves in the richest fifth of the income distribution (Women's Unit 1999: 2 and Table 1.4. See also Sutherland 1997; Jenkins 1998; Webb 1993).

The comparison of women's and men's incomes should not blind us to differences *among* women. For example, in 1996/7 the average (mean) gross individual weekly income of Pakistani and Bangladeshi women was £73, less than half the average for White and Black Caribbean/African women (DSS 1999a). Clearly, there remain significant differences between women and men and among women in their access to economic resources – it is these that the present report seeks to explore.

Focusing on women's lifetime *incomes* gives this report a unique perspective on economic inequality between women and men as it allows us to go beyond an analysis of the gender pay gap of those who happen to be employed at a given moment. By studying lifetime incomes we can look at women's relationship with the labour market over the life course and study both the family and the state as sources of income.

Our analysis of incomes, rather than earnings, is essential in order to encompass women's experience over the life course and diversity within this. Earnings constitute an average of 61% of women's individual incomes, but represent just 37% of total income for those who are currently lone mothers and only 3% of the incomes of single pensioners (Women's Unit 1999 Tables 2.1, 2.3 and 2.4).

In addition, we consider the distribution of lifetime incomes, rather than the risk and incidence of poverty. By including women at a number of points in the income distribution, differences among women can be explored and the hypothesis that women's experiences are becoming increasingly polarised examined. Further, while the over-representation of women among the poor is clear evidence of economic inequality between men and women, their under-representation among the rich also signals gender inequality. Finally, by focusing on *lifetime* incomes we move beyond looking at a simple snapshot of women's incomes to consider the long-term economic impacts of key life events, such as caring for children and divorce. The lifetime focus is discussed more thoroughly in Section 1.2 below.

Although income is our chosen measure, we recognise its limitations. Firstly, a different picture of the distribution of income arises depending on whether income is measured at the level of the individual or the household (for example, a household which on aggregate commands a high level of income may contain members with a low individual income). While we are primarily concerned with women's individual incomes, our lifetime perspective means that we also must consider their living arrangements. Childbearing, childrearing and family life are, for the majority of women, key determinants of their lifetime income. We therefore consider the family and men's incomes, alongside women's engagement with the labour market. We use individual income as a measure of independent access to resources while recognising the *potential* importance of the income of other household members in contributing to an individual's economic resources (these issues are explored in Chapter 4).

Secondly, income operates only as an imperfect proxy of standard of living or well being. Clearly well-being can be derived from goods and services that fall outside the money economy. Standard measures of income such as those employed here do not measure, for example, the value to individual or family well-being of unpaid time spent providing childcare, cleaning or provisioning a household. The important questions of how unpaid labour might be valued and how far increases in women's participation in the labour market have meant a more equitable distribution of domestic labour, or, alternatively, the imposition of a double burden on women, remain beyond the scope of this report although they are considered briefly. We nevertheless signal them as areas of future research.

Thirdly, income tells us what an individual or household has, not what *is* or *can be* done with it. Income does not accurately measure what individuals or households consume and the ability to translate income into a certain level of well-being depends upon needs (a single person household has distinct needs from that of a couple and four children). Although information on the distribution of income does not tell us about the distribution of well-being, it does provide us with crucial information about access to economic resources, allowing us to assess the degree of economic independence afforded to individual women and men.

1.2 Why look at incomes over the lifetime?

We focus on incomes over the lifetime for good reason. A century ago, Rowntree's analysis of the lifecycle of income showed how incomes may fluctuate over an individual's lifetime, making any one-off snapshot of income potentially misleading (Rowntree 1901). More recently, interest in the dynamics of income has led to studies of transitions in and out of poverty and between labour market states (see, among others, Jarvis and Jenkins 1998, Hills 1998, Hills 1999 and Liesering and Walker 1998). Such studies confirm that wherever income varies over the life course, a snapshot of someone's income is not necessarily informative of what their income has been or will be in the future.

There are many reasons for taking a long-term perspective on income. For example, studies of returns to education and prospects of pension adequacy are best conducted taking a lifetime perspective. For women in particular, family-related fluctuations in earnings over their lifecycle mean that women's incomes at any moment in time have traditionally borne a more complicated relationship to their lifetime incomes than do men's. For all women, the lifetime perspective allows us to examine the income consequences of different marital histories and the cumulative impact of the pay gap over the lifetime. For women with children, lifetime incomes can show the long-term consequences of childbearing on earnings and income. In this case, the lifetime perspective is particularly useful as the consequences of having children may extend across the working life and into old age. In addition, looking over the whole lifetime means we can show whether taxes, benefits and pensions smooth women's incomes over their lifetimes and how the family itself may redistribute lifetime income towards women.

1.3 Outline of the report

The report is structured as follows:

- **Chapter 2** considers women's and men's experience of paid work. It explores continuing differentials between women and men in the type of paid work they undertake (including a consideration of job segregation), and examines the changing profile of the pay gap. In reviewing current statistical evidence on the labour market and pay, this chapter provides a picture of the contemporary British labour market and gives a context within which to situate the simulations of women's and men's lifetime incomes that follow.

- **Chapter 3** introduces the model used to simulate lifetime incomes in the rest of the report. Here we explore the assumptions employed and the standard lifetime biographies used to illustrate a variety of family and labour market experiences. The patterns of labour market participation, lifetime earnings and lifetime incomes for women of three different skill levels are set out. We also examine the magnitude and impact of the pay gap extrapolated over the lifetime.

- The impact of partnership and partnership breakdown on projections of women's lifetime incomes provides the focus of **Chapter 4**. Here we consider the interaction between partnership status and economic status and examine the potential contribution of a partner to a woman's incomes, and, conversely, the economic consequences of divorce.

- In **Chapter 5** we analyse the economic consequences of parenting and caring for others. We examine the relative importance of being a woman and being a mother on lifetime earnings. We first consider how having and raising children affects women's lifetime incomes, and we provide an estimate of the lifetime earnings and incomes cost of having children. We then consider the lifetime earnings and incomes of teenage mothers and assess the additional penalty that arises from early motherhood and absence of a partner. Lastly, we look at the connection between women's incomes and the risk that their children will be in poverty.

- **Chapter 6** looks at incomes in later life. We examine differentials between women and men and among women in the level and source of income in later life, and estimate the impact of having children on pension income. We also use this chapter to examine the impact of a spell of unemployment in later life and of early retirement on lifetime income.

2. GENDER DIFFERENTIALS IN PAID WORK

2. GENDER DIFFERENTIALS IN PAID WORK

This chapter reviews current literature and statistics to draw a picture of women in the contemporary British labour market and to give context to the simulations of women's and men's lifetime incomes that follow in the remainder of the report. Section 2.1 examines differences in the educational attainment and educational choices of men and women, looking at how these influence the level and type of labour market participation. We explore patterns of women's and men's labour market activity in the context of the changing British labour market in Section 2.2, paying particular attention to the types of paid work that women and men do. We look at differences among women by ethnicity and examine throughout how far women's experience of the labour market is captured by standard classifications of employment status. We then turn our attention to job segregation (Section 2.3). The effects on women's and men's wages of 'sex-typing' of occupations and of barriers to career progression are explored. In Sections 2.4 and 2.5 we look at the pay gap. First, we explore the changes in the pay gap since the early 1970s and the patterns of pay across ethnicity and region. We then consider the causes of the pay gap, and separate out the impact of motherhood on pay from the pay disadvantage that is attributable to gender alone.

2.1 EDUCATION, TRAINING AND SKILLS

To understand the relative position of women and men in the labour market, information on gender differentials in education and training is essential. Measures of 'human capital' (an important element of which is education) are commonly used to understand labour demand and supply, as well as the wages that an individual commands. Educational choices influence career and job choices (and thereby earnings), while training offered while in work can affect the chances of promotion and future earnings.

Against a backdrop of continuing improvements in educational attainment, advances in women's qualifications have been particularly noticeable. Indeed at secondary school level, attention is focusing increasingly on boys' 'underachievement'. However, looking below the headline figures, and at the whole British population, continuing differences in educational attainment appear. Further, gender differences in subject choice, already evident at GCSE level, open up markedly at A level and beyond. From the perspective of lifetime incomes, persistent differences in educational attainment and educational choice are important because they affect women's and men's access to the labour market, their choice of jobs and career advancement.

2.1.1 Gender differences in basic skills

One way of looking at how changes in educational attainment reflect genuine changes in the skills base of the population is to look at the distribution of basic skills. The 1997 Adult Literacy Survey divided literacy into three aspects – prose, document and quantitative (see Carey et al. 1997 for details). It found that while women and men exhibited little difference in their levels of prose literacy, women were more likely than men to perform poorly on tests of document and, particularly, quantitative literacy. For document literacy, all other things being equal, women were 1.31 times more likely to have the poorest literacy score, and for quantitative literacy this figure was 1.64 times greater (Carey et al. 1997, Table 5.4, p. 60). While these differences may well be set to reduce over time with the increases in women's educational attainment noted below, the research points to important differences within the basic skills of the current population, differences that may be of particular importance when considering issues such as financial planning (see Section 6.1).

2.1.2 Educational attainment

The qualification level of British women has continued to improve relative to men. At secondary school level, 51% of girls achieved five A*– C grades at GCSE level in 1996–7, compared with 41% of boys. The proportion of young women leaving school with at least two A levels or equivalent almost doubled between 1980 and 1995–6 to 23%. By 1995–6, young women had overtaken young men, of whom only 20% reached this level of attainment (ONS 1998a, Table 2.6).

Figure 2.1 compares the educational levels of men and women between the mid-1970s and the mid-1990s. The cumulated level of qualifications among adults of working age improved for both sexes over the period, with greater change among women. The figure reveals the falling numbers of, and narrowing gender differential among, those with no qualifications. In 1974–5, 61% of women aged 30–39 had no qualifications compared to 46% of men, while in 1995 the percentage of unqualified women in this age group had fallen to 20%, and to 18% for men. Nevertheless, 11% of male and female 20–29 year olds remained without qualifications in 1995. The connection between lack of educational qualifications and low lifetime income is well documented. For example, a recent government report focused on the 9% of 16–18 year olds not in education, employment or training and identified such non-participation as a 'fast-track' to low incomes and social exclusion in many cases (The Social Exclusion Unit, 1999a). The report found gender differentials among this group of non-participants – women are slightly over-represented in this group and approximately a third of them are registered as economically inactive and caring for a child or others.

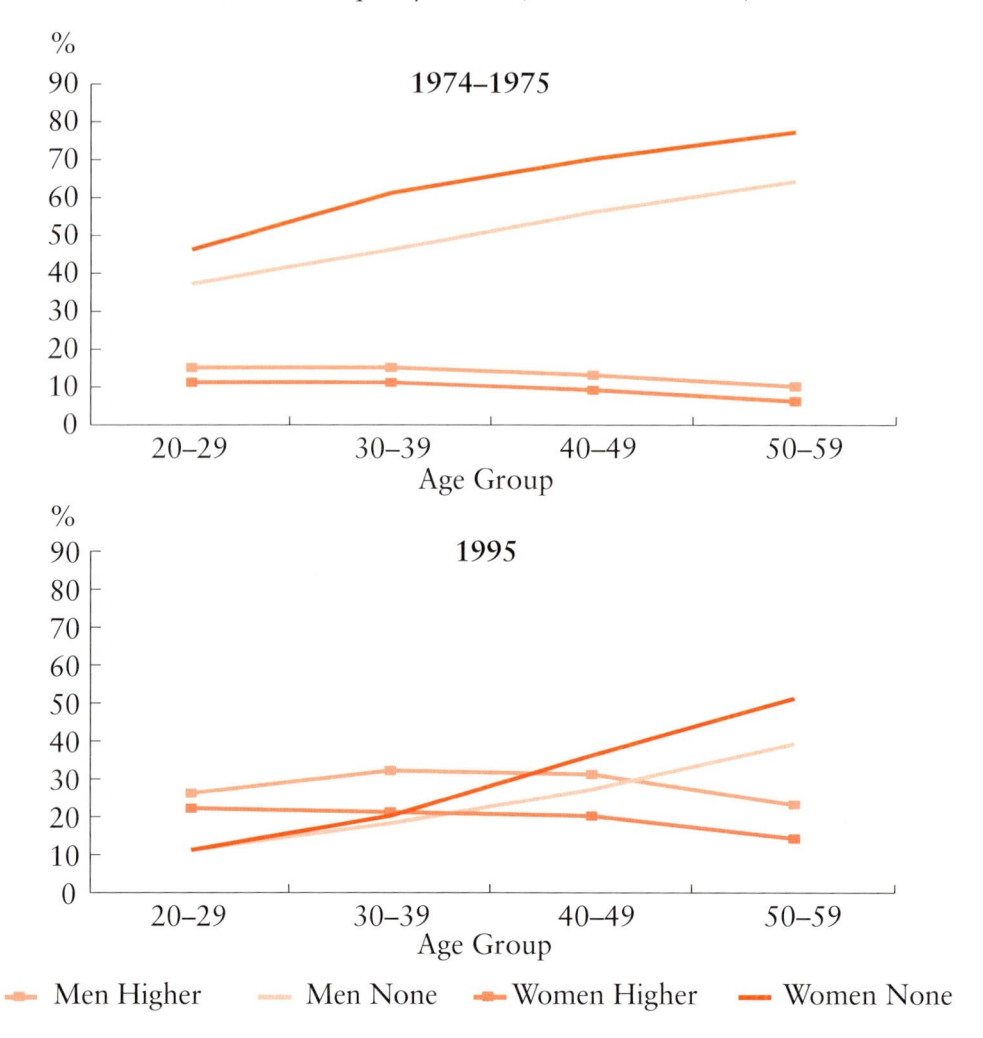

Figure 2.1: Percentage of men and women with higher and no educational qualification (1974/5 and 1995)

[Chart: 1974–1975 — % vs Age Group (20–29, 30–39, 40–49, 50–59)]

[Chart: 1995 — % vs Age Group (20–29, 30–39, 40–49, 50–59)]

■— Men Higher   — Men None   ■— Women Higher   — Women None

Source: General Household Survey

Among those studying for higher (tertiary) qualifications, in 1980/81 there were 57 females per 100 males enrolled as students in higher education; by 1995/6 the figure was 108. For postgraduate courses, men remain the majority of students (86 female enrolments per 100 male) despite the large growth in the female postgraduate population since the 1970s (ONS 1998a Table 2.7). Yet, as Figure 2.1 shows, amongst 20–29 year olds the average level of higher qualifications was still higher for men (26%) than women (22%) in the mid 1990s.

Taking a slightly different perspective, Table 2.1 shows the changes over the period 1974/6–1993/5 in the educational attainments of those in employment. The table reveals a noticeable increase in the percentage of employed women and men with higher educational qualifications that has, in nearly all cases, been more rapid for women. The percentage of employed women with higher vocational qualifications has risen by 423% (compared to 154% for men), while the percentage of women in employment with a degree has risen by 356% (165% for men). At the other end of the scale, the percentage of women in employment without qualifications has fallen by 59% (57% for men). Despite the much faster increase in the educational level of employed women than of employed men, the educational level among the stock of employed men exceeds that of employed women. For example, in 1993/95 15% of employed men had a degree compared to 10% of women, while 21% of men and 24% of women had no qualifications.

Table 2.1: Percent of employed in specific education groups (1974/76–1993/95)

	1974–76	1979–81	1984–86	1989–91	1993–95	Percentage Change[1]
Men						
Degree	6	8	11	12	15	165
Higher Vocational	5	7	10	11	12	154
Teaching	1	1	1	1	1	-3
Nursing	0	0	0	0	0	115
2 + A Levels	2	3	3	4	4	74
1 + A Level	1		2	2	2	146
Voc. Middle	4	6	8	9	10	123
Some Quals.	31	32	28	34	34	11
No Quals.	50	43	35	27	22	-57
Women						
Degree	2	4	6	8	10	358
Higher Vocational	1	1	2	3	4	423
Teaching	3	3	4	3	3	-17
Nursing	3	3	5	5	5	96
2 + A Levels	2	3	3	4	5	118
1 + A Level	1		2	2	3	212
Voc. Middle	0	1	2	3	4	870
Some Quals.	30	35	39	43	43	46
No Quals.	58	49	37	30	24	-59

1 Percentage change defined as [(1993/5 − 1974-6)/1974-6] x 100
Source: Harkness and Machin 1999, Table I (derived from the General Household Survey).

2.1.3 Educational choice

As with educational attainment, looking at the subject choices of women and men presents us with a picture of change combined with enduring gender differentials. At GCSE level, there has been considerable narrowing of differences between girls and boys. Nevertheless, as Table 2.2 reports, boys continue to dominate a small range of subjects (Chemistry, Economics and Computer Studies), while other subjects that were previously dominated by boys – e.g. Physics, Design and Technology – are becoming increasingly mixed. Girls continue to dominate Home Economics, Social Studies and Vocational Studies with the concentration of girls in the latter two subjects increasing over time (Arnot et al. 1998).

Table 2.2: Changes in the gender gap in entry to different subjects at GCSE (1984-1994)

Size of Gap in 1994	Boys predominate	Balanced entry	Girls predominate	Trend in gap over last decade
Large (30%+)	Physics			Decreasing
	CDT			Decreasing
	Economics			Increasing
			Home Economics	Decreasing
			Social Studies	Increasing
			Vocational Studies	Increasing
Sizeable (15–30%)	Chemistry			Increasing
	Computer Studies			Increasing
Small (5–15%)	Technology			Decreasing
	Geography			Decreasing
			Mod. Foreign Languages	Decreasing
			English Lit.	Decreasing
No gap (less than 5% either way)	Science			Decreasing
			Biology	Decreasing
		English		No change
		Mathematics		No change
		History		No change
		Art & Design		No change

Source: Arnot et al. 1998, Table 1.3.

At A level, the picture is quite distinct. Gender differentials in subject choice are more persistent, with only one A level – History – showing equivalent numbers of male and female entrants. In many subject areas the gap in entrants is actually increasing (Table 2.3). Looking at the traditional under-representation of girls in maths and sciences, Cheng et al. (1995) found that 56% of male students were taking some science or maths based subject compared to 40% of female.

Table 2.3: Changes in gender gap in entry to different subjects at A-Level (1984–1994)

Size of gap in 1994	Boys predominate	Balanced entry	Girls predominate	Trend in gap over last decade
Large (30%+)	Physics			Increasing
	Mathematics			No change
	Computer Studies			No change
	Technology			Increasing
	Economics			Increasing
	CDT			Increasing
			English	Decreasing
			Mod. Foreign Languages	Decreasing
Sizeable (15–30%)	Chemistry			No change
	Geography			No change
			Biology	Decreasing
			Social Studies	Increasing
			Art & Design	Decreasing
Small (5–15%)	none		none	
No gap (less than 5% either way)			History	Decreasing

Source: Arnot et al. 1998, Table 1.3.

Gender segregation in subjects studied persists at degree level. If we again look from the perspective of the educational qualifications of those in employment, Table 2.4 shows that the proportion of employed men with science/engineering degrees was nearly double that of women, whilst for those with degrees in the arts the situation was reversed with the proportion of women twice that of men. Nevertheless, there has been some change. For example, in 1980/2 15% of employed women had a science/engineering degree and by 1993/5 this had grown to 24%.

Table 2.4: Percent of the employed with degrees by degree type (1980/2–1993/5)

	1980–2	1984–6	1989–91	1993–5
Men				
Arts	15	13	13	12
Science/Engineering	41	42	45	47
Social Science & Business	26	27	28	27
Other	18	19	14	15
Women				
Arts	38	35	30	25
Science/Engineering	15	16	19	24
Social Science & Business	22	23	27	25
Other	25	27	23	26

Source: Harkness and Machin 1999, Table XI (derived from the General Household Survey).

2.1.4 Educational attainment and participation in the labour market

The difference in participation rates of women with different qualification levels has widened over the past 15 years. The Labour Force Survey shows that for women with higher qualifications (equivalent to A levels or above) rates of labour market activity have grown steadily: from 78% in 1984 to 86% in 1998. Those with no qualifications have seen their activity rates fall from 59% to 50% during the same period. Educational attainment has a stronger influence on women's labour market activity[3] than it does on men's. The equivalent figures for men were 66% and 92%.

The difference among women by level of educational qualification is particularly strong when there are young children present. From Figure 2.2 we see that three-quarters of women with high levels of qualification are active in the labour market when their youngest child is under five compared to just over a quarter of those with no qualifications. The differential between women narrows for those mothers with older children, although even when the youngest child is aged 16–18 the rate of labour market activity among women with high educational qualifications is 25 percentage points higher than that for women without educational qualifications.

---

[3] We prefer the term labour market activity to term 'economic activity'. Although economic activity is commonly used in statistical reports, the notion that women who are not in the labour market are economically inactive undervalues the contribution that unpaid caring labour makes to the economy. This is discussed in more detail in Section 2.2 below.

Figure 2.2: Women's labour market activity by age of youngest dependent child and level of highest qualification held (1998)

Percent of women active in the labour market

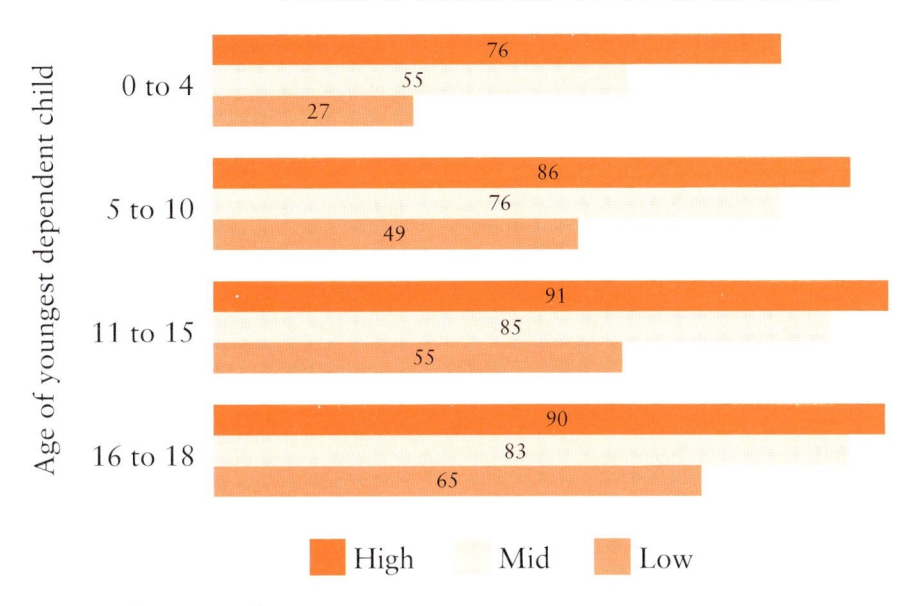

Age of youngest dependent child	High	Mid	Low
0 to 4	76	55	27
5 to 10	86	76	49
11 to 15	91	85	55
16 to 18	90	83	65

Source: Labour Force Survey.

2.1.5 Training

Alongside education, training received while in employment has a positive impact on wages. Any differential in access to training is likely to show up as differential earnings further down the road. Table 2.5 shows the percentage of women and men employed full- and part-time who received training while in employment. Although the percentage of all working age women receiving training is higher than that of men, this overall average disguises important differences among women. Notably, only 11% of women working part-time were in receipt of training compared to almost 17% of women working full-time.

Looking at a range of determinants of training, Arulampalam and Booth found that being on a temporary contract, working where there is no union coverage and working part-time all have a negative impact on the likelihood of receiving training. The lower incidence of training among part-timers is of particular importance for women – Arulampalam and Booth found that overall 33% of women and 36% of men had experienced training in the previous 12 months, but for women working part-time this figure dropped to 23% (Arulampalam and Booth 1997, Table 1). Callender and Metcalf found that being employed part-time, being married or cohabiting and having a child aged under five (and especially under two) all reduced the probability of receiving training. In addition they found that women were less likely to have access to employer funded training. Black women, women from lower occupational groups and lower educational qualifications, women working outside the public sector and in small firms, and women with young children all had lower access to employer-funded training (Callender and Metcalf, 1997).

Table 2.5: Incidence of training among full- and part-time employees by sex (1999)

	% receiving training[1]
Women working full-time	16.9
Women working part-time	11.2
All women	14.5
Men working full-time	12.6
Men working part-time	12.8
All men	12.6

1 Employees receiving job-related training in the four weeks prior to interview as a percentage of all employees of working age (men aged 16–64 and women aged 16–59).

Source: Labour Force Survey, Summer 1999.

2.2 EMPLOYMENT, UNEMPLOYMENT AND UNDEREMPLOYMENT

2.2.1 The changing labour market

Understanding changes in women's labour market activity requires an understanding of changes that have affected the British labour market in recent years. In broad terms, the decline in the manufacturing sector has reduced employment for men more than for women and growth in service sector jobs has led to an increase in women's employment opportunities. The service sector now accounts for 76% of all employment (compared to 66% in 1983) and women occupy 57% of all service sector jobs.[4] By contrast, the share of jobs found in manufacturing now stands at 18% (having fallen from 25% in 1983), with the majority of these job losses concentrated among men (Table 2.6). One consequence of these changes in the structure of the economy is that much future labour market growth will be accounted for by jobs currently done by women. Projections suggest that 1.7 million new jobs will come into existence before 2011 of which an estimated 1.4 million will be taken by women (ONS 1998a).

---

[4] This calculation combines part-time and full-time employment. For further commentary, see Dex 1999.

Table 2.6: Labour market change (1983–1997)

	1983		1987		1997	
	% total employment	'000s	% total employment	'000s	% total employment	'000s
Manufacturing	24.5		22.3		18.0	
Men – all		3,862		3,547		2,880
Women – all		1,556		1,502		1,121
part-time		336		302		204
Services	65.8		69.2		76.0	
Men – all		6,110		6,379		7,197
Women – all		7,060		7,868		9,696
part-time		3,346		3,774		4,908
Public administration	7.1		6.8		5.9	
Men – all		835		831		658
Women – all		717		746		646
part-time		218		231		192
Total – %	97.4		98.3		100	
– 000s		20,572		21,080		22,236

Source: Dex 1999, derived from Employment Gazette, Historical Supplement June 1992 100 (6) Labour Market Trends, Feb 1998

Changes in the structure of the labour market have been accompanied by changes in the nature of paid work. The number of part-time jobs has grown as has the number of individuals working on temporary or casual contracts. Further, the notion of a normal working life extending from the age of leaving education to retirement age is changing. Extended periods in education are squeezing this norm from one end, low rates of labour market activity before retirement age is pushing it at the other.

2.2.2 Labour market activity

Figure 2.3 shows the narrowing differential in labour market activity rates for women and men since 1971. This narrowing has been driven slightly more by an increase in women's labour market activity than by a decrease in men's. For men, labour market activity rates have fallen from 91% in 1971, to 88% in 1985 and 84% in 1998. The equivalent rate for women stood at 57% in 1971 and, following a period of rapid growth in the 1980s (women's labour market activity rate increased from 63% in 1980 to 72% in 1990), has stabilised around that level in the 1990s, standing also at 72% in 1998.

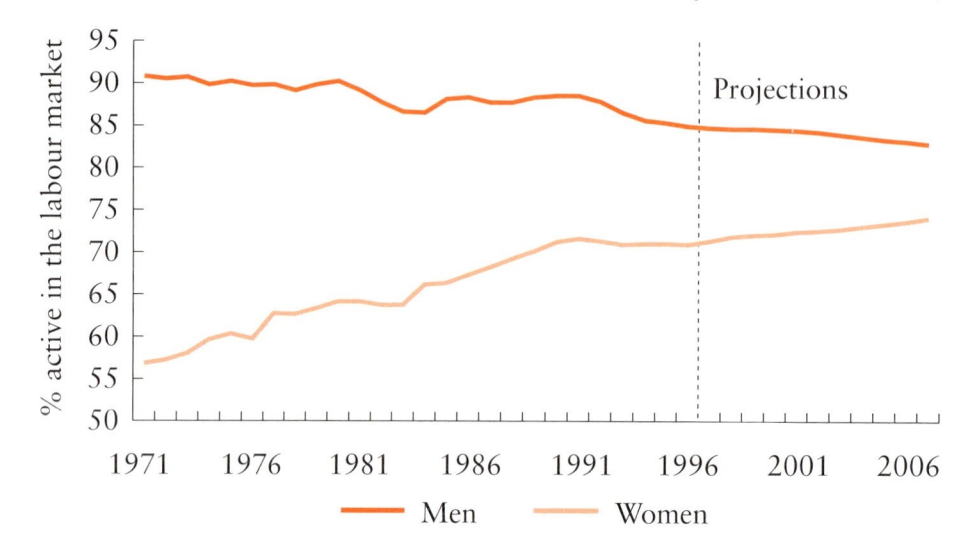

Figure 2.3: Women's and men's labour market activity rates (1971–2006)[1]

[Line chart showing % active in the labour market from 1971 to 2006, with Men declining from about 91% to 83% and Women rising from about 57% to 73%, with projections after 1996.]

Source: ONS 1997.

1 The definition of the labour force changed in 1984 when the former Great Britain civilian labour force definition was replaced by the ILO definition which excluded members of the armed forces.

Change in labour market activity rates has been greatest among mothers. The proportion of mothers employed full time has risen since the mid 1980s, notably those remaining continuously employed following maternity leave (Callender et al. 1997). The proportion of women who had been employed while pregnant who were actually in work nine months after the birth was 25% in 1979, 45% in 1988 and 68% in 1996, and the higher the level of qualification the more likely continuous employment. The key determinant of mothers' labour market activity is the age of their youngest child. Mothers with a child under five have the lowest economic activity rates (see Figure 2.2). However, since 1980, the proportion of British mothers of children under five who have paid work has seen a spectacular increase – from under one-third at the start of the 1980s to over one-half in the mid 1990s. The employment rates of mothers with a child under age 5 were 28% in 1979, 30% in 1985, 43% in 1991 and 53% in 1996/7 according to the General Household Survey. Rates of full-time employment have grown most among the group with the lowest base, mothers with a child under five, from 6% in 1979 to 16% in 1996/7.

While descriptions of labour market activity are very useful in tracing change over time, the raw labour market activity rate disguises a number of important features of women's work:

1. The exclusive association of economic activity with paid work overlooks the economic contribution made by those outside the paid labour force (see, for example, Murgatroyd and Neuberger 1997, Davies et al. 1999 and Jenkins and O'Leary 1996 and 1997). Time budgets show that men and women do about the same number of hours of total work, but that women do nearly twice as much unpaid domestic work as men. They take the major, though usually shared, responsibility for childrearing and most other household tasks. The categorisations of women bringing up children or caring for older relatives as 'economically inactive' contributes to the under-valuation of their unpaid work.

2. Those without paid work are categorised as economically active *only if* they meet the criteria for being classified as unemployed.[5] The notion of unemployment as a temporary break from an otherwise permanent labour market attachment is not suited to the chequered history of many women's lives and increasingly inappropriate for men's labour market activity also.[6] Women's caring responsibilities mean that they are less likely to be identified, or to identify themselves, as unemployed and hence end up in the catch-all category of 'economically inactive'. In the labour force statistics we find that the category of economically inactive contains individuals with widely different levels of labour market attachment. For example, in spring 1998, 1.4 million women (29% of those women classified as economically inactive) said they would like to work. For women with dependent children classified as economically inactive, 35% (854,000) said they would like to work. However, of these, only 6% were actively looking for a job. Of the remaining 800,000, nearly three-quarters described themselves as looking after the family/home, and of these, 60% had a child under 5 and a further 24% a child under 10 (Authors' calculation from Thair and Risdon 1999, Table N).[7]

---

[5] The use of claimant counts of the unemployed is known to be problematic for women – where there is little immediate pecuniary advantage for women to "sign on" as unemployed they are unlikely to do so. In recognition of this, Government statistics now use the International Labour Office definition of the unemployed where unemployment status is based upon meeting two criteria – being available to start work in the next two weeks and having actively looked for a job in the previous four weeks.

[6] In particular, growing numbers of men are spending extended periods out of the labour market prior to the official retirement age. For some, this is a period of high labour market attachment in which they are actively seek work, while others have effectively ceased labour market activity (Campbell 1999).

[7] The category 'economically inactive' also includes many men who would like to be in the labour market – 1 million men or 33% of men classified as economically inactive say they would like to work. Of these almost 13% are actively seeking work, and of the remaining 875,000 not searching for a job, only 8% describe themselves as looking after family/home (Authors' calculation from Thair and Risdon 1999, Table N).

3. Women's engagement in paid work takes a great variety of forms and differs from men's employment patterns on a number of dimensions (the next section considers these in detail). Accurately describing women's participation is therefore a complex task, and headline statistics on economic activity can hide as much as they reveal.

2.2.3 Types of paid work

In analysing gender differentials in paid work attention needs to be paid to:

- the number of hours performed and whether the job is considered part or full-time;

- the type of employment contract (permanent vs. temporary);

- the length of service with the employer;

- the type of employment undertaken (employed; self-employed etc.);

- the nature of the job (including occupational and industrial classification). This point is considered in Section 2.3.

Part-time and full-time work

Figure 2.4 shows trends in women's and men's full and part-time employment since 1987. In 1999, 43% of women's employment is accounted for by part-time work compared to just 8% for men. Since 1987, the increase in women's jobs has come in roughly equal numbers from full- and part-time jobs. While the number of part-time jobs for men has almost doubled over this period (with the number of full-time jobs fluctuating around the same level), for each man in part-time work in spring 1999 there were 4.2 women.

Figure 2.4: Women and men's full and part-time employment (1987–99)[1]

In employment ('000s)

	Women			Men	
1987	5,854	4,334	1987	13,407	635
1988	6,159	4,434	1988	13,865	675
1989	6,370	4,594	1989	14,253	649
1990	6,520	4,596	1990	14,294	723
1991	6,418	4,596	1991	13,861	732
1992	6,302	4,670	1992	13,200	817
1993	6,245	4,711	1993	12,910	867
1994	6,229	4,775	1994	12,948	955
1995	6,318	4,771	1995	13,104	979
1996	6,330	4,938	1996	13,109	1,071
1997	6,450	4,979	1997	13,297	1,151
1998	6,519	5,020	1998	13,471	1,159
1999	6,639	5,052	1999	13,551	1,190

■ Full-time   ▫ Part-time

1   Employment for women aged 16–59 and men aged 16–64. Numbers include all in employment who stated whether they work full- or part-time.

When taking a lifetime perspective, a further important gender differential emerges. The snapshot picture of part-time working among women and men of different age ranges given in Table 2.7 shows that for men part-time work is particularly concentrated among the young (many of whom will be students), while for women part-time working is common at much later ages as it allows women to accommodate caring responsibilities – three-fifths of employed women with children work part-time compared to a third of women without dependent children. Hence, 46% of part-time male employees are aged under 25, compared to 36% of female, and only 18% of part-time male employees are between the ages of 35 and 55, compared to 50% of female.

Women's propensity to work part-time is strongly affected by the age of their youngest child. In spring 1998, 50% of women whose youngest child was under 5 were in employment, of whom 65% were working part-time; for those with a youngest child aged 11–15, 74% were in employment of whom 53% were in part-time work (calculated from Thair and Risdon 1999, Table C).

Table 2.7: Employees who work part-time by age (1999)

United Kingdom	Percentages	
	Women	Men
16-19	9	32
20-24	5	14
25-34	20	11
35-44	28	9
45-54	22	9
55-59	8	7
60-64	4	8
65 and over	2	10
All aged 16 and over (=100%) (Millions)	4.9	1.1

Source: Labour Force Survey, Spring 1999, Office for National Statistics

Part-time work is often a long-term state for women, while for men it is frequently a stepping stone to full-time employment or a transitory stage prior to unemployment or early retirement. A study examining three consecutive waves of the British Household Panel Study found that on a year-on-year basis, 41% of men working part-time moved to full-time work while 19% moved to inactivity/unemployment. By contrast, only 12% of women working part-time moved to full-time work, while 10% became 'inactive'. Over the three year period, 15.6% of all women were in part-time work in all three years compared to under 1% of men (Booth, Garcia-Serrano and Jenkins 1996).

While the disaggregation of employment into part- and full-time work tells a very interesting story, it *still* may not be enough to capture the true extent of variation among women and between women and men. Classifications of part-time work are not objective, but based on a notion of 'normal' economic activity that may not reflect the norm for women, or increasingly for men. Statistical sources, such as the Labour Force Survey, traditionally classify full-time workers as those who work 31 or more hours per week, and part-time workers as those working fewer than 31 hours. In other countries the norms can be different. However, it may be more appropriate to think of working hours as a continuum – with jobs with 'long part-time hours' (e.g. 21–30) sharing more characteristics with full-time jobs than those with very short hours (e.g. under 20 hours). Table 2.8 shows the usual hours of employment of women and men and reveals that 8% of women work fewer than 10 hours per week and 26% fewer than 20 hours (compared to 5% of men). At the other end of the spectrum the prevalence of the 'long hours culture' is confirmed by the fact that the majority of men (56%) work 40 or more hours a week as do 20% of women. It is difficult to know what this distribution of hours signals about under-employment among women (or, indeed, over-employment among men) – 78% of women working part-time say they do so because they do not want a full-time job (this figure is 92% for women with dependent children working part-time) (Thair and Risdon 1999, Table H). Nevertheless, and crucially, current labour force data do not tell us whether individuals, particularly those on very short hours, would like to work longer part-time hours, or indeed whether those working very long hours would like to reduce their hourly burden. They also do not tell us about when the hours are worked nor whether the employee has any choice about when as well as how many hours to work.

Table 2.8: Usual weekly hours of work of employees[1] (1997–98)

United Kingdom	Percentages	
Hours per week	Women	Men
10 or fewer	8	2
11 to 20	18	3
21 to 30	16	2
31 to 40	38	35
41 to 50	16	39
51 to 60	3	14
Over 60	1	5
All employees	100	100

1 Women aged 16–59, men aged 16–64.
Source: Labour Force Survey, Winter 1997–98, Office for National Statistics.

Permanent and temporary work

A further important qualitative difference between women's and men's jobs is whether employment is on a permanent or temporary basis. There are currently more women employees on temporary contracts (872,000 compared to 722,000 men) and they account for just over 8% of all female employees. While the numbers and percentage of men on temporary contracts are lower overall, men have experienced a considerable increase in the prevalence of temporary work in the past 10 years. Temporary work accounts for over 40%

of the growth in the number of male employees since 1987 compared to just under 13% of the growth in female employees (calculated from Thair and Risdon 1999: Table A).

Length of service

Women's and men's experience of the labour market is clearly differentiated by the length of time they have spent with their current employer. Length of service with an employer gives some indication of labour market turnover and, for the individual, has a number of direct and indirect consequences for access to statutory and occupational benefits. Those with short job tenure may not meet the requirements for benefits (e.g. for Statutory Maternity Pay 26 weeks' continuous employment is needed to make a claim), and may be excluded from occupational benefits, such as membership of occupational pension schemes requiring a minimum number of years of service. Indirect costs also arise where chances of promotion and pay prospects are linked to an individual's length of service within the company – this is explored more fully in Section 2.3.2 below. As Figure 2.5 shows, 35% of female employees (and 39% of those with children under 5) compared to 30% of males have been with their employer for less than two years. Men are more than twice as likely to be with their employer for 20 years or more – almost 3 times as many male employees (2,095,000) fall into this category as female (733,000).

Figure 2.5: Length of time in current employment (1998)

Percent in employment

Women aged 16–59

| 6 | 20 | 19 | 20 | 13 | 22 |

Men aged 16–64

| 15 | 21 | 16 | 18 | 11 | 19 |

■ 0–11 months   □ 12–23 months   ■ 24–59 months
■ 60–119 months   ■ 120–239 months   □ >240 months

Source: Labour Force Survey, Spring 1998, Office for National Statistics.

Employment and self-employment

Women are much less likely to be self-employed than men – of women active in the labour market, 7% are self-employed compared to 14% of men, with men making up 74% of the total number of self-employed (Thair and Risdon 1999: Table A). The distribution of hours worked is slightly different for the self-employed – the proportion of men working very long hours is higher among the self-employed, while self-employed women have a greater tendency to work either very short or very long hours than female employees (ONS 1998a: 35).

Unemployment

As discussed above, measuring women's unemployment may be problematic. Nevertheless, comparing levels of unemployment reveals gender differentials both in the rate and duration of unemployment (the important differences in unemployment between women of different ethnic minority groups are discussed below). Overall women have lower rates of unemployment than men, and their unemployment tends to last a shorter period of time. In spring 1999, 3.8% of all working age women and 5.2% of those classified as economically active were unemployed; equivalent figures for men were 5.7% and 6.8%. Table 2.9 shows that 62% of the female unemployed had experienced unemployment for less than 6 months while 11% had more than 2 years of unemployment – for men the figures were 50% and 22% respectively.

Table 2.9: Unemployment[1] and duration of unemployment (1999)

	All women (000s)	per cent	All men (000s)	per cent
All ILO unemployed(=100 per cent)[a]	643	100	1,079	100
Duration of unemployment[b]				
Less than three months	277	43	335	31
Three months but less than six months	125	19	200	19
Six months but less than 12 months	104	16	169	16
One year but less than two years	66	10	141	13
One year or more	137	21	373	35
Two years or more	71	11	232	22

1 ILO unemployment for people of working age, not seasonally adjusted.
a Includes those who did not state their duration of unemployment.
b The shorter of time seeking work and time since last job.
Source: Labour Force Survey, Spring 1999, Office for National Statistics.

2.2.4 Employment and ethnic minority women

An important axis of variation among women is their ethnic origin. This affects employment and unemployment rates, as well as hourly pay (see below). The employment rate varies widely among ethnic minority groups, but the variation in employment rates is particularly wide for women (Sly et al. 1999). As Table 2.10 shows, the percentage of women active in the labour market varies from those with high levels of participation – 77% of women who classify themselves as Black, Other are active in the labour market as are 74% of White women and 72% of Black Caribbean women – to those with low levels of labour market activity – 20% of Bangladeshi women and 30% among Pakistani women.

Table 2.10: Economic status by sex and ethnic origin (1998–99)

	% active in the labour market[a]	% employed[a]	% unemployed[b]
Women			
White	74	70	5
All ethnic minority groups	56	49	12
Black[c]	68	58	14
Black Caribbean	72	63	12
Black African	59	49	16
Other Black[c]	77	66	*
Indian	61	56	9
Pakistani/Bangladeshi	27	22	21
Pakistani	30	25	18
Bangladeshi	20	14	*
All other groups	60	53	12
Chinese	59	54	*
Other/mixed origins[d]	61	53	13
Men			
White	80	75	6
All ethnic minority groups	66	57	13
Black[c]	73	62	15
Black Caribbean	76	66	13
Black African	68	57	16
Other Black[c]	78	63	19
Indian	71	65	9
Pakistani/Bangladeshi	50	40	19
Pakistani	51	42	18
Bangladeshi	46	36	22
All other groups	66	58	12
Chinese	59	55	8
Other/mixed origins[d]	68	59	13

Source: Sly et al. 1999, Table 1 (derived from the Labour Force Survey).
Notes: Figures are an average of summer 1998 to spring 1999.
* Annual estimates less than 6,000 are too small to be reliable and are excluded from the tables.
a Working age women (16–59) and men (16–64).
b ILO unemployment for all aged 16 and over.
c Excludes Black mixed.
d Includes Black mixed.

Rates of part-time working also vary across ethnic groups. A larger percentage of White women employees (43%) than Black women employees (31%) work part-time, with the highest rates of part-time employment being found among Pakistani women (52%). (Labour Force Survey, Summer 1999).

Of those that are classified as 'economically inactive' (see discussion above) there is a wide variation in the numbers who want a job – in 1997, more than two-fifths of Black women classified as economically inactive wanted to work, compared to less than a third of White women and less than one-sixth of Pakistani and Bangladeshi women (Labour Force Statistics, quoted in Sly et al. 1999). This reinforces the point made earlier that the category of "economic inactivity" may disguise variation among individuals with widely different attachments to the labour market.

A comparison of the labour market activity rate and employment rate shows us that the two rates are much closer for White women than women from all ethnic minority groups. This reflects the higher unemployment rates of women from ethnic minority groups, which stand at 21% for Pakistani and Bangladeshi women compared to just 5% for White women.

Figure 2.6: Employment and ILO unemployment rates for women by ethnic group (1984–99)

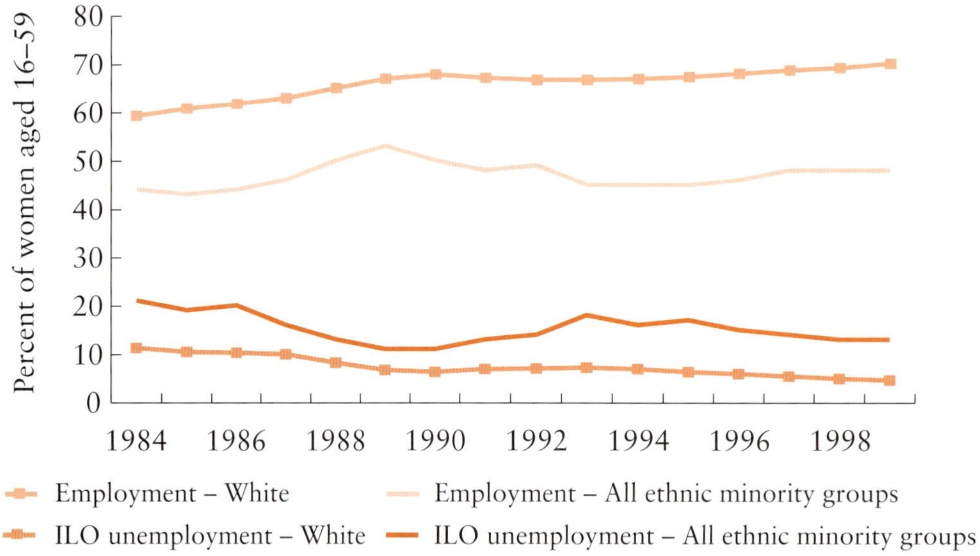

Note: Calculated for women of working age (16–59) in the spring of each year.
Source: Sly et al. 1999: Tables 3 and 4 (derived from the Labour Force Survey).

The experience of labour market change is also distinct for White women and those from ethnic minority groups (Figure 2.6). For women from all ethnic minority groups the employment rate has fluctuated around 48% since the early 1990s, but for White women the employment rate stood at 70% in 1999, three percentage points higher than it was in 1990. The unemployment rate for

White women has fallen steadily from 1984 (11.2%) to 1999 (4.6%), while that of women from all ethnic minority groups has been more sensitive to changing macro-economic conditions (although not as sensitive as the unemployment rate for men from ethnic minority groups). Thus, the unemployment rate fell from a high of 21% in 1984 to 11% in 1990. It then increased in the early 1990s (to 18% in 1993), but has fallen again to 13% in 1999. The unemployment rate for women from all ethnic minority groups was 2.8 times higher than that of White women in 1999.

2.2.5 Employment status and income

Figure 2.7 gives a cross-sectional picture of women's and men's individual gross incomes by employment status. As the figure demonstrates, in each employment status men's median income is higher. The gender gap in income is smallest among the unemployed and widest for the self-employed, with self-employed men having almost double the gross individual incomes of self-employed women.

Figure 2.7: Employment status and median gross individual income by sex (1996–97)

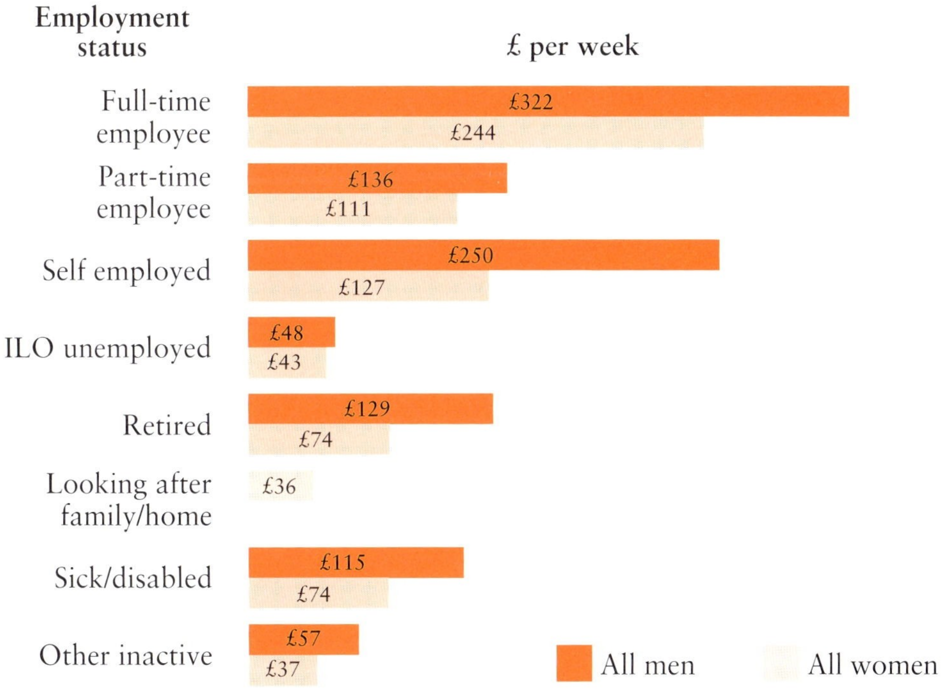

Employment status	All men (£ per week)	All women (£ per week)
Full-time employee	£322	£244
Part-time employee	£136	£111
Self employed	£250	£127
ILO unemployed	£48	£43
Retired	£129	£74
Looking after family/home		£36
Sick/disabled	£115	£74
Other inactive	£57	£37

Source: Women's Unit 1999, Figure 5.1.

2.3 JOB SEGREGATION

This section considers how the structure of the labour market affects gender inequality in earnings. The section examines the extent and impact of two forms of labour market segregation:

1. Where women and men are crowded into particular occupations they become sex-typed as 'women's jobs' and 'men's jobs'. For example, women account for 96% of those employed in secretarial occupations, while men constitute the same percentage of drivers and machine operators (Thair and Risdon 1999, Table I). This is referred to as occupational or horizontal segregation.

2. If within any occupation men and women reach different levels of seniority the occupation is segregated vertically. Blocks on women's promotion through 'glass ceilings' and the over-representation of women in the lowest level jobs ('sticky floors') are both examples of vertical segregation. To illustrate, evidence for the vertical segregation of teaching as a profession can be found in the fact that 88% of primary school teachers are women but only 55% of primary school headteachers are women.

3. The impact of both these forms of segregation on the gender differential in pay is examined below.

2.3.1 Men's jobs, women's jobs

The British labour market is far from unique in demonstrating high levels of occupational segregation. A wide range of measures have evolved to capture different aspects of the gendered structure of the labour market. One such measure is the concentration of women or men within an occupation and the ranking of occupations according to how 'feminised' or 'masculinised' their workforce is. A recent OECD study estimated that in 1995 60% of all British women were employed within the ten most feminised occupations[8] and within these occupations the workforce was 80% female (OECD 1998: 22 and Table A.1). Earlier analysis found that men experience higher levels of gender concentration in their workplace than women. In 1990 34% of males and 23% of females worked in establishments where they represented at least 75% of the workforce (Millward and Woodland 1995). The OECD study presents some evidence that occupational segregation has been falling over the last decade. However the process of desegregation may not be evenly spread across the labour market suggesting

---

[8] The top ten most feminised occupations were, in descending order of degree of feminisation: Sales assistants; Cleaners, domestics; Other secretaries, personal assistants; Other clerks; Accounts, wages clerks etc,; Nurses; Care assistants; Primary, nursery teachers; Counter clerks, cashiers; Retail cash-desk operators. (OECD 1998, Table B.1).

a further source of polarisation among women. High-level jobs are becoming increasingly open to women, at the same time as low-level, and particularly part-time jobs, are becoming increasingly segregated (Rubery and Fagan 1993; 1994).

Highly feminised occupations are distinct from the rest of the labour market in a number of respects:

- They have a higher than average share of part-time workers. 55% of the labour force in the top ten feminised occupations were working part-time compared to a UK average of 44%.

- Women working in highly feminised occupations experienced a higher than average wage shortfall.[9] For the UK, the wage ratio[10] was 57% for women employed part-time in the 'top ten', while for full-timers the ratio was 78%. This compares particularly poorly to women working outside the most feminised occupations who experienced a much smaller pay gap – 68% for part-timers and only 92% for full-timers (OECD 1998, Table 2.2).

Looking at average pay in feminised occupations is revealing, but this average may disguise a great deal of variation within these occupations. As Table 2.11 shows, although low-paid occupations tend to be highly feminised, there is no simple relationship between female concentration and low pay. Some high paid occupations contain significant percentages of female employees (e.g. health professionals) and some of the lowest-paid occupations are male dominated (e.g. agricultural jobs). Other low-paid jobs have varying degrees of female concentration (under two-thirds in catering compared to almost nine-tenths in hairdressing and related occupations). Some highly feminised occupations are high skilled and enable women to earn wages above the average for women (for example, teaching and nursing). Others are concentrated in the low-skilled sector and combine high levels of part-time work with wages considerably below average. For example, the OECD study found that in the UK 76% of sales/shop assistants were women and they earned 44.4% of average male wages (OECD 1998: Table 2.4).

This level of variation among highly feminised occupations suggests that while occupational segregation may exert a downward pressure on the wages of some

---

[9] There is evidence that men working in feminised occupations also experience a wage penalty – for example Millward and Woodland estimate that, compared to men working in male dominated sectors, men working in occupations where the workforce is over sixty per cent female experience a wage penalty of 24% (Millward and Woodland 1995).

[10] The wage ratio is female average hourly pay expressed as a percentage of male average hourly pay.

women, for others, segregation may protect women against competition from unemployed men and give them greater access to promotion. Further, while the extra pay penalty to working in a feminised occupation reflects the current reality of pay structures, desegregation no doubt would impact on pay structures – for example, the pay advantage that women currently experience by working outside the top ten feminised occupations might not persist if more women were to move into these occupations as the very process of 'feminisation' of an occupation can put a downward pressure on wages (see, for example, Rubery and Fagan 1993 and 1994; Bruegel 2000).

Table 2.11: Average hourly earning of full-time employees in highest/lowest paid occupations (1998)

	Pay (£)	Female % of employees
General managers – government, large organisations	20.21	34
Legal professionals	19.45	41
Health professionals	18.94	45
Specialist managers	18.88	32
Business and financial associate professionals	18.18	34
Other occupations in agriculture etc	5.15	22
Sales assistants and check-out operators	5.01	75
Catering occupations	4.94	63
Hairdressers, beauticians and related occupations	4.84	89
Other occupations in sales and services	4.72	74

Note: Data are shown at minor occupation group level. There may be some high/low paid occupations for which data are not available.
Source: EOC 1999a, derived from the New Earnings Survey, Table A12; Labour Force Survey, Spring 1998.

2.3.2 Glass ceilings and sticky floors

'Glass ceilings'

Unequal access to promotion, and unequal rewards to promotion, both affect women's earnings across their lifetime. It is difficult to demonstrate that women and men have differential access to promotion and to identify any blocks to career progression. However, recent qualitative research on the attitudes of line managers revealed surprisingly traditional attitudes towards the career ambitions of women and men, especially among older male managers (EOC 1999b). Statistics show that vertical segregation has lessened over time (and this has no doubt contributed to the diminution in the pay gap), but nevertheless remains a persistent feature of women's and men's working lives. In 1980 44% of women and 2% of married men had a female supervisor. By 1994 the figures were 50% of women and 10% of men (Martin and Roberts 1984, King et al. 1996).

A study of nursing looked in detail at the characteristics of women and men across nursing grades that affected promotion (Finlayson and Nazroo 1998).[11] The study found that the few men who entered this female-dominated occupation had a higher chance of promotion than women. For registered nurses the chances of being in Grades F/G (ward-based management posts) were similar for men and women. However, men were eighty per cent more likely to be in a grade H post and three times as likely to be in the top, grade I post (both H and I being non-ward based management) (Finlayson and Nazroo 1998: Table 2.2). Using more sophisticated modelling of the probability of promotion they found that if controls were entered for human capital factors traditionally thought to be associated with promotion (e.g. age, qualifications, years spent nursing etc.), they revealed that the probability of men being promoted increased. Comparing similarly qualified men and women, the probability of men reaching grade G was 1.54 times higher than it was for women, while men were almost six times as likely to reach the highest grade, I.[12] They also examined other explanatory factors such as career orientation to see if this gender differential was reduced. They found that career orientation was positively associated with grade, but it did not alter the differential between women and men in the chances of being at a higher grade.[13]

Another study of the pay effects of promotion looked across all occupations and had the advantage of using five years of data from the British Household Panel Study (Booth et al. 1998). While the study of women and men working full-time found that there was no differential in the rate at which women and men were promoted, the pay rewards to that promotion were distinct. Men who had been promoted received wages 20.4% higher than men who had not received

[11] The study was cross-sectional and although it asked some questions about work history – particularly about the timing and length of career breaks – it was not able to capture the impact of changes in an individual's characteristics on their promotion.

[12] As with all statistical estimates, their results are subject to error. Even when possible error is taken into account, men are between 3.8 and 8.7 times more likely to reach grade I and between 1.3 and 2.9 times more likely to reach grade H.

[13] Of interest to the discussion above of job segregation, an important factor that did reduce the gender differential was the speciality chosen within nursing. Within nursing, there is evidence of gender segregation as male nurses are much more likely to specialise in areas such as mental health while women are more likely to be in areas like obstetrics. The chances of career progression appear to vary between these specialisms, and this accounts for some of the differences between women and men (Finlayson and Nazroo 1998: Table 5.3).

promotion but the equivalent wage premium for women was 9.8% (less than half that of men). The study further found that while men continued to gain wage increases from the promotions they had experienced 3–5 years before, women did not. The cumulative effect of this differential is obviously large – if an identical man and woman experienced three promotions in a five year period, the man would experience real wage growth of almost 32% compared to only 7% for the woman (Booth et al. 1998: 21). Even with similar rates of promotion, the differential impact of promotion on wages will put an upward pressure on the pay gap between women and men.

'Sticky floors'

Women are at particular risk of getting stuck at the bottom of the pay distribution or in a 'low-pay, no-pay' cycle[14]. Further, and closely associated with this, a number of studies have identified the loss of promotional chances and/or experience of downward occupational mobility on returning to the labour market after having children (Brannen et al. 1997; Callender et al. 1997; Jacobs 1995, 1997 and 1999; Joshi and Hinde 1993; McRae 1991 and 1993; Blackwell 1998). The risk of downward occupational mobility is high for those who take part-time work when their children are young and particularly acute where finding this part-time work means a change of employer. There is evidence that the impact of childrearing on occupational mobility is decreasing over time as more recent cohorts of mothers are more likely to maintain full-time employment with the same employer. However, as the hypothetical illustrations in the remaining chapters demonstrate, this appears to be confined to women of higher educational attainment and is thus becoming a further source of polarisation among women.

Women have been found to remain for longer periods with very low pay. For example, McKnight et al. (1998) found that women were more likely to be in and remain in jobs where they earned below the National Insurance Lower Earnings Limit (McKnight et al. 1998; see also McKnight 1998). While studies that have focused just on wages have shown higher wage mobility among women (Gosling et al. 1997), analysing spells of no pay, low pay, and low pay-no pay cycles takes into account women's greater likelihood of spending time out of the labour market. For example, analysis of the Department of Social Security's Lifetime Labour Market Database reveals that in each of the five years between 1990-94, 13% of women experienced low-pay in every year, 14% no pay in every year and 22% of women experienced nothing other than low pay or no pay in each year. In each case the percentage of men affected was considerably lower, with the equivalent figures for men being 2%, 11% and 8% (Endean 1999: Table 1).

[14] Where individuals are caught in a revolving door of low-paid employment followed by unemployment or 'inactivity' rather than moving up the pay ladder.

2.4 THE CHANGING PAY GAP

One of the central issues differentiating women's from men's incomes is the gap between their hourly pay. Unequal pay may reinforce the domestic division of labour between men and women. For example, on the arrival of a new baby any consideration about who should take care of the child and whether a partner should leave paid employment or reduce their labour market participation may be influenced by the relative wages of the couple. Where they face traditional differences in pay (as many do – see below) the economic impetus will favour a traditional domestic division of labour, as any loss of wages from the lower earning woman will be felt less keenly than the loss of male wages. Hence, unequal pay affects wages directly and indirectly by influencing women's and men's labour market behaviour.

Inequality in pay may be generated by discrimination or by differences in the characteristics of male and female workers, including different levels of education and different labour market histories. A key issue explored below is the element of the pay gap that is not accounted for by differences in women's and men's characteristics (e.g. the gender gap) and the element that arises from women's experience of motherhood and the ensuing changes in labour market histories (e.g. the mother gap). These issues are explored below, and taken up again, using evidence from the simulation model, in Chapters 3 and 5.

2.4.1 The pay gap over time

It is a quarter of a century since Equal Pay legislation came into force. It appeared to make an impact at the time, but the trend towards closing the gap between men's pay and women's has been neither gradual nor complete. Changes in the pay gap need to be set in the context of the growth in wage inequality over the past 20 years (Harkness, 1996; Gosling et al. 1994; Goodman et al. 1997; Hills 1995). The changing structure of the labour market, de-regulation and a move away from centralised to individually negotiated and performance related pay and the privatisation of erstwhile public sector jobs have all contributed to this growth (Disney et al. 1998). Increasing wage inequality has a distinct effect on women's wages. On the one hand, increasing wage inequality reduces the relative earnings of those with below-average skills, and given women's concentration in this group, growth in wage inequality has had a disproportionately negative effect on women's wages. On the other hand, those women with above average skills are able to benefit from growth in wages. Thus, growing wage inequality is a force for polarisation among women as it is for the workforce as a whole (Harkness 1996; Blau and Kahn 1992).

Figure 2.8 covers both manual and non-manual hourly earnings, from a few years before the Equal Pay Act to 1999. After a peak at 74% in 1977, the ratio of women's and men's hourly pay at the median[15] for all full-time jobs has climbed more steadily, reaching 84% in 1999. We discuss the relativity for women in part-time jobs below.

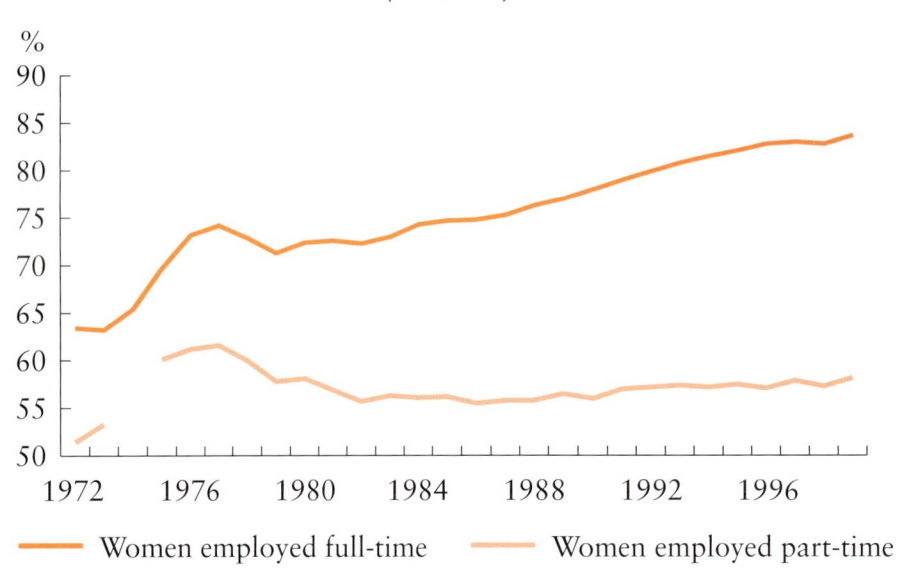

Figure 2.8: Women's hourly pay relative to men's full-time hourly pay (1972–99)

Source: New Earnings Survey.
Note: The calculations are based on median hourly earnings for women and men in all occupations. The ratio for part-time workers in 1974 is omitted because of a change in the way in which New Earnings Survey data were collected from that year onward.

Relative hourly pay of the two sexes in full-time work is not the same at all ages. The age profile of relative pay is shown in Figure 2.9 for 1976, 1986, 1996 and 1999. In all years, the pay gap widens for older workers. There was little change in this profile between 1976 and 1986, but in the decade from 1986 to 1996, relative pay improved for women under 40. The age group showing the biggest change since 1986 is the 25–29 group, whose wages in 1996 had reached 94% of their male contemporaries and 95% in 1999. Similar results are found for a sample of 26 year-olds in 1996 (Joshi and Paci 1997). For women aged over 40 relative pay remained the same or deteriorated between 1986 and 1996, but they seemed to have inched up lately, reaching 77% for women aged 40–49 in 1999. It remains to be seen whether, and how many of the more recent cohorts can carry their unprecedented pay advantages into middle age.

[15] In view of the skewness of the distribution of hourly pay, we prefer to use the median rather than the mean to represent the central tendency.

Figure 2.9: Women's hourly pay relative to men's, by age (1976–99)

[Chart showing women's hourly pay as percentage of men's across age groups 18–20 to 60–64 for years 1976, 1986, 1996, and 1999]

Source: New Earnings Survey. Calculations based on average hourly pay excluding overtime.

Part-timers, who account for a large minority of the employed women, face especially low wages.[16] In contrast to the converging gender rates among full-timers, the relative pay of female part-timers to male full-timers has fallen since the mid 1970s (see Figure 2.8). It stood at 58% in 1999 and much the same rate has held since the early 1980s. The gap between the median hourly pay of women employed full-time and women employed part-time actually grew wider: increasing from 74% in 1986 to 69% in 1999.

2.4.2 Pay by ethnicity

The pay of women and men varies by ethnicity. Table 2.12 shows that for all ethnic minority groups combined, men experience lower average rates of hourly pay than White men while women across ethnic minority groups have higher rates of hourly pay than White women. As a consequence, the hourly pay gap for all ethnic minority groups is narrower than it is for White women. However, the figure for all ethnic minority groups disguises important variations between different ethnic minorities. For example, women from the Indian sub-continent, particularly Pakistanis and Bangladeshis, earn lower than

---

[16] Since there are (or have been) so few males in part-time employment, the New Earnings Survey report on male wages is usually confined to males in full-time jobs. The New Earnings Survey data on female part-time earnings are not ideal, because those on very low earnings are incompletely captured in the sampling frame.

average hourly wages – £6.84 and £6.33 respectively compared to £7.50 for White women. Looking at the gender differential within ethnic minority groups, low wages among Pakistani and Bangladeshi men mean that gender differentials are narrow while higher than average wages for Indian men mean that this group experiences the largest gender differential in wages. Both Chinese men and women have a higher average hourly wage than White men and women and, interestingly, experience the lowest gender differential of any ethnic group. Black women experience higher hourly wages than all women, while lower than average wages among Black men mean a narrow gender differential in pay among this group also.

Table 2.12: Pay by ethnicity (1998–99)

Hourly pay of employees by sex, ethnic group and whether working full or part-time

	Full-time			Part-time	
	Men	Women	Relative pay[1]	Women	Relative pay[1]
All persons	9.27	7.51	81	5.74	62
White	9.29	7.50	81	5.73	62
All ethnic minority groups	8.66	7.66	89	5.91	68
Black (includes Black mixed)	8.25	7.78	94	6.06	74
Indian	9.34	6.84	73	5.82	62
Pakistani/Bangladeshi	6.87	6.33	92	5.48	80
Chinese/Other	9.62	8.81	92	5.96	62
– Chinese	9.66	9.42	98	6.81	71
– Other	9.61	8.61	90	5.70	59

1 Women's hourly pay relative to the hourly pay of men working full-time.
Source: ONS, Labour Force Survey. Four quarter average taken over Spring 1998 to Winter 1998–99. NB Ethnic minority data in this table are based on small samples and so should be treated with caution.

2.4.3 Pay differentials in England, Scotland and Wales

Pay differentials also vary by region – as Table 2.13 shows, the hourly, weekly and annual differences in women's and men's pay is slightly wider in Scotland than Britain as a whole, while lower men's wages in Wales mean that women experience a smaller pay gap than either Scotland or Britain as a whole.

Table 2.13: Average pay of full-time employees in England, Scotland and Wales, 1999

		Hourly	Weekly	Annual
England	Women	£8.80	£331	£16,706
	Men	£10.89	£448	£23,726
	Relative pay[1]	*81*	*74*	*70*
Scotland	Women	£8.03	£298	£15,001
	Men	£9.83	£406	£21,791
	Relative pay[1]	*82*	*73*	*69*
Wales	Women	£8.76	£298	£14,882
	Men	£9.22	£384	£19,901
	Relative pay[1]	*95*	*78*	*75*
Great Britain	Women	£8.70	£327	£16,481
	Men	£10.75	£442	£23,412
	Relative pay[1]	*81*	*74*	*70*

1 Women's hourly pay relative to men's.
Source: New Earnings Survey 1999. Table A19 and A20.

2.5 THE CAUSES OF THE PAY GAP

2.5.1 Differences in characteristics or differences in rewards?

One approach to the study of wages is to attribute differences in hourly pay to the observable characteristics of workers. This identifies determinants of a person's earning power in their educational level and length of employment experience (or human capital), and assesses the rate at which education and experience are rewarded. Where characteristics are rewarded differently, this is taken as evidence for unequal treatment or discrimination. Hence, the observed pay gap between men and women may be divided into the following elements:[17]

- differences in women's and men's characteristics which mean that the two groups are differently composed (e.g. men still have, on average, higher education than women and more experience);

and

- differences in the rates at which such attributes are rewarded (i.e. unequal treatment).

Because women's pay is so different in the part-time sector, attempts to explain the factors underlying unequal pay need to consider the full- and part-time wage

---

[17] The method for decomposing the pay gap into these two components is explained in Appendix I.

separately. People in part-time jobs receive a lower hourly wage than workers in full-time jobs who have identical measurable characteristics. We refer to this as the 'part-time penalty'.

The data we use here[18] are from the period after the Equal Pay Act, when the relative wage in full-time employment was rising, the relative wage of female part-timers was stagnating or falling, and the composition of the female workforce was changing in favour of full-timers. Figure 2.10 summarises these results, which are given in greater detail in Appendix I. Other estimates of wage functions are also available;[19] for the most part these use data for earlier years than we discuss here.

The estimates of discrimination amongst full-timers are depicted (measured in logarithms in part (a) of the figure) on the left-hand side of each stack. They can also be expressed as the proportion by which the average woman's pay would rise if she were paid at men's rates (shown in part (b) of the figure). Thus, a 32 year old in 1978 would expect to see her wages rise by 24% if she were paid the same as an identically qualified man while a 33 year old in 1991 would expect a rise of 17%. For married women of all ages, the equivalent rise would be of the order of 19% in 1980 and in 9% in 1994. The figure shows that differences in human capital (right-hand side of stack) have dwindled for persons in their early thirties (but remain similar for the samples of married/partnered). This is a result of a narrowing in differences between women's and men's employment experience and their educational attainment. Part (b) of the figure shows that, whereas in 1980 over 40% of the raw gender pay gap for employed married men and women could be attributed to discrimination in full-time jobs, by 1994 this had fallen to under a quarter.[20] These analyses all imply that despite the changes associated with the Equal Pay Act a considerable degree of pay discrimination has remained.[21] Underlying these analyses is also a measure of the penalty to part-time employment. In

---

[18] We use data for 1978 and 1991 from the National Birth Cohort Studies for men and women at a particular age, and for adults of all working ages from the 1980 Women in Employment Survey and the 1994 wave of the British Household Panel Study.

[19] Other recent estimates of earning functions include Miller (1988), Wright and Ermisch (1991), Harkness (1996) and Blackaby et al (1997). The estimates we obtained using BHPS data for 1994 (Davies et al. 1997) are rather different from those obtained with the 1992 BHPS data by Harkness (1996), but are very similar to those she obtained from the 1994 BHPS (seminar presentation, City University, April 1997).

[20] The 1994 figures refer to partnered men and women.

[21] Zabalza and Arrufat (1985) reached a different conclusion: that the pay gap remaining after the Equal Pay Act was largely attributable to women's greater 'home time', but this has not been confirmed in subsequent studies. The interpretation of unequal remuneration as discrimination rests upon the defensible assumption that there is no systematic bias in favour of males in all the relevant attributes which we are unable to measure.

1980 the part-time penalty lowered the average pay of all married part-timers by 16%; in 1994 this had increased to 35%. For partnered women, and all part-timers, the analysis also shows that the payoff to accumulating employment experience has risen a little in women's wages in full-time work. These widening disparities among women need to be seen as part of the increase in wage dispersion in a less regulated labour market.

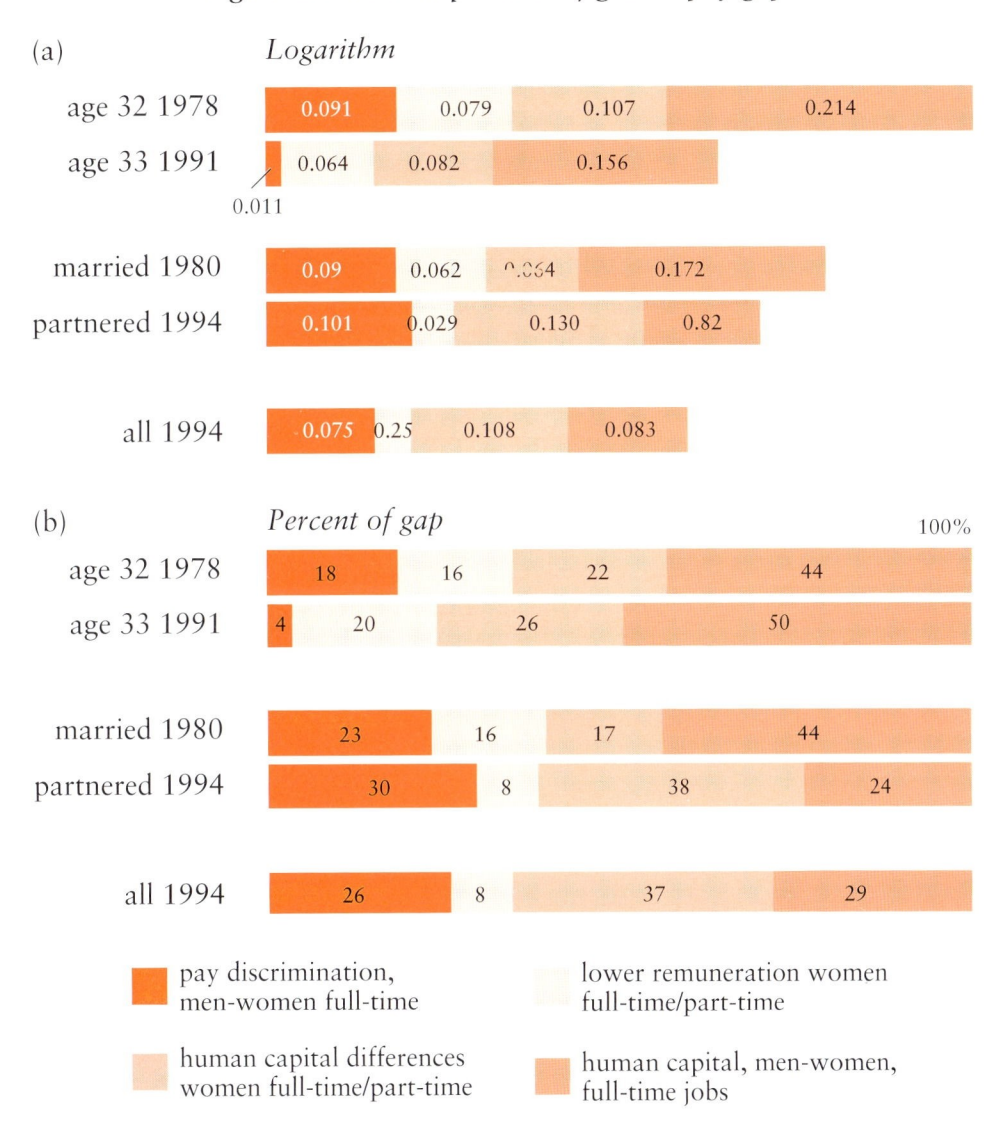

Figure 2.10: Decomposition of gender pay gaps

(a) *Logarithm*

age 32 1978	0.091	0.079	0.107	0.214
age 33 1991	0.011	0.064	0.082	0.156
married 1980	0.09	0.062	0.064	0.172
partnered 1994	0.101	0.029	0.130	0.82
all 1994	0.075	0.25	0.108	0.083

(b) *Percent of gap* 100%

age 32 1978	18	16	22	44
age 33 1991	4	20	26	50
married 1980	23	16	17	44
partnered 1994	30	8	38	24
all 1994	26	8	37	29

- ■ pay discrimination, men-women full-time
- ▫ lower remuneration women full-time/part-time
- ▪ human capital differences women full-time/part-time
- ▪ human capital, men-women, full-time jobs

Sources: *Cohort Studies:* Joshi and Paci (1998). Sample contains workers of the specified ages only. *Women and Employment Survey:* Ermisch and Wright (1992). Sample of married women under 60 and their spouses. *British Household Panel Study:* Davies et al. (1997). Samples covers all working ages, and not just those with partners.

The low pay of part-timers is linked to their relatively low human capital and to structural features of the labour market. Part-time workers are more concentrated in small firms, within certain, predominantly private sector, industries where the workforce is frequently highly feminised (see discussion above) and less likely to have union coverage – all these factors contribute to the lower pay of part-time workers (Paci et al 1995). Furthermore, part-timers may not find that it pays them to travel more than a short distance to work. They may therefore suffer a lack of bargaining power in the face of labour monopsony[22] (Joshi and Paci 1998). The hypothesis that the domestic responsibilities of part-timers accounted for their low pay was investigated by Joshi et al. (1999a). They found that among the sample of 33 year olds in 1991, domestic responsibilities did not account for the low pay of part-timers, as motherhood was not necessarily penalised in the pay of all full-timers, and part-timers suffered pay penalties even if they did not have children.

2.5.2 Motherhood as a source of low pay

It is often suggested that Equal Pay policy cannot eliminate gender differences in pay, because women with family responsibilities will continue to receive less. Current family responsibilities might reduce pay for a number of reasons: less effort or more fatigue, restricted choice of jobs within a travelling time consistent with other obligations, employee preference for flexible features of job contracts, employer preference for unencumbered employees, less interest in promotion or time for training, for example. There is also the effect of less past work experience, and a possible spurious correlation between low pay and motherhood if less skilled women are more likely to be mothers (as is the case in samples of women in their early thirties). We here explore evidence of how far motherhood, rather than gender *per se*, is a source of the pay gap (this issue is picked up again in Chapters 3 and 5, particularly Section 5.4).

The wages of women with and without children in two birth Cohort Studies[23] were analysed by Joshi and Paci (1998) using a method similar to the analysis of men and women. Mothers aged 26 in 1972, aged 32 in 1978 and 33 in 1991 would all have been paid about 20% more if there were no direct pay penalties to motherhood. This would mean no lower employment experience, no greater chance of part-time employment and, explicitly in the study of the earlier cohort, no job downgrading on return to the labour market. Analysis of the 1991 data revealed that the pay consequences of motherhood (20%) were

---

[22] Monopsony – literally "single buyer". Manning (1996) suggests that monopsony applies to women's low wages generally.

[23] The MRC National Survey of Health and Development (MRC) and the National Child Development Study (NCDS) are national longitudinal surveys which have followed up everyone born in a week of March 1946 (MRC) and March 1958 (NCDS).

about as great as the gender penalty on mother's wage rates (what mothers would receive if paid as men: 22%). At the earlier dates the gender penalty had been even more important: in 1972 (before the Equal Pay Act) it was 76%, though it had declined to 34% in 1978. Thus the gender penalty had fallen, but still remained important, but the pay penalties of motherhood seemed unchanged.

The 'fatigue' hypothesis suggests that motherhood leads to lower productivity and as a consequence women shouldering a 'double burden' are paid lower wages. The hypothesis implies that there would be a direct effect of family responsibilities on wages, even after human capital and the part-time nature of many mothers' jobs had been taken into account. However, Joshi and Paci's analysis of the 1991 data showed no evidence for this, nor for the notion suggested by Becker (1991) and Hakim (1996), for example, that mothers who chose part-time jobs are of a selectively uncommitted type with low productivity. What the analysis did clearly show was that the part-time pay penalty was a growing component of the low pay of mothers, just as it is of the low pay of women as a whole. Although Joshi and Paci could not rigorously distinguish the reasons for low pay in part-time jobs, the notion that low pay was a result of asymmetrical bargaining power between employer and employee was consistent with the fact that part-time jobs tend to be in smaller firms, nearer home and less unionised (Joshi and Paci 1998).

Joshi and Paci also investigated whether mothers who had gone back to work within a year of their first giving birth (which, in the majority of cases, would be a return to the same employer) after their (presumed) statutory maternity leave were paid better than other mothers.[24] The 1991 data revealed that if employed full-time, the 'maternity leavers' benefited from a premium, leaving them as well paid as childless women with the same human capital, and better paid than other mothers. Mothers who interrupted their careers were penalised. This might reflect the direct impact of a change of employer, lower training, a lower chance of promotion, or poorer job match in the labour market. The analysis showed that there is a pay penalty to motherhood amongst otherwise identical full-timers which only affected those who did not maintain continuous employment over their first child's birth. The analysis suggests that the pay penalty to motherhood was becoming diversified, worse for some, less for the better-qualified women on a career track. However, this is not to say that childless women (and women who took maternity leave) are treated like men as they continue to experience a gender penalty in pay.

---

[24] See also Joshi et al (1999a), Joshi, Dex and Macran (1996), and Dex et al. (1998), show that the women with minimal employment breaks at the time of their first birth had stronger labour force attachment thereafter.

In sum, when all else is held constant, motherhood *in and of itself* does not appear to lead to one woman being much worse paid than another with no children. However, where motherhood reduces a woman's employment experience or puts her in the part-time sector, a pay penalty follows. The pay gap experienced by mothers is affected by changes that are pushing the pay gap in opposite directions. On the one hand, the penalty to part-time work is growing. On the other, employment breaks following childbirth are becoming less common and, where taken, are becoming shorter.

In the simulation model used later in this report, the pay consequences of motherhood are expressed in a separate pay equation for part-time work, and in the link between current pay and past experience, which is affected by family building. Job downgrading on return to the labour market is not modelled explicitly, but is implicitly captured by the drop in pay from full-time to part-time within a skill level (see Sections 3.4 and 5.2).

2.6 CHANGING EARNINGS AND CHANGING INCOMES

Our focus above on hourly pay reflects concern with equality of opportunity in the labour market for women and men. However, hourly pay does not tell us about equality of outcome. Weekly or annual earnings give us a clearer picture of an individual's returns from their labour market participation and, in addition, determine the relative share of partners in a couple's earnings, giving us some measure of the inequality that may exist within the household. The gap between men's and women's weekly earnings is bigger than that in hourly pay, because male full-timers work longer hours on average than female full-timers. According to the New Earnings Survey the ratio of average (mean) hourly pay of full-timers (over 21) rose from 75% in 1976 to 80% in 1996 and 82% in 1999. However, the ratio of average (mean) weekly earnings rose from 66% in 1976 to 73% in 1996 and 74% in 1999. The ratio of weekly earnings is consistently, and considerably, lower than that of hourly pay.

Alternative estimates of men's and women's wages can be drawn from household surveys, averaging all women's pay across full-timers and part-timers. Estimates from the Family Expenditure Survey (FES) show that women's hourly pay was around 60% of men's at the end of the 1960s, when there were relatively few part-timers, and there was not much of a pay penalty for working part-time. By 1977 the ratio had risen to 70% after which the gap opened again with the ratio standing at 67% in both 1986 and 1990 (Davies and Joshi 1997). This is shown in the final row of Table 2.14.

Table 2.14: The sex composition of employment and earnings (1968–90)

	1968	1977	1983	1986	1990
Percent of:					
All employees who are female	37	42	44	45	48
All earnings earned by females	20	26	27	28	31
Paid hours done by females	29	33	36	37	40
Ratio of women's to men's pay (percentage)					
Per week	42	47	46	48	48
Per hour	60	70	66	67	67

Notes: Self-employed excluded.
Source: Family Expenditure Survey, analysed by Davies and Joshi (1998).

Table 2.14 shows that although women increased as a proportion of employees from 37% in 1968 to 48% in 1990 (just over one-third to nearly one-half), their share in earnings remained well below their share of employment, rising from 20% to 31%. In 1990 women were nearly half the workforce but received less than one-third of the earnings. This imbalance in men's share of paid work mirrors their minor share of unpaid work (as noted above).

When we come to look at the earnings and incomes of men and women in couples it is not surprising to find that women are the minor earners on average. The proportion of couples' joint gross earnings brought in by the woman showed some increase in the 1970s and then stabilised around 30% in the 1980s (Family Expenditure Survey figures quoted in Joshi 1989). For two earner couples where the woman is aged 24–55, women's share of joint earnings was 28% in 1970–81 and 31% in 1989–91 (Harkness et al. 1996). The proportion of couples where the woman earns more than her partner remains low, but has risen from 7% in 1980 to 18% in 1996-7.[25] In 7% of the 1996–7 sample the partners earned within 5% of each other, and in 75% of cases, as is traditional, the woman earned less. Similar patterns of asymmetry in couples' incomes were apparent in a study of 33 year old women in 1991, where 10% of the women earned at least 55% of joint income, 12% earned 45-54%, and 78% were clearly minor contributors (Joshi et al. 1995). What this reveals is that if we assume that couples share their incomes, the majority of women in couples can be presumed to be, at least partly, financially dependent on their partner's wages.

---

[25] The 1980 figure comes from WES (Martin and Roberts, 1984: 99), the later number from Family Resources Survey, quoted in Table 4.8, ONS 1998a.

2.7 CONCLUSIONS AND KEY FINDINGS

This chapter has reviewed the literature and current empirical evidence on gender differentials in paid work. A picture of narrowing, but still persistent, gender differentials has emerged on a number of levels:

- Despite overall improvements in women's educational attainment, differences in the subjects studied persist. Given the impact of occupational segregation on wages, there are important consequences of educational choices on future career and lifetime earnings.

- There is considerable differentiation *among* women in their experience of paid employment, with educational attainment having a strong influence on labour market activity. For example, in 1998, 76% of mothers with a child under five and qualifications of A level equivalent or above were active in the labour market compared to just 27% of mothers without qualifications.

- Ethnicity is another important dimension of variation among women. Women from ethnic minority groups experience lower rates of employment and lower rates of hourly pay. However, there is enormous variation between women from different ethnic minorities. 20% of Bangladeshi women and 30% of Pakistani women are classified as active in the labour market with full-timers (averaged across both groups) earning £6.33 an hour (£1.20 less than the average for White women). By contrast, 72% of Black Caribbean women are classified as economically active, and average pay for all Black women working full-time is £7.78. For White women, high employment rates are matched by low unemployment rates (4.6% in 1999) while women from all ethnic minority groups experience higher levels of unemployment (13% for all ethnic minority groups, and 21% for Pakistani and Bangladeshi women).

- Despite the dramatic changes in women's employment over the past 30 or so years, women's rates of labour market activity remain lower than men's (respectively 72% and 84% in spring 1999), and they remain employed in different types of jobs – for example, for each man in part-time employment there are 4.2 women.

- Occupational segregation has decreased over time, yet it remains an important feature of the British labour market: 60% of all British women work in ten occupations within which the workforce is 80% female.

- Although high-skilled women increasingly have access to desegregated occupations, many women (especially those working part-time) remain in highly feminised occupations, which attract lower pay and have higher rates of part-time working.

- The association of feminised occupations and low wages is strong (although not universal). The gender ratio of wages in the 'top ten' feminised occupations was 78.4% for women working full-time (59.6% for part-timers) while women outside these occupations earned 92.0% of the average male wage (67.8% for part-timers). Part-time jobs, in particular, are both highly feminised and low paid.

- The link between part-time jobs and low pay and the concentration of part-time work in low-skilled occupations is both a reflection of the quality of these jobs and of the fact that there are limited opportunities available to work part-time in higher grade occupations.

- Women continue to experience restricted access to promotion (the 'glass ceiling' effect) and tend to be over-represented at the bottom of the occupational ladder (the 'sticky floor'). For example, men were almost six times as likely to reach the highest nursing grade as similarly qualified women. This evidence, in combination with the traditional attitudes that prevail among many line managers, suggests that we cannot rule out the contribution that discrimination, however unknowing, continues to make to vertical segregation.

- Men appear to reap greater pay rewards from promotion. One estimate suggests that if an otherwise identical man and woman were to experience three promotions over a five year period, the man's wage would be raised by about a third, while the woman would experience a pay increase of less than ten per cent.

- Since the Equal Pay Act, the gap between the hourly wages of men and women working full-time has narrowed (although change in recent years has been slow) but for women working part-time, the pay gap has remained unchanged since the early 1980s, and is now wider than it was in the mid 1970s. Younger cohorts of women appear to be experiencing a narrower pay gap.

- The percentage of the pay gap attributable to discrimination has fallen for those employed full-time. The proportion of the pay gap attributable to discrimination was estimated to be 40% in 1980 and 25% in 1994. However, in the same period the part-time penalty has increased. In 1980, working part-time lowered average wages by 16%, but by 1994 this penalty had more than doubled to 34%.

- Although the gender pay penalty has narrowed over time, pay penalties associated with motherhood have remained more or less constant over the past twenty years, and stand at around 20% of average wages.

- The fact that women spend fewer hours in the labour market, in combination with their lower wages, means that the increases in women's share of employment are not matched by an equivalent increase in the share of earnings. For example, the proportion of employees who were female grew from 37% in 1968 to 48% in 1990, while the proportion of all earnings earned by women rose from 20% to 31%.

In the following chapters, we will use the tool of our simulation model to explore how the advantages and disadvantages within the British labour market translate into lifetime incomes, and periods of dependency on either family or state.

3. WOMEN'S INCOMES OVER THE LIFETIME

3. WOMEN'S INCOMES OVER THE LIFETIME

This chapter presents the simulation model of women's lifetime incomes that informs the remainder of this report and presents findings for the standard cases used in the model. Section 3.1 reviews the methods and assumptions employed in building the simulation model, and reflects on how closely these match the actual experiences of women in contemporary Britain. The hypothetical lifetime biographies of women of three different educational levels are presented. The lifetime labour market participation and earnings of the women provide the focus of Section 3.2, and allow us to reflect on the differences in labour market participation and lifetime earnings of women of different skill levels. Section 3.3 examines how the tax-benefit system affects the incomes of these women across their lifetimes. In Section 3.4 an estimation is made of the absolute and relative lifetime costs of the gender pay gap and the consequences this has for women's share of family earnings.

3.1 SIMULATING LIFETIME INCOMES – METHODS AND ASSUMPTIONS

3.1.1 Why use a hypothetical model of lifetime income?

There is no empirical data source which tracks the incomes of individuals in Britain over their whole lifetime.[26] Even if we had a source of complete

[26] The General Household Survey, Family Expenditure Survey and Family Resources Survey have extensive data on income and other variables, but they are cross-sectional surveys, with information about the sampled individuals and households in only one year. The Department of Social Security's Lifetime Labour Market Database does have information on the earnings history of individuals (from administrative records) but this is only available for earnings above the Lower Earnings Limit for National Insurance for a limited number of years. Furthermore, this dataset lacks information on other variables of great interest – especially education, fertility and partnership. The ONS Longitudinal Study contains much interesting data on individuals, potentially over a thirty-year period, but it has no data on income. Britain has an extraordinarily valuable longitudinal data resource in its Birth Cohort Studies, (MRC 1946 Cohort, NCDS, BCS70) but these are not suitable for our purposes either. They relate only to relatively young people. Since all the members of a cohort are of the same age, and since successive waves of the surveys are separated by several years, they do not enable us (yet) to build up a good picture of the relationship between age and income. Lastly, the British Household Panel Study (BHPS) enables incomes to be tracked for a few years, but collecting complete lifetime histories from this source would require waiting for many years, by which time the information from the early years would be rather out of date.

life histories of individuals, giving their education, employment, earning, fertility and partnership histories, this would still not present us with complete answers. By its nature, such a source would be retrospective and the data on the early years of people now in their sixties and above would relate to the circumstances of thirty or more years ago. Valuable though such a data source might be, our purpose here is prospective not retrospective. We are more interested in looking at the income prospects of today's younger generations than in looking backwards at the history of older generations. No dataset could, on its own, give us such information directly. To trace out likely trajectories of income over the lifecycle requires modelling, rather than merely description of the data. Here we use a simulation model to construct earnings and incomes of hypothetical, stylised individuals. We do not neglect the data, however. The simulation model is constructed around evidence on individual's behaviour, and other data inform our choice of stylised biographies for the simulation.

3.1.2 The development of the simulation model

The simulation model used in this report is developed from a previous model that drew its data from 1980. Data on the lives and employment of British women in 1980 revealed several important relationships. Motherhood reduced women's participation in the labour market and often confined their hours of work to part-time jobs. Hourly pay was lower in part-time jobs and lower for those with interrupted employment than those with a more continuous work history. Over a lifetime, therefore, mothers would earn less than childless women through having fewer years of earnings, lower hours of work when employed and lower rates of pay. Estimates were made of the forgone earnings of a hypothetical mother with various numbers of children (Joshi 1990).
On this reckoning, the typical mother of two children earned only about half as much as her counterfactual earnings from the age of childbearing to retirement, the missing half representing the earnings opportunity cost of motherhood.

The models were subsequently elaborated to look at women with a range of educational levels, to simulate taxes, pensions and their contributions, and the pooling of net income costs with a spouse. They were applied to the economics of fertility, of divorce and of daycare. They were also compared with analogous simulations for other European countries (Joshi, Davies and Land 1996 summarises a number of other papers including Davies and Joshi 1992, 1994a, and 1995, and Joshi and Davies 1992).

In the earlier model, the central case of a British mother with middle-level qualifications – 'Mrs Typical' – did not appear to be typical across countries (according to retrospective data for 12 European countries collected by Kempeneers and Lelievre, 1991). Her earnings profile was similar to those for West Germany and the Netherlands, and to that of lower skilled women in France and Britain, but much more disrupted than those of her Swedish counterpart, of women in France with a high initial labour force attachment, and of graduates in Britain. The latter all achieved greater if not complete employment continuity, presumably facilitated by maternity leave, public or private daycare and other supportive policies.

The lifetimes simulated in all this previous work take place in a time warp where the participation, hours and pay parameters observed in 1980 are frozen in perpetuity. The present report brings this story up to date. As in previous work, we here adopt the device of calculating income profiles for illustrative hypothetical individuals. We synthesise hypothetical, simplified biographies for hypothetical characters set in a simplified world in hypothetical time. The individuals are case studies, representing people with the specified features. They are not an average over the many types of person in the real world, nor are their lives as complicated as any real person's would be. These are stereotypical distillations of reality, upon which they throw back some light.

3.1.3 The components of the model

Our model has several components which we now discuss. The elements which go into the calculation of an individual's own income are represented schematically in Figure 3.1 (we also model the potential sharing of household income – this is fully discussed in Chapter 4).

To begin the modelling process we first specify characteristics of the hypothetical individuals – for example, their levels of education, the age at which they marry, the education of their spouses and the ages at which they bear children. Next, using statistical relationships estimated from 1994 BHPS data[27] we predict labour market participation and wages for these hypothetical people for each year of their lifetime. The underlying equations allow for feedback from previous labour market experience and, for women, for the impact of husbands' earnings on their own participation and earnings. At this stage we constructed a profile of each person's gross earnings for each year of their working life. We then make assumptions about the pension scheme membership of each of our hypothetical people, and thus use the earnings to model pension contributions and receipts. Modules for income tax, National Insurance Contributions (NICs) and the main Social Security benefits, enable us to extend the model from earnings to both gross income (including pensions and state benefits) and net income (deducting Income Tax and NICs from gross income).

[27] The timescale of this project precluded re-estimation of our equations with more recent data.

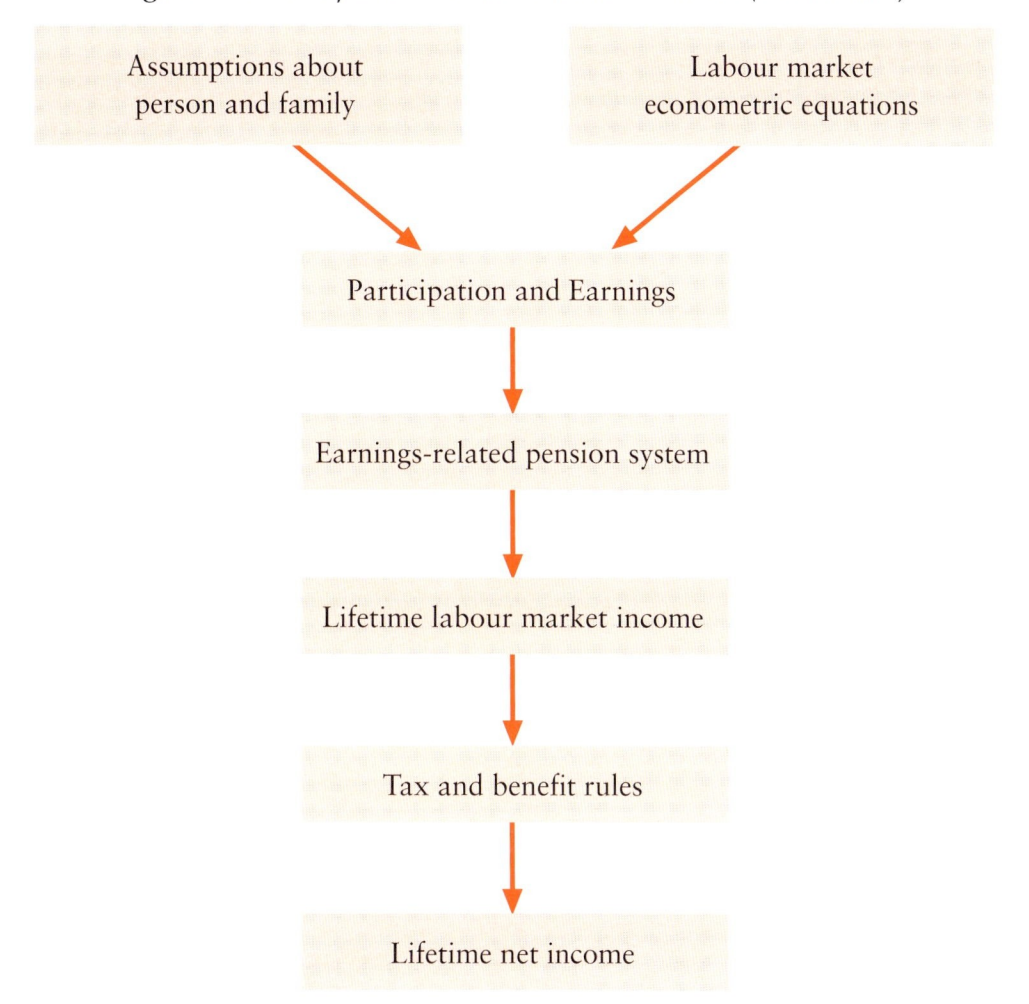

Figure 3.1: The lifetime income simulation model (individuals)

```
┌─────────────────────┐      ┌─────────────────────┐
│  Assumptions about  │      │    Labour market    │
│  person and family  │      │ econometric equations│
└──────────┬──────────┘      └──────────┬──────────┘
           │                            │
           └─────────────┬──────────────┘
                         ▼
              ┌─────────────────────┐
              │ Participation and Earnings │
              └──────────┬──────────┘
                         ▼
              ┌─────────────────────┐
              │ Earnings-related pension system │
              └──────────┬──────────┘
                         ▼
              ┌─────────────────────┐
              │ Lifetime labour market income │
              └──────────┬──────────┘
                         ▼
              ┌─────────────────────┐
              │   Tax and benefit rules   │
              └──────────┬──────────┘
                         ▼
              ┌─────────────────────┐
              │   Lifetime net income   │
              └─────────────────────┘
```

It is important to realise that the projected lifetime incomes produced by the model are not forecasts. To keep matters simple, it is assumed that there is no economic growth, no inflation and personal saving outside pensions. Earning levels are calibrated to 1999 levels, with assumed rules for tax, benefit and pension schemes, with the exceptions discussed below, being those facing someone entering the labour market in April 1999. The simulations take into account a number of new pieces of legislation – the Working Families' Tax Credit introduced in Autumn 1999, the Children's Tax Credit due to come into being in April 2001, pension sharing after divorce,[28] child support payments according to the new rules set out in the July 1999 White Paper, and the

---

[28] Provision for pension sharing was set out in the 'Welfare Reform and Pensions Act'. Draft regulations were under consultation of the time of going to press.

equalisation of the pension age to 65 that will only come fully into force in 2020 (for details see Appendix II).

While the personal profiles of the hypothetical people are chosen so as to reflect recent social and demographic trends, they are also designed to capture a wide range of family histories and socio-economic circumstances. A key feature of the model is that it allows for family building scenarios which are differentiated by socio-economic group or skill level.

3.1.4 The hypothetical individuals

The simulation allows for three occupational levels, determined by educational attainment. At each of these levels, we construct a number of hypothetical women, distinguished by their marital and fertility histories.

- Our central figure, "Mrs Mid", has some schooling beyond the minimum (O levels or GCSE equivalent) and works in a clerical occupation: think of her as a secretary.

- We compare her with a graduate, "Mrs High", who is perhaps a teacher.

- Finally, "Mrs Low" left school with no qualifications and takes only low-skill jobs, such as a shop assistant.

The model allows us to simulate different fertility histories for each type of woman. The age at marriage and at childbirth varies with the woman's occupational level – the more highly qualified the woman, the older she is assumed to be when she marries and has children. We assume that our hypothetical women marry men of the same educational level.

The emphasis on equally educationally matched couples is broadly supported by GHS data for 1996 (ONS 1998b: Table 7.5). This shows that more men and women have partners of similar qualification level than of different educational attainment. Also, a wide sample of partnered women from the 1994 British Household Panel Study (see Table 3.1) showed that about half had the same educational level as their partners, and in 30% of cases the men were more highly qualified than the women. Where the women were under 35, almost as many of them (25%) had the higher qualification in the couple as vice versa. Cases where the woman is more qualified than her husband are thus no longer rare.[29] Among the equally matched couples where the woman was under 35,

---

[29] Lifetime simulations for educationally mixed couples were also produced as part of the research, but constraints on space mean that we do not present the findings for these couples here.

about two-fifths had high (post-school) qualifications and a similar proportion had mid ('O' and 'A' level) qualifications. About one-fifth of these couples had low or no qualifications.

Table 3.1: The educational levels of women and men in couples (1994)

All couples

Man's educational level	Woman's educational level			
	Low	Mid	High	Total
Low	16	9	4	29
Mid	10	14	8	32
High	8	13	18	39
Total	34	36	31	100

Couples where woman aged under 35

Man's educational level	Woman's educational level			
	Low	Mid	High	Total
Low	8	11	3	22
Mid	9	19	11	39
High	5	14	20	38
Total	22	44	34	100

Notes:
Authors' analysis of the 1994 wave of the BHPS (as referred to in Davies et al. (1998)). Sample of 2126 partnered women under 60 not in full-time education, with information available on educational level of both partners. These results refer to a 3-fold classification of educational qualifications similar to that employed in the simulation exercise: post school, A- or O-level, below O-level.

The marriages in our standard cases are lifelong partnerships: even today, 59% of marriages in Britain are not expected to end in divorce. We also consider examples of divorce and unmarried teenage parenthood – these are discussed in Chapters 4 and 5 respectively.

In each case, the man is assumed to be two years older than his wife. Men are assumed to live up to age 78, and women up to age 81.[30] The husband's earnings may affect a woman's earnings indirectly by influencing her participation in the labour force. More importantly, the husband's earnings will affect the possibility of income redistribution within the partnership, and the woman's pension in widowhood.

---

[30] We have abstracted from social differences in life expectancy.

3.1.5 Marriage and fertility patterns of the hypothetical individuals

The family histories used here assume the continued social differentiation among married women of the timing rather than the number of births. Common to all our hypothetical individuals is the arrival of a first child two years after marriage and the others at three-year intervals. Hence:

1. Mrs Low, who has no qualifications, marries at the age of 21, and has her first and second child at 23 and 26. If she goes on to more, she will have her third child at 29 and fourth child at the age of 32.

2. Mrs Mid, who has a middle level of skill and qualifications, marries at the age of 26, and has her first and second child at the ages of 28 and 31. She is set to complete a family of four children at age 37.

3. Mrs High, who has a high occupational level, marries at the age of 28. She is assumed to have her first child at 30 and subsequent births at three-year intervals.

How do the family sizes we have simulated relate to the size of British families? Among the cohorts born in the 1930s and 1940s, around 90% of women became mothers. However, since the 1940 cohort the proportion remaining childless has nearly doubled to 21% (Pearce et al. 1999: 35-37). Increasing childlessness, and falling family size (see below), have reduced the total fertility rate so that the average number of children born to a woman at current rates now stands at 1.7 (ONS 1999: Table 2.2). Completed family sizes by birth cohort of women are shown in Figure 3.2 opposite.

The average family size is around two, but has been falling. Two-child families are by far the most frequent, one-child families have never been popular. Thus, our discussion focuses on mothers with two children. In simulating scenarios with one, two and four children, we are more or less covering the range of current completed family sizes. Although the missing intermediate case of the three-child family is the second most popular, we simulate the case of the four-child family to give a more graphic illustration of the large family.

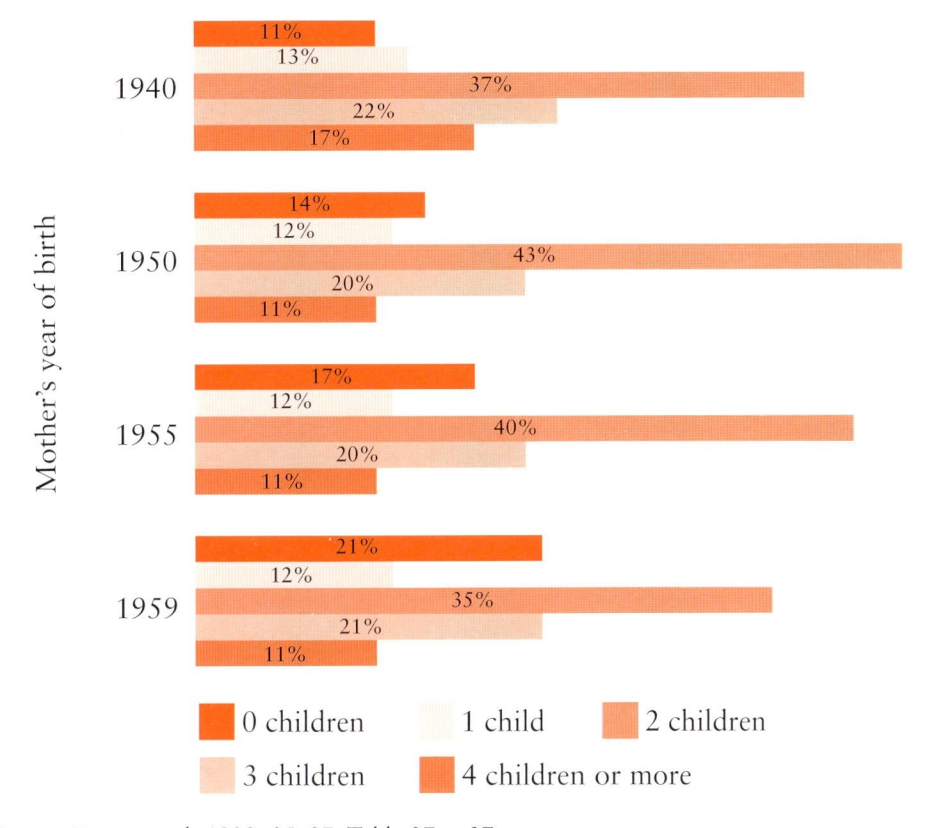

Figure 3.2: Distribution of completed family sizes by birth cohorts of mothers

1940
- 11%
- 13%
- 37%
- 22%
- 17%

1950
- 14%
- 12%
- 43%
- 20%
- 11%

1955
- 17%
- 12%
- 40%
- 20%
- 11%

1959
- 21%
- 12%
- 35%
- 21%
- 11%

Mother's year of birth

■ 0 children   ■ 1 child   ■ 2 children
■ 3 children   ■ 4 children or more

Source: Pearce et al. 1999: 35–37; Table 37, p.37.

These illustrative family histories for married women also reflect two other key trends of the 1990s, namely:

- The rise in the mean age of first marriage and of motherhood.

- The fact that fertility rates have been falling for younger women and rising for older women, so that since 1992, women in the age group 30–34 are more likely to give birth than women aged 20–24.[31]

---

[31] In 1997, rates per thousands for women in the age group 30–34 and women in the age group of 20–24 stood at 139.2 and 49 respectively, with women aged 25–29 still having the highest rates at 145.1.

The ages at marriage and the age difference between partners assumed in the model are consistent with recent data. Indeed, the average age at first marriage for women in Britain in 1996 was 26.3 (also the EU average), while for men it was 28.5, the median being roughly the same.[32] The mean age of motherhood for all births rose from 28.1 in 1984 to 28.8 in 1997. Within marriage, the mean age of giving birth rose from 28.1 in 1987 to 30.3 in 1997, with the mean ages of mothers in that year for birth orders 1, 2, 3 and 4 being 29, 30.5, 31.5, and 32.4 (OPCS 1997: Table 1.6). We have not attempted to model the distinction between marriage and cohabitation. In our model 'marriage' stands for all partnerships.

However, childbearing at younger ages is still common, and these overall trends continue to be differentiated by socio-economic classes and educational level. Births to women aged over 30 are more concentrated in families in the upper social classes (defined by registration statistics by the Registrar General's scheme (RG)), while births to younger women are more typical in the lower skill classes. In the early 1990s, the mean ages of the mother at first, second and third live births within marriage were about three years greater for women married to men from occupational classes I and II, than for those married to men in classes IV and V (OPCS 1997: Table 11.4).[33] Likewise, the distribution of births by age and RG occupational class of mother shows that 6% of births to mothers under 20 were to women from occupational groups I or II, compared to 37% from the less skilled groups IV and V. In contrast, among births to mothers aged 35–39, 57% were to women in classes I and II, compared to 10% in classes IV and V.[34]

There is similar differentiation of age of motherhood by educational level. In 1996, of women aged 16–59, the modal (and median) age group at which mothers with higher educational achievement had had their first child was 25–29, while it was 20–24 for those with low or no qualifications. Women who had had their first child when they were under 20 formed 6%, 16% and 26%

---

[32] In 1996, median ages at marriage for all, rather than first, brides and grooms were at 28.6 and 30.6, with the means at 31.1 and 33.6. Tables 3.15, 3.16, and 3.17, p.17, in Marriage, Divorce, and Adoption Statistics 1996. The data can also be found on http:\\www.statistics.gov.uk/Statbase/datasets.asp the sub-theme of "Population, Census, Migration and Vital Events".

[33] For women married to men from classes I and II the average ages were 30.2, 31.9, and 33, while for those married to men from classes IV and V the corresponding figures were 27.6, 29, and 29.8. For occupational classes IIIN and IIIM, the ages at first birth in 1997 were 28.4 and 28.8. Similarly, Table 11.3 shows that while the overall median interval of marriage to first birth is 28 months, it ranges from 32 months for social classes I and II to 24 months for social classes IV and V. Note that the 1987 median level stood at 18 months.

[34] Botting and Cooper 1993: 31, Table 8, based on a 10% sample of birth registrations.

of mothers with high, medium, and low or no qualifications (see Figure 3.3). The issue of young motherhood is taken up again in Chapter 5.

Figure 3.3: Age of mother at first birth by highest educational qualification (1986 and 1996)

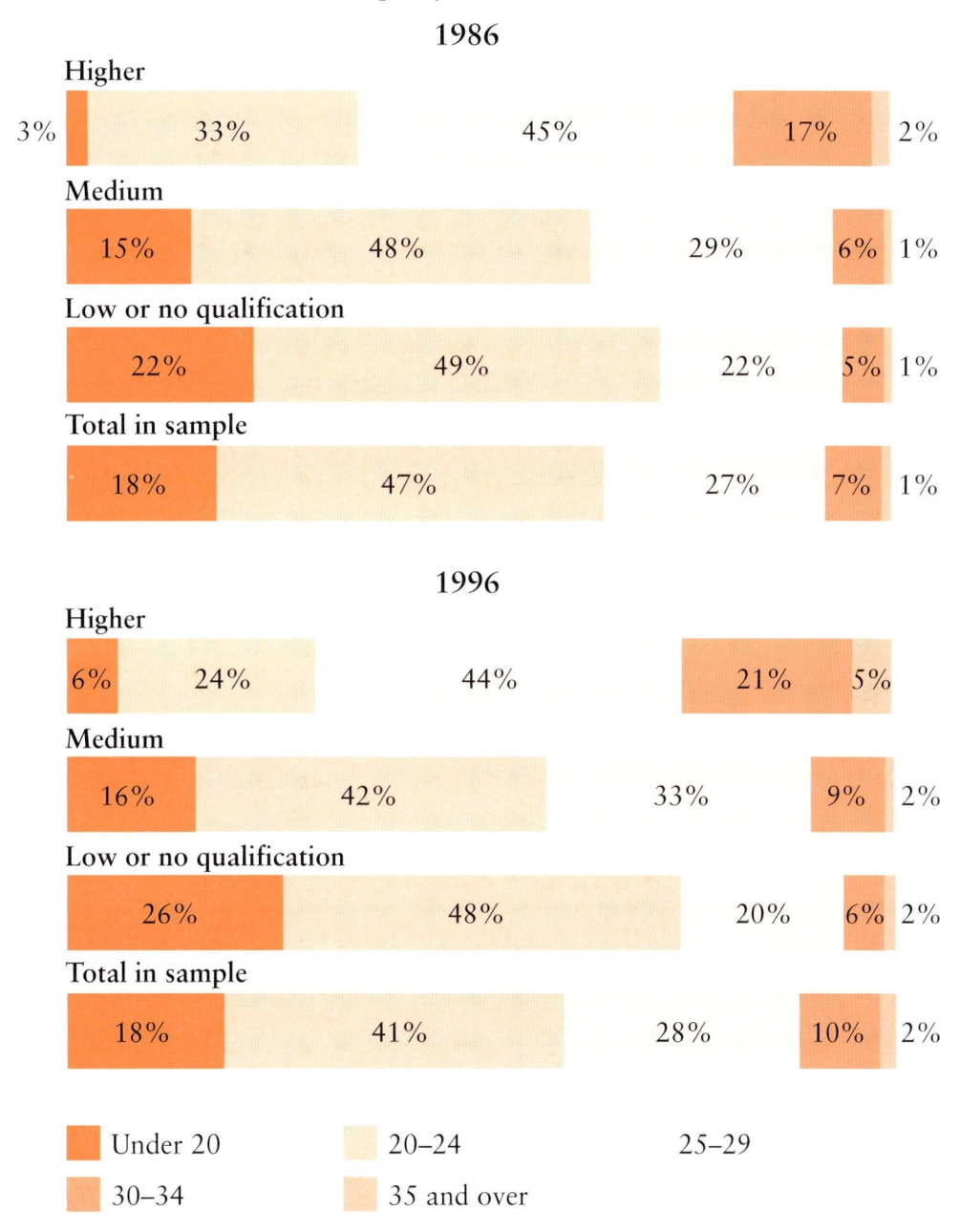

1986

Higher
3% | 33% | 45% | 17% | 2%

Medium
15% | 48% | 29% | 6% | 1%

Low or no qualification
22% | 49% | 22% | 5% | 1%

Total in sample
18% | 47% | 27% | 7% | 1%

1996

Higher
6% | 24% | 44% | 21% | 5%

Medium
16% | 42% | 33% | 9% | 2%

Low or no qualification
26% | 48% | 20% | 6% | 2%

Total in sample
18% | 41% | 28% | 10% | 2%

■ Under 20 ■ 20–24 ■ 25–29
■ 30–34 ■ 35 and over

Source: Authors' analysis of the General Household Survey.

On the other side of the scale, of women with high educational attainment, 26% were aged 30 and over at first birth, which represents a slight rise over the 19% observed in the 1986 sample. In contrast, there has been a slight decline in the proportion of these women giving birth at younger ages, with the percentage of highly educated mothers aged 25 or under at first birth declining from 36% to 30%. Between 1986 and 1996, the proportion of women with low or no qualification in the sample as a whole fell significantly from 47% to 33%. In this group, the percentage of mothers aged 25 or under at first birth inched up from 71% to 74%. Although the percentage of those becoming mothers at age 30 and over rose from 6% to 8%, this was still less than a third of the rate experienced by their more qualified counterparts.

Hence our family building scenarios allow for early marriage and earlier births to be associated with lower earning power, and for later marriage and childbearing to be associated with women in or married into the upper skill classes. We will also examine some counterfactual cases of histories that differ from that typical for a given skill group, including women who experience lone motherhood either through unmarried teenage childbearing (see Chapter 5, Section 5.5) or after divorce (see particularly Chapter 4, Section 4.4).

Our assumptions about ages of marriage and childbirth for the standard cases are summarised in Table 3.2

Table 3.2: Hypothetical individuals: assumed ages at key family events

Age at event		Skill level		
		Low	Mid	High
Marriage		21	26	28
Births	1st	23	28	30
	2nd	26	31	33
	3rd	29	34	36
	4th	32	37	39

3.1.6 Labour market behaviour of the hypothetical individuals

Since the main subject of interest is the implications of child rearing for women's lifetime earnings, the only interruptions to earning histories that we usually consider are those due to childcare. Our standard cases make no allowance for sickness or unemployment, so that in their hypothetical world, uninterrupted male careers are the norm. We do, however, consider the implications of examples of unemployment and early retirement in Chapter 6.

Other aspects of the labour market are modelled by econometric equations which encapsulate recent behaviour in the British labour market (equations and further details in Appendix III). If employment is more likely than not in a given year, considering the woman's earning power and circumstances, she is assumed to be employed in that year. The model also predicts whether she is more likely to be in a part-time or full-time job. The woman is assumed to drop out of employment whenever the model predicts that staying at home is more likely than going out to work.

Hours of full-time paid work depend on sex and occupational grade, reflecting hours reported in the BHPS. Men are assumed to work somewhat longer hours than female full-timers (as shown in Chapter 2, see also Appendix III). For the part-timers, hours are assumed to increase with the probability of full-time relative to part-time employment.[35] Hourly earnings for female participants are obtained from separate wage equations for full-time and part-time jobs. Apart from a few special cases, men are assumed to be employed continuously. All the econometric equations were estimated on the assumption that fertility is exogenous, i.e. decided upon outside the model.

Hourly wage rates are explained by equations of a standard "human capital" type. The level of education and the amount of work experience attained to date are the principal determinants of wages within gender. Work experience has a positive effect on wages, though the effect of a year's extra experience is lower at higher levels of experience. For women of low and mid-skill, the hourly wage reaches a plateau in mid-life. The possibility of outlying 'high flyers' of any educational level making big career advances in their forties and fifties is not captured in our cross-sectional average for women. Perhaps they are (still) too small a minority to show up. This plateau may be thought of as a 'glass ceiling' to women's upward mobility. However, it should be noted that women with high educational qualifications experience less of a ceiling in earnings than those with lower qualifications.

Time out of the labour force reduces wages. For women this mainly reflects time spent in domestic work (principally childcare). The median length of time out of employment for women providing evidence for the wage equation is about four years. (For men, it is about four months, mainly reflecting spells of unemployment.)

---

[35] Our investigations of hours of work had shown these not to be very sensitive to economic variables within the full- and part-time sector (Davies et al. 1999). The procedure adopted here, and in earlier work, has the effect of adjusting hours of part-time work to the age of the youngest child.

Words of caution

A few words of caution about the method are in order. Our system of assigning employment status to our illustrative individuals appears to produce some upward bias in their labour market histories if we compare these to actual participation rates for mid-age to older women in the 1990s. This is a result of three assumptions we make in order to construct scenarios:

1. The decision rule that anyone with a probability of employment over 50% is counted as employed, even though she might have up to 49% chance of being out of paid work.

2. This decision rule generates a cumulative upward bias as simulated employment experience feeds into the next period's imputed wage which in turn raises the probability of being counted as employed.

3. For the majority of the report, we have made the simplifying, but unrealistic, assumption that there are no sources of absence from a job other than childrearing (and derived wage effects). Thus any scenario with sickness, unemployment, elder care, etc. would have lower employment probabilities than any of our illustrative people. This would affect earnings and pension for a scenario without children as well as for mothers.

Although these assumptions boost lifetime incomes, their effects on the costs of motherhood are not obvious, and could be either way or neutral. We explore these issues in Chapter 6 where we deviate from our initial assumptions and look at the impact of unemployment and early retirement of lifetime income.

We must emphasise that our illustrative people are not representative of everybody. They are not an average as we could not generate an average without generating a whole population of thousands of individuals. Furthermore, our scenarios do not cover the most chequered employment histories. As a result many people would have lower lifetime earnings than the (near) central case picked here. Others, perhaps not so numerous, would have higher lifetime earnings. It is best, therefore, to think of our scenarios as an upper limit on a central case.

3.1.7 The tax-benefit environment of the model

Our model calculates the major components of the tax, benefit, and pension systems as they apply to the hypothetical individuals. The simulations take place in a timewarp: a lifetime income is constructed assuming current institutional arrangements and determinants of behaviour apply in perpetuity.[36]

---

[36] This is essentially the same premise that actuaries and demographers use in constructing lifetables.

Our general approach is to take the tax and benefit rules and rates as they were at April 1999: our timewarp assumes that the system is frozen at these values and that individuals are treated as though they spent their whole lives in this static tax-benefit environment. As our focus is on the long-term view of income, it is appropriate to ignore various transitional arrangements. We have made a few exceptions from our general rule of using April 1999 rates for the imminent policy changes concerning Children's Tax Credit, Working Families' Tax Credit, pension sharing and child support. The modelled tax-benefit environment is discussed fully in Appendix II.

3.2 WOMEN'S LIFETIME LABOUR MARKET PARTICIPATION AND EARNINGS

We now turn to the results of our simulations for the labour force participation patterns and earnings of our standard cases and include, for comparison, the case of childless married and unmarried women.[37]

3.2.1 Projected participation probabilities

Figure 3.4 plots the simulated probabilities of employment for the different types of couples, contrasting the mother of two with the childless married woman. As we are assuming a State Pension age of 65, but our evidence is necessarily drawn from the period when it was 60, we have assumed that the participation probabilities simulated at age 59 will continue at ages 60–64, which accounts for the horizontal line at these ages. First, consider the women who never have children. They are projected to have high rates of full-time labour force participation for almost all of the years after they leave education. The projected rates of participation vary with the women's educational level and, hence, earning power. The projected participation rate of the graduate childless woman levels off at a rate of over ninety-five percent, with almost all of the participation being full-time rather than part-time. Among childless married women of lower educational levels there is a slightly lower overall chance of employment, but it remains at over 80% until the woman reaches her fifties. The low-skilled childless woman is more likely to be in part-time employment from the age of 59.[38]

[37] We have not considered the self-employed separately. Though there is a trend towards increased self-employment, the data available on the incomes and hours of work of the self-employed are much less reliable than those on employees.

[38] The employment trajectories for unmarried childless women (not shown here) differ from those of married childless women only where the women are low-skilled. Unmarried low skilled women are simulated to stay in full-time employment until State Pension age, rather than moving to part-time employment in their late fifties.

Figure 3.4: Probabilities of participation in any or full-time employment for childless women and mothers of two by skill level

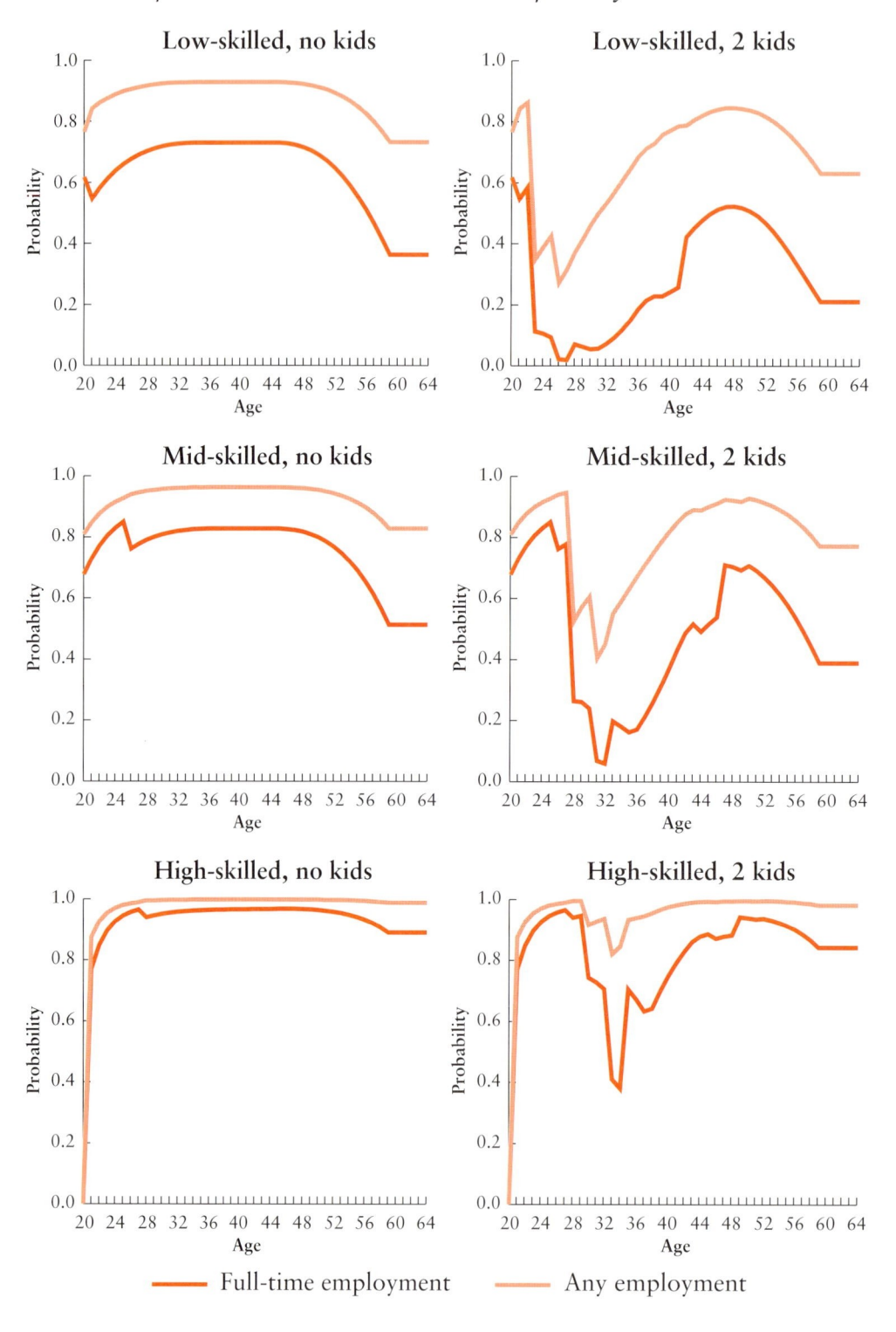

Against this hypothetical standard, we assess the impact of childbearing by comparing the employment probabilities for women who have children, focusing particularly on mothers of two.

Mrs Low (who is bearing children when she is 23 and 26) experiences a steep drop in the chances of employment, particularly full-time, at the time of her first child. Her probability of any employment remains below 50% until her second child is 6 (and oldest 9). Any employment while the children are at school (up to 16 in this case) is part-time. Although she has another spell more likely to be full-time in mid-life, she is also likely to resume part-time employment between age 55 and 64. This is a classical pattern for British mothers, leaving employment for a long gap that includes all births, and returning to employment part-time when the children are of school age. This pattern is seen in much empirical data (Dex 1984, Kempeneers and Lelievre 1991), and was dubbed 'typical' in our earlier work based on the 1980 Women and Employment Survey (Joshi et al. 1996).

The simulation produces a distinctive pattern of employment for the mid-skill mother of two. The probability that Mrs Mid will be in employment drops around the time of her births (28 and 31). However, the probability of employment does not plummet but remains close to the balancing point of 50%. This implies that about as many mothers of young children stay in employment as do not, as indeed was reported in the 1996 Maternity Rights and Benefits Survey (Callender et al. 1997).

Thus, in our simulation Mrs Mid remains in full-time employment during the year of the first birth, and continues in employment, part-time, until the second birth, when the balance of probabilities takes her out of employment for two years and brings her back to part-time employment (for 10 years). Over the period when her children are young, the mid-skilled woman does not sustain full-time employment for long. For the rest of her career she is most likely to be employed full-time, although this probability drops over the last 15 years of her working life. The apparent paradox of the mid-skill mother being in full-time employment while she has a baby under a year can be explained by the practice of taking maternity leave. The data that generate this scenario capture the fact that women on leave from full-time contracts tend to report themselves as being in full-time employment, and to return to their original job, at least for a short time.

Mrs High, the graduate who starts childbearing at 30, has her probability of employment barely perturbed by the two births. The probability of being employed full-time drops while the children are young, particularly around the time of the second child, but the balance of probability keeps her in full-time employment throughout, apart from a year's part-time employment following the second birth. We think of the three years of full-time employment following the birth of her first child as containing, and having been assisted by, maternity leave. At the end of Mrs High's career, the probability of full-time employment continues almost undiminished.

Changing the number of births changes the length of the simulated employment break roughly *pro-rata* for the low-skilled women: 4 years for one child, 9 for two, and 17 in the case of four children. For the mid-skilled mother, the employment break disappears if there is only one child and rises disproportionately (from years 2 to 9) if there are four births rather than two. Mid and low-skilled mothers of four are also projected never to return to full-time work. The high-skilled mothers are simulated to have employment continuity whatever number of births. With employment between births, the old pattern of scale economies in forgone earnings is disappearing, and British patterns will look more like those we estimated for France in the 1980s (Davies and Joshi, 1994).

3.2.2 Women's lifetime earnings

For the employment histories (from age 20) shown in Figure 3.4, year-by-year imputed earnings are depicted in Figure 3.5. The childless women have the highest trajectory throughout. Note that the vertical axes are on different scales to accommodate the much higher overall level of earnings of the high-skilled woman. The earnings trajectory of the mid-skilled woman is, in turn, somewhat higher than that of the low-skilled. The trajectories for most of the mothers are, in varying degree, below childless women. Among the high-skilled, mothers show very little shortfall compared to childless women – indeed, there is no difference between the earnings of the high-skilled mother of one, and her childless counterpart.[39] The three years of part-time work that the high-skilled mother of four spends between the births are, nevertheless, visible. The earnings gap widens out for women with middle and especially lower skills, especially if they have four children.

---

[39] This is assuming, as before, that any maternity leave taken is paid.

Figure 3.5: Women's earning over the lifetime by skill level and number of children

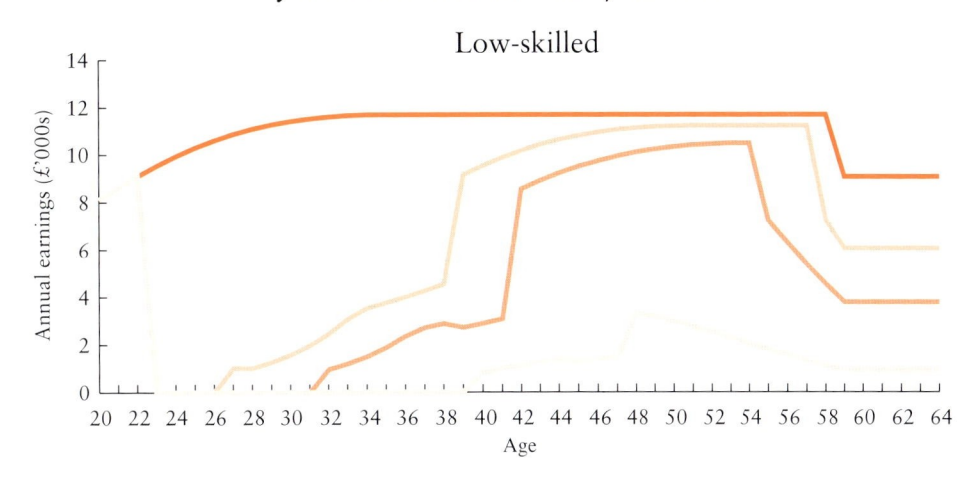

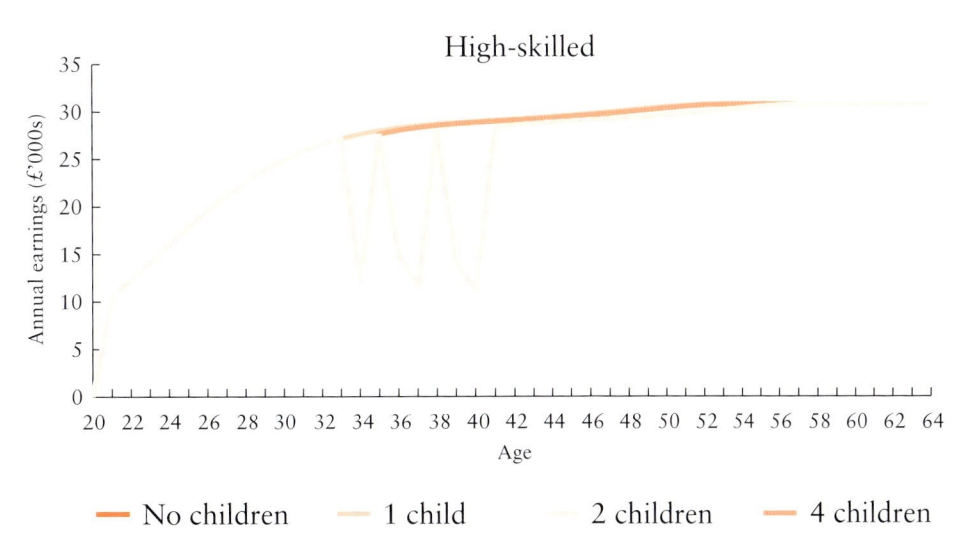

The simulated earnings of these women (including the unmarried childless cases) totalled over the whole of their working lives are given in Table 3.3.[40] The earnings profile of the mid-skilled childless woman is only modestly above and modestly steeper than that of the low-skilled (earnings of the mid-skilled woman reach a plateau of around £15,000 per annum, compared with around £12,000 for the low-skilled woman). However, the total gross earnings for Mrs Mid and Mrs Low with two children are sharply different at £510,000 and £249,000 respectively, a much wider difference than the gap between their childless counterparts, estimated at £650,000 and £518,000. Mrs High's earnings, by contrast, soar to more than double that of Mrs Mid and result in total gross earnings of £1,171,000, which is only some £20,000 less than her childless counterpart. The gap between the earnings profile of a childless woman and that of a mother can be thought of as the forgone earnings of the mother or the gross earnings cost of motherhood – this is discussed in full in Chapter 5, Section 5.1.

Table 3.3: Women's gross lifetime earnings

Skill level	Women by family building type (£000s)			
	Unmarried childless	Married childless	Married mother of 2	Married mother of 4
Low	534	518	249	93
Mid	650	650	510	237
High	1,190	1,190	1,171	1,100

Note: Earnings from labour market, whole working life.

3.3   FROM EARNINGS TO INCOME – THE IMPACT OF THE TAX-BENEFIT SYSTEM

So far we have looked at women's labour force participation, and hence at their gross earnings. Gross earnings do not tell the full story about lifetime incomes, however. This is for three reasons: life continues into retirement, people pay taxes on their income and they get state benefits.[41] We now look at these three factors and their influence on women's lifetime incomes. A person's income may also be affected by how they share their life and income with a partner – we will take this up in Chapter 4.

[40] In our simulations, we did not impose the National Minimum Wage, but our simulated hourly earnings never fall below the National Minimum Wage (which stood at £3.60 for those aged 21 and over in 1999) even for Mrs Low.

[41] The simulations abstract income from capital. For most people, their two most important assets are their house (from which they commonly derive no direct financial return) and their pension. The simulation only takes account of pensions.

To calculate the impact of taxes and state benefits we first need to decide what they include. For our purposes, the basic pension is considered as a state benefit but State Earnings Related Pension Scheme (SERPS) is considered to be deferred earnings (this accounting allows us to calculate the pension consequences of motherhood in Chapter 6). Similarly, we count the part of National Insurance Contributions (NIC) attributable to SERPS as a pension contribution, while we count the rest of the NIC in with Income Tax. Adjusting for pensions and taxes and state benefits enables us to go from gross earnings to net lifetime income (and from the gross earnings cost of motherhood to the net income cost as discussed in Chapter 5, Section 5.1).

The relationship between gross earnings and net lifetime income is shown for the high-skilled unmarried woman in Figure 3.6. The line which starts on top represents her gross earnings, which end when she retires at age 65. The line labelled 'Labour market income' is adjusted for earnings that are, in effect, being deferred through pension contributions (hence, while she is employed and contributing to her pension, the line representing labour market income is below gross earnings). In retirement, she receives an earnings-related pension, which we treat as labour market income. The third line shows what happens after taxes (Income Tax and other NICs) and benefits (here state basic pension) are taken into account. During her working life, her net income is somewhat less than three-quarters of her gross earnings (about 72%). In retirement, net income is close to her occupational pension – the state basic pension comes close to offsetting the effect of Income Tax.

Figure 3.6: Lifetime income profile: high-skilled unmarried woman

The shape and relative position of these curves will vary from case to case. In the case of the low-skilled mother of two, for example, the state makes a net positive contribution to the woman's income while the children are small and labour force involvement is low (see Figure 3.7). While she is employed gross earnings and labour market income are very close, separated only by small SERPS contributions and hardly distinguishable in the graph. In retirement, net income exceeds the woman's own earnings-related pension (regarded here as deferred labour income), as her basic pension and survivor's pension exceeds her Income Tax liability.

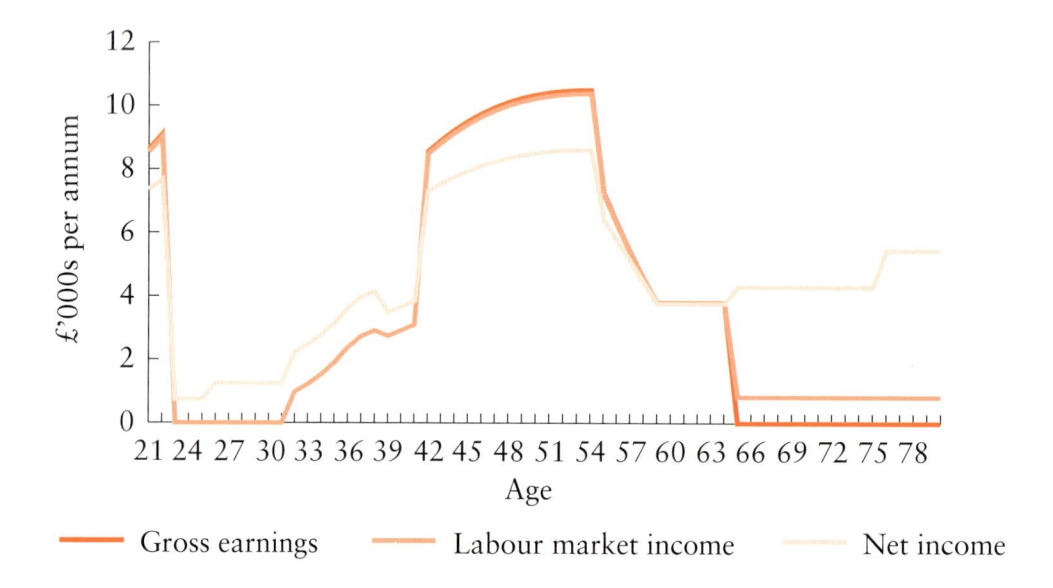

Figure 3.7: Lifetime income profile: low-skilled mother of two

Table 3.4 shows the impact of the tax-benefit system on lifetime incomes. The tax-benefit system goes a little way in modifying the differences in lifetime labour market income (earnings plus earnings-related pension contribution and receipt) and the differences in original income (labour market income plus survivor's pension). For example, a high-skilled married, childless woman has net income of 80% of original income. For the low- and mid-skilled childless woman the figures stand at 93% and 90%. As the table also demonstrates, the tax-benefit system redistributes more strongly towards women with children, an issue that is further explored in Chapter 5.

Table 3.4: The impact of the tax-benefit system on the lifetime income of women by skill level and family characteristics

	Unmarried	Married	Married	Married	Married
Number of children	0	0	1	2	4
	\multicolumn{5}{c}{Amounts (£'000s)}
Low-skilled woman					
Labour market income	518	502	312	226	62
Original income	518	508	318	232	68
Net income as % of original income	93%	94%	108%	122%	266%
Mid-skilled woman					
Labour market income	591	591	501	446	161
Original income	591	625	536	481	196
Net income as % of original income	90%	89%	95%	100%	143%
High-skilled woman					
Labour market income	1,353	1,353	1,353	1,336	1,270
Original income	1,353	1,409	1,409	1,392	1,326
Net income as % of original income	80%	79%	81%	81%	84%

Note: Lifetime lasts from wedding until woman's death.

3.4 THE PAY GAP OVER THE LIFETIME

3.4.1 The gender gap in lifetime earnings

As the simulation generates a lifetime earnings profile for women and men, we are here able to provide an estimate of the gender gap in *lifetime* earnings. We calculate the gender gap as the difference between the earnings of childless women and men of the equivalent educational level – the gender gap in earnings is, therefore, that which affects women and men regardless of whether they have children. Our estimates give us some understanding of what the lifetime 'cost' of the gender pay gap may be for women of different skills levels. In Chapter 5 we take this analysis further and look at what additional earnings gap is generated by the experience of motherhood, and this allows us to compare the absolute size and relative impact of the 'gender' and 'mother' gap in earnings (see Chapter 5, Section 5.2).

Table 3.5 sets out the estimates of the gender gap in lifetime earnings. The childless mid-skilled woman has lifetime earnings £241,000 (or 37%) below that of the equivalently skilled man. Given lower earnings among the low-skilled, the absolute difference between the woman and man is lower – £197,000 – but represents an equivalent relative loss (the earnings of the low-skilled woman are also 37% below his). For the high-skilled childless woman the gender gap is both absolutely and relatively smaller. The graduate woman has lifetime earnings 12% lower than the equivalently skilled man, a loss of about £143,000.

Table 3.5: The gender gap in lifetime earnings

	Skill level		
Lifetime earnings in £'000s	Low	Mid	High
Man	731	891	1333
Childless woman	534	650	1190
Difference-absolute	197	241	143
Difference – percent relative to woman	37	37	12
Contribution to the % difference in lifetime earnings from:			
Difference in hours	24	16	5
Difference in rates of pay	11	18	7
Interaction	3	3	0

Note: The gender gap in lifetime earnings is calculated as the difference between the man and the childless woman with the same qualification level.

The gender lifetime earnings gap arises for two reasons: unequal pay and unequal hours, the contribution of which to the difference in lifetime earnings of men and childless women are given in the bottom rows of Table 3.5.[42] For the mid-skilled woman, a differential of 16% comes from her lower hours in the labour market. This may be seen either as a gain (of leisure) or as a loss (of money) for the woman. However, a differential of 18% is attributable to a lower rate of hourly pay for identical attributes – this clearly represents a pay penalty for being female. The pay penalty varies with the level of qualifications. It is less for the low-skilled (11%) and lowest for the high-skilled (7%).

Hourly earnings of the mid-skilled man and the childless woman averaged over a lifetime were £8.11 and £6.86, giving the man an 18% differential above women's wages. This can be compared with the average gender premium of 8.6% estimated from 1994 data (Davies, Peronaci, and Joshi 1998, Table 2).

[42] The effect of a change in hourly wages on weekly earnings depends on the number of hours as an increase in hourly wages has a bigger effect on weekly earnings if the number of hours is high. To allow for this, the decomposition also contains an interaction term.

Figure 3.8: Hourly wages of men and childless women by age

The higher lifetime average rate of pay penalty arises because the pay gap opens out with age for the mid- and low-skilled (see Figure 3.8). The simulations give equal weight to all ages, whereas the observed sample of full-time female employees is concentrated on younger ages. The results here imply that, if women were to be paid at the same rate as men are currently, our mid-skilled childless woman would see a gain of about 18% in her lifetime gross earnings.[43]

The age profile of these gender gaps in pay also varies. For the low-skilled, it opens up from age 29, but only slightly. Between the highly-skilled individuals, the wage gap converges over time, if anything. The hours gap is greatest for the least skilled where men's hours of work are particularly high and smallest for the highly qualified cases in accordance with the evidence of the hours reported in BHPS. By reason of both pay and hours, the overall total of lifetime earnings is closest for the highly skilled.

3.4.2 Women's share in family earnings

Our lifetime earnings simulations also enable us to derive the woman's share of a couple's lifetime earnings. Results for childless couples and couples with two children are shown in Table 3.6.

Table 3.6: Percentage contribution of wife's earnings to couple's joint lifetime earnings

	Low-skilled	Mid-skilled	High-skilled
No children	41	42	49
Two children	24	35	47

Note: Lifetime runs from marriage until first retirement.

What stands out here is the contrast between the relatively small difference between the woman's contribution in the childless cases, and the very large differences in the cases with children. In the high-skilled couple with two children, the woman's percentage contribution is almost twice what it is in the low-skilled couple, and is scarcely less than what it would be without children. The 35% contribution from the mother of two in the mid-skill couple is quite close to the figure obtained from the Family Expenditure Survey and the NCDS.[44]

---

[43] In the absence of discrimination, men's wages might fall, with the common wage ending up somewhere between those currently paid to men and to women.

[44] See Chapter 2 and Joshi et al. 1995, Tables 5.1 and 5.3.

3.5 CONCLUSIONS AND KEY FINDINGS

Our analysis of labour market participation and earnings of women and men of three skill levels has uncovered a number of important findings:

- Women's labour market participation is now relatively unaffected by marriage alone, in contrast to most of the rest of the 20th Century. By contrast, the impact of having children is very large for some women – low-skilled mothers of two are estimated to spend nine years out of the labour market and 28 years in part-time work.

- The effect of children on employment patterns varies enormously by qualification level. Unlike low and mid-skilled mothers, women with high qualification levels have their probability of employment barely affected by having children. Thus, high-skilled mothers of two are estimated to remain continuously employed, with one year of part-time work following the birth of their second child.

- The differences in women's earnings by qualification level are striking. Married, childless women are estimated to earn £518,000 over the entire lifetime if they have no qualifications, £650,000 if mid-skilled and £1,190,000 if graduates.

- The tax-benefit system goes some way in modifying the differences in lifetime income before taxes and benefits. For example a high-skilled married, childless women has net income of 80% of original lifetime income. For the low- and mid-skilled childless woman the figures stand at 93% and 90%.

- The simulated benefits paid to the low- and mid-skilled mothers outweigh the lifetime taxes paid. The benefits include Child Benefit, Children's Tax Credit and Working Families' Tax Credit and the Basic Pension.

- The lifetime gender pay gap (the gap that exists above and beyond any penalties attached to motherhood) is estimated to 'cost' the mid-skilled woman just under a quarter of a million pounds over her lifetime. Her lifetime earnings are 37% below those of an equivalently skilled man – attributable about equally to spending fewer hours in the labour market (16%) and lower hourly pay (18%).

- The mid-skilled mother of two contributes about 35% of the couple's joint lifetime earnings. This figure rises to 42% if she remains childless. Again, the contribution varies across educational levels, from 24% for the low-skilled mother of two to 47% for the high-skilled. These figures suggest that for some women, especially those of lower skills, economic dependence on a man's wage remains a reality.

Having set out the standard cases in our simulation, the subsequent chapters both examine these in more detail and add to the range of hypothetical cases by altering our base assumptions (e.g. by introducing divorce, lone motherhood, unemployment and early retirement).

4. PARTNERSHIP AND PARTNERSHIP BREAKDOWN

4. PARTNERSHIP AND PARTNERSHIP BREAKDOWN

In this chapter, we consider the interaction between partnership status and economic status and examine the potential contribution of a partner to a woman's income, and, hence, the financial consequences of divorce. While partnership formation and having children are clearly related, we here attempt to disentangle the impact on women's lifetime incomes of marriage and divorce from that of having children (discussed in Chapter 5). Section 4.1 contains a discussion of changing patterns in family formation and dissolution. Section 4.2 considers income sharing within the 'standard' families discussed in Chapter 3. In Section 4.3 we look at the relative contribution of the family, the labour market and the state to the incomes of the hypothetical individuals at different stages in their lifecycles. Section 4.4 looks at the implications of divorce for lifetime income.

4.1 PARTNERSHIP AND ECONOMIC STATUS

We here briefly consider current patterns of partnership and partnership breakdown and the consequences this has for the types of household in which individuals live. The relationship between partnership and economic status runs both ways – a partnership may affect an individual's economic well-being, and conversely economic status affects the likelihood of partnership formation and breakdown.

4.1.1 Changing patterns of partnership formation and dissolution

The key changes over the past thirty years in patterns of partnership formation and dissolution have been:

- later age at first marriage (as discussed in section 3.1.5);

- falling rates of marriage but slightly increasing rates of remarriage;

- increasing rates of divorce;

- rising rates of cohabitation.

As Figure 4.1 illustrates, the number of marriages has halved since its peak in the early 1970s. Over the same period, the number of divorces has almost trebled, with a notable rise in divorce rates following the introduction in 1971 of the Divorce Reform Act. At the same time there has been a more steady growth in remarriages, growing around 60% since the early 1970s, with men more likely to remarry following divorce than women (Haskey 1999a).

Figure 4.1: Marriages and divorces (1961–98)

[1] For both partners   [2] Includes annulments   [3] For one or both partners

Source: Office for National Statistics; General Register Office for Scotland; Northern Ireland Statistics and Research Agency.

Looking in more detail at the characteristics of divorce and remarriage reveals that:

- At present, 1 in 13 men and 1 in 12 women are divorced. If current rates persist, 2 in 5 couples will ultimately divorce (Haskey 1999a: 18-19).

- In 1997, the median duration of marriage at divorce was 9.9 years, with marriages lasting 5-9 years being the largest group, accounting for 28% of divorces, followed by 18% for those lasting 10-14 years.

- The median and mean ages of divorce for females have risen by 4-5 years since the early 1980s, and were at 35.1 and 37.7 in 1997. The corresponding figures for men were 38.4 and 40.1.[45]

---

[45] The evidence for this and the preceding bullet point was extracted from both Table 4.9, Marriage, Divorce, and Adoption Statistics 1996, pp. 82-83 and the dataset called "Divorce by duration of marriage", freely available on the ONS's on-line database at http:\\www.statistics.gov.uk/Statbase/datasets.asp under the sub-theme "Population, Census, Migration and Vital Events".

- The risk of divorce is higher for those who marry young – on one estimate, the probability of a marriage dissolving in its first year if the woman was aged 18 at the time of marriage is 10.4%, while for a marriage starting at age 23 that probability drops to 7.4% (Böheim and Ermisch 1999, Table 3).

- Remarriage after divorce is either speedy or occurs after 6-12 years. The DSS/PSI Lone Parent Cohort study shows that 32% of the 1991 panel had partnered by 1998. While only 3% of the panel had married in 1993, this rose to 19% in the 1998 sample. The number of divorced mothers in the sample declined from 34% in 1991 to 22% in 1998, tentatively indicating that one in three divorcees can expect to remarry within 7 years. Nevertheless, the analysis of the 1993 cohort suggested that between one in four or one in five of lone mothers can expect to experience a spell in that state lasting at least 9-10 years.[46]

A driving force behind the falling rate in marriage is the increase in cohabitation, which has shown notable increases particularly since the early 1980s (Kiernan 1999). Current estimates suggest that more than one in five adults were cohabiting in 1995-97 with 34% of single women aged 25-34 and 35% of divorced women in a cohabiting union (ONS 1998a, Table 1.9). Cohabitation may either be a precursor or, increasingly, an alternative to marriage. Of first unions, 40% are marriages without pre-marital cohabitation, 40% marriages with pre-marital cohabitation and 20% are continuing cohabitation that have not (yet) led to marriage (Haskey 1999b). Another contributor has been the rise in the proportions of women and men who have never married – projections of the 1964 cohort suggest 10% of women and 16% of men will not have married or formed a cohabiting union by the time they reach 50 (Evandrou and Falkingham 2000). Thus, later and fewer marriages and rising divorce contribute both to increasing rates of both lone parenthood (discussed in Chapter 5) and of living in a single person household. Given women's greater longevity, solo living among the older population affects women more than men (see Chapter 6) and is set to increase as the cohorts to have experienced increasing rates of divorce move into old age. As the figures on those who have never married/cohabited suggest, the experience of solo living is also increasing among younger cohorts, either as a period prior to cohabitation/marriage or as a more permanent state. The proportion of women in single person households is higher, at around 16%, than that of men (ONS 1998a, Table 1.10).

4.1.2 Partnership and economic status

Mean individual gross incomes and source of income for women and men without dependent children by marital status are shown in Figure 4.2. The figure shows that for both women and men, widowhood and being single is associated with a lower mean income. Even in the absence of children, divorced and

---

[46] Unpublished tabulations supplied by Dr Alan Marsh.

separated women have lower mean incomes than their male counterparts and rely slightly more on state benefit as a source of income. The age profile of these different groups is distinct, and will explain some of the difference in mean incomes – for example, the differences between the incomes of married and cohabiting couples without dependent children reflects the younger age profile of the latter group who are more likely to be of working age and in the labour market. Interestingly, if individual income of couples with dependent children is examined this picture is reversed, as women and, especially, men in cohabiting couples with dependent children have lower mean individual incomes than their married counterparts. Cohabiting men have a mean individual gross weekly income of £268 compared to £406 for married men; for women the figures are £137 and £165 (Women's Unit 1999, Tables 4.20 and 4.21).

Figure 4.2: Individual gross income by marital status and source of income; women and men without dependent children (1996–97)

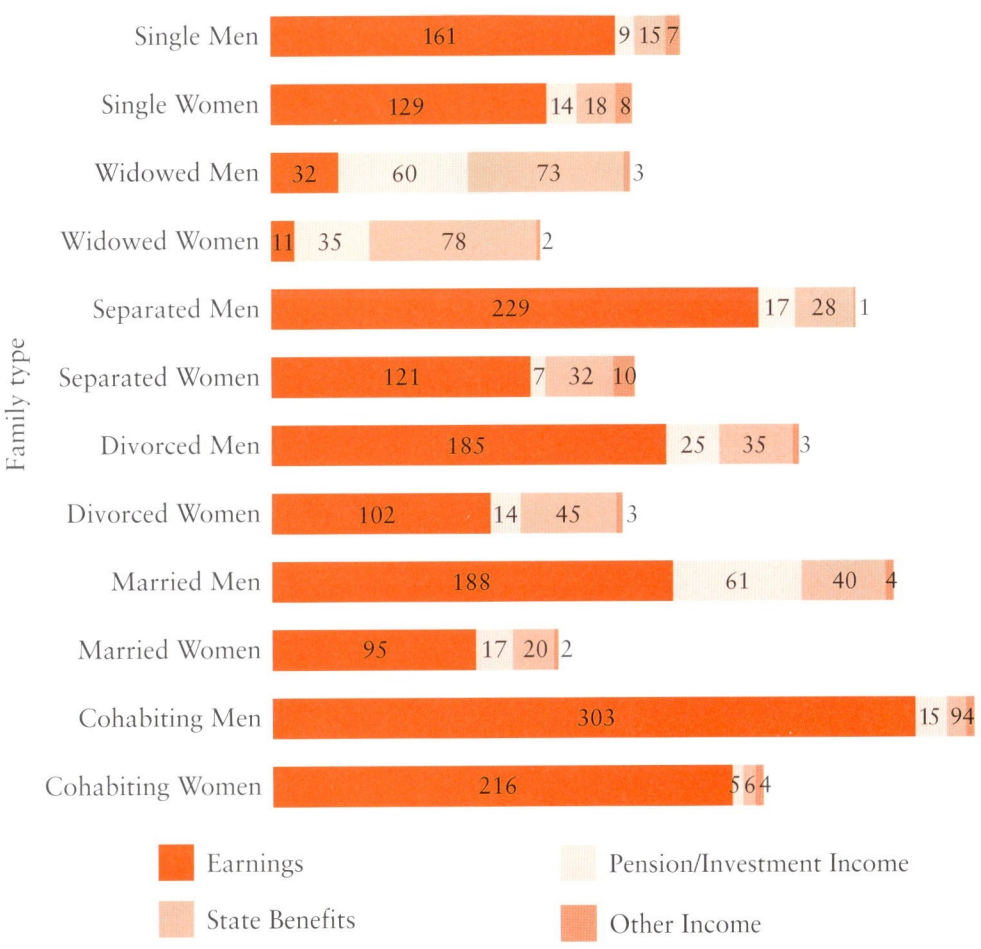

Family type	Earnings	Pension/Investment Income	State Benefits	Other Income
Single Men	161	9	15	7
Single Women	129	14	18	8
Widowed Men	32	60	73	3
Widowed Women	11	35	78	2
Separated Men	229	17	28	1
Separated Women	121	7	32	10
Divorced Men	185	25	35	3
Divorced Women	102	14	45	3
Married Men	188	61	40	4
Married Women	95	17	20	2
Cohabiting Men	303	15	9	4
Cohabiting Women	216	5	6	4

Source: Women's Unit 1999, Figures 4.6, 4.7 and 4.8.

There is evidence that economic status also affects the likelihood of partnership breakdown. Higher earnings among the male partner decrease the risk of partnership dissolution, while higher female earnings have the opposite effect and increase risk of dissolution. Furthermore, favourable financial surprises appear to decrease the risk of partnership dissolution, while unfavourable ones have no significant effect (Böheim and Ermisch 1999).

4.2 SHARING WITHIN PARTNERSHIPS

Considering individuals within the partnerships they form means that we must consider the sharing that may occur within partnerships.[47] Partnerships offer individuals the possibility of sharing income and sharing in domestic labour or household production. The division of domestic labour and the amount of goods and services that a household produces are very important determinants of individual well-being (see, for example, Davies et al. 1999; Jenkins and O'Leary 1996 and 1997), and a continuing source of labour market inequality between women and men. Nevertheless, the main focus of this report is on income, and we therefore limit our focus below to the sharing of income within households, without attempting to value unpaid work or the sharing of its output.

4.2.1 Sharing income

Many analyses of the income distribution use family (or benefit unit, or household) income and implicitly assume that income is shared within the unit. It is almost certain that some degree of sharing takes place within couples – indeed it is almost implicit in the concept of a co-residential partnership. However, as economists have become more interested in the family, the view that income is equally shared within the household has come under scrutiny. The hypothesis that income is equally shared among family members has been questioned on both theoretical and empirical grounds. The weight of empirical evidence is currently against an assumption of equal sharing – Lundberg and Pollak (1996) survey this literature and Lundberg et al. (1997) provide empirical evidence that husbands and wives do not share their incomes equally in the UK. Empirical analysis also reveals that the measurement of women's position in the income distribution is highly sensitive to the assumptions made about the degree of income sharing. For example, data from the Family Expenditure Survey has been used to compute men's and women's incomes under two extreme assumptions of full and minimum sharing[48] (Davies and Joshi 1994b). On the full sharing assumption, 15% of married women would have fallen into the poorest fifth of the income distribution in 1986, but on minimum sharing over half (55%) would have done. In 1968, women's assumed dependence on sharing within the marriage was even greater. Hence, at least

---

[47] Sharing may also occur outside partnerships with non co-resident family or friends. It is beyond the scope of this report to look at this largely unstudied area.

[48] 'Full sharing' is the conventional equal sharing assumption, while under the minimum sharing assumption, the couples share only housing costs.

hitherto, the assumed transfer from their husbands would have been an important part of women's income. As this analysis reveals, the assumption about the extent of sharing is a crucial factor in the estimation of the income available to women. It should be noted, however, that estimates of women's incomes are less sensitive to the assumptions made about sharing where the difference between the incomes to which men and women are individually entitled is small.

Although evidence suggests that equal sharing is far from universal across couples, and that sharing assumptions make a big difference to women's position in the income distribution, it is very difficult to discern how people actually distribute their income within a partnership. In the absence of such information, assumptions have to be made about how income is shared. For the purposes of this simulation, the conventional assumption that income is shared equally among the adults in a family – here at most two – is adopted. Our analysis goes beyond that offered by most in that it explicitly quantifies the amount assumed to be shared. We do not, however, make any allowance for any economies of scale in consumption (encapsulated in the idea that 'two can live as cheaply as one') that may be realised by sharing living arrangements, nor for the needs of any children. Later in this chapter, we also look at what happens when a partnership breaks down.

4.2.2 Income sharing among the hypothetical couples

The role of the income sharing assumption is illustrated in Figure 4.3, which shows the income of both partners. The top line depicts the man's net income, while the bottom depicts the woman's. Although both parties are of the same skill-level, the man's earnings are projected to be higher because of unequal hourly pay and longer hours of paid work (discussed in Chapter 3 and Appendix III). If income is shared equally within the partnership then both partners enjoy the fruits of the average of their two incomes – shown as the line running between the two individual income lines. This implies a transfer of purchasing power from the partner with the higher income to the one with less (in practice most commonly from the man to the woman): we refer to this transfer of purchasing power as the 'family transfer'. By this term we do not intend to suggest that the transfer is entirely altruistic or unreciprocated.

The sharp jump in the woman's income at age 76 arises from the survivor's occupational pension she receives following the assumed death of her husband. Although this can be thought of as a 'posthumous family transfer' it has a different status from the family transfer *inter vivos*. The widow has a legal right to the survivor's pension, and it is counted as part of her income for legal and statistical purposes – for example, it is subject to Income Tax. The family transfer *inter vivos*, on the other hand, is a hypothetical construct: although some income sharing almost certainly takes place in many marriages, we do not know its extent, and it is not taxed.

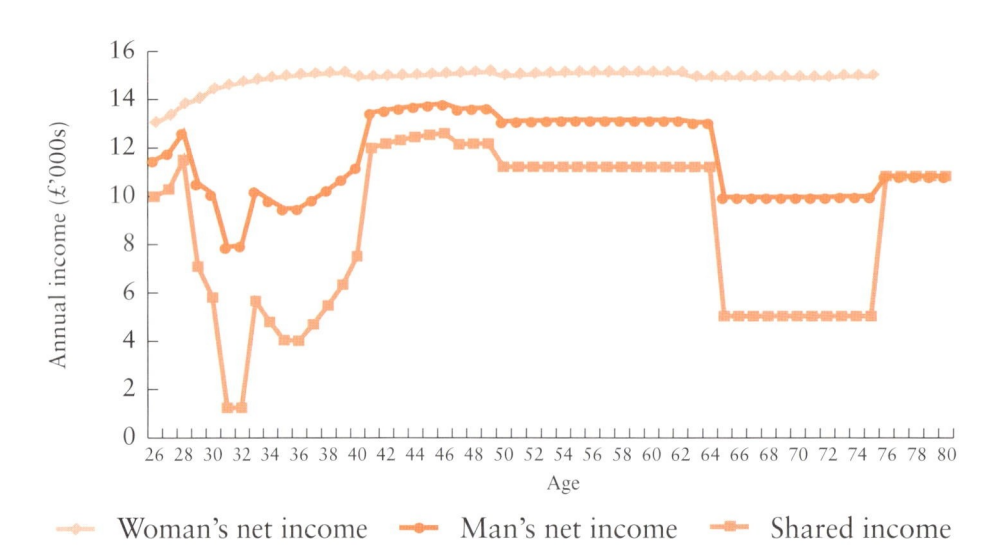

Figure 4.3: Income sharing in partnership: mid-skilled married couple with children

4.3 SOURCES OF INCOME ACROSS THE LIFECYCLE

4.3.1 Sources of income over the whole lifetime

We can look at a person's income over the lifecycle as deriving from three sources:

1. the labour market;

2. the state;

3. any transfer from a partner.

Table 4.1 shows the contributions which the labour market, the state and the 'family transfer' make to the lifetime incomes of our hypothetical women. The income concept we use here ('woman's portion') is net income calculated on the assumption that equal sharing takes place between the spouses. The labour market and the state are the only sources for our hypothetical single women: for the married women, however, we must also include the 'family transfer'. A negative number for the state indicates that the woman pays more in taxes than she receives in benefits.[49] A positive number for the 'family

---

[49] Remember that we are taking no account of the state's expenditure on goods and services- defence, health, education etc. from which people also benefit.

transfer' indicates that the woman is (assumed to be) receiving a flow of purchasing power from her husband: where the family transfer is negative, the woman is calculated to be transferring purchasing power to her husband. For the purposes of this table, as in Table 3.4, we count only the years after a woman marries. For the unmarried women (shown for comparability) we cover the same ages as for the married women of the same skill level – for these women, their portion is just the same as their own net income. Note that the age coverage is therefore different for women at different skill levels.

Table 4.1: Sources of women's income over the lifetime (as percent of 'woman's portion')

	Unmarried	Married			
Number of children	0	0	1	2	4
		in percent			
Low-skilled					
Labour market	107	91	64	49	15
State	−7	−5	6	13	28
Family transfer	0	14	30	37	57
Woman's portion (£'000s)	*£484*	*£549*	*£485*	*£459*	*£404*
Mid-skilled					
Labour market	112	87	77	70	30
State	−12	−10	−4	0	18
Family transfer	0	22	27	30	53
Woman's portion (£'000s)	*£530*	*£675*	*£653*	*£638*	*£545*
High-skilled					
Labour market	125	116	115	113	109
State	−25	−25	−23	−22	−19
Family transfer	0	9	8	9	10
Woman's portion (£'000s)	*£1,082*	*£1,166*	*£1,178*	*£1,177*	*£1,165*

Perhaps the first point to note concerns differences among unmarried women: the lifetime incomes (as calculated here) of the high-skilled women are twice as large as those of the mid-skilled women – a similar ratio to that for lifetime earnings (see Table 3.3).

The table shows that most of these women derive well over half their lifetime portion from the labour market. The 'labour market income' is gross earnings *less* earnings related pension contributions *plus* earnings related pension – we here treat earnings-related pension (including SERPS) as deferred labour market income. The women who are net beneficiaries from the state are predominantly mothers with low skills.[50] The extent to which hypothetical women gain from the 'family transfer' (if it is indeed made) varies quite considerably. Whereas the women in the couples where both partners have high skills are calculated to get 10% or less of their income from the family transfer, other women are still reliant on the putative family transfer for a large fraction of their income. The mother of two in the mid-skilled couple, for example, although she has the same level of skill as her husband and is only out of employment for two years during her child-rearing years, is calculated to get (potentially) 30% of her lifetime income from this source.

4.3.2 Sources of income at four different stages of the lifecycle

It is interesting to look at where women's income comes from at different stages of the lifecycle. We divide the lifecycle into four segments (after marriage):

- the period while there are dependent children;

- the rest of the working life;

- retirement (while the husband is still alive);

- widowhood.

These stages of the lifecycle are illustrated for the mothers of two who are married to men at the same skill level in Figure 4.4. Table 4.2 shows the contributions of these different sources to the incomes of our hypothetical women during the first two (pre-retirement) stages of the lifecycle. We will discuss the retired stages of the lifecycle in Chapter 6.

Consider the childrearing years. During these years, the low-skilled women are net beneficiaries from the state. Their receipts of state benefits exceed their payments in Income Tax and NICs, for example the low-skilled mother of two derives about 14% of her income from the state during these years. The mid-skilled mothers are net beneficiaries if they have large families but almost exactly break even if they have two children. The high-skilled women make net payments to the state, even while they have dependent children. The table also shows the contribution of the 'family transfer' and calculates women's income if such a transfer does indeed take place (labelled the 'woman's portion' in the table). The 'family transfer' is an extremely important potential source of income for the low-skilled women in these years. On the equal sharing assumption, the low-skilled mother of one or two would receive over 60% of her portion from the family transfer.[51]

[50] Note that we generally assume that any WFTC is paid to the husband (see Appendix II). If we altered this assumption, mothers in families receiving WFTC would receive more from the state, and less from the assumed family transfer.

[51] If the assumption about who gets WFTC were altered, so would the balance between the contributions of the state and the family transfer, but the total portion would be the same.

During the rest of the working life, the great majority of the simulated women shown are net taxpayers, and the family transfer plays a much smaller role in their income than during the child-rearing phase. As we have already seen, the high-skilled women take very little time away from paid work while rearing their children, and so there is very little difference in the composition of their income during these first two stages of the lifecycle.

Table 4.2: Sources of women's income over the working life

	As percentage of woman's portion for relevant stage of lifecycle							
	A) While have dependent children			B) Rest of Working life				
	Married			Unmarried		Married		
Number of children	1	2	4	0	0	1	2	4
		in percent				in percent		
Low-skilled								
Labour market	27	16	5	122	104	94	82	36
State	10	14	38	−22	−18	−15	−11	−2
Family transfer	64	70	57	0	14	20	29	66
Woman's portion (£'000s)	£122	£144	£199	£405	£460	£279	£232	£136
Mid-skilled								
Labour market	81	71	31	126	110	109	108	57
State	−6	−1	19	−26	−23	−22	−22	−4
Family transfer	25	30	50	0	13	13	14	48
Woman's portion (£'000s)	£212	£240	£270	£442	£507	£276	£234	£120
High-skilled								
Labour market	122	119	112	133	126	126	126	126
State	−26	−23	−19	−33	−31	−31	−31	−31
Family transfer	4	4	7	0	5	4	5	4
Woman's portion (£'000s)	£398	£466	£592	£771	£814	£427	£359	£221

Note: Income is expressed as a percentage of the 'women's portion' for the relevant edge of the lifecycle.

Figure 4.4: Sources of income by stages of lifecycle: mothers of two

Low-skilled

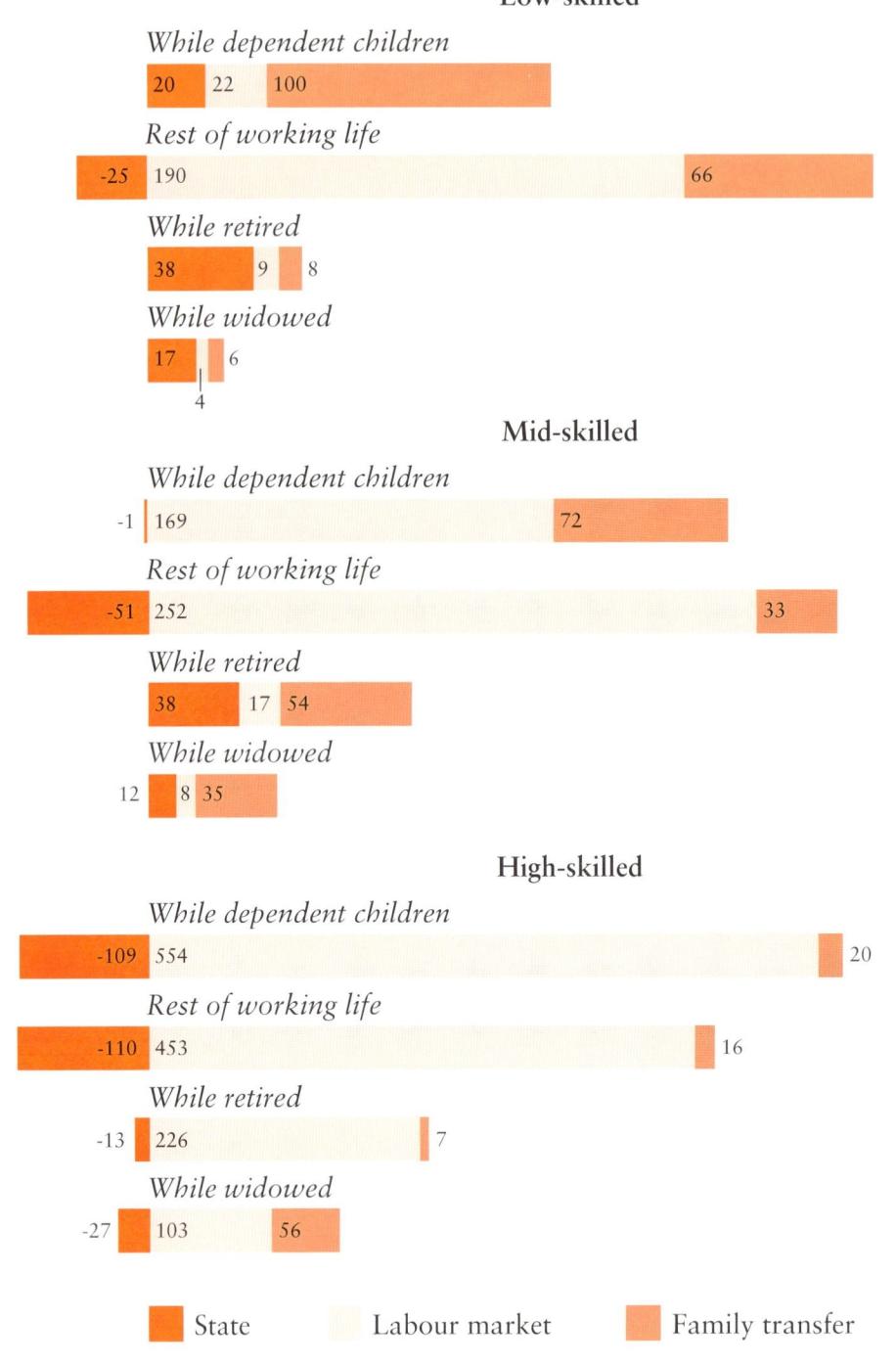

While dependent children
| 20 | 22 | 100 |

Rest of working life
| -25 | 190 | 66 |

While retired
| 38 | 9 | 8 |

While widowed
| 17 | 4 | 6 |

Mid-skilled

While dependent children
| -1 | 169 | 72 |

Rest of working life
| -51 | 252 | 33 |

While retired
| 38 | 17 | 54 |

While widowed
| 12 | 8 | 35 |

High-skilled

While dependent children
| -109 | 554 | 20 |

Rest of working life
| -110 | 453 | 16 |

While retired
| -13 | 226 | 7 |

While widowed
| -27 | 103 | 56 |

■ State   □ Labour market   ■ Family transfer

Note: Income is totalled over the relevant stage of the lifestyle and expressed in £'000s.

4.4 THE IMPACT OF DIVORCE ON LIFETIME INCOME

4.4.1 The timing of divorce

The changing characteristics of divorce were laid out above (Section 4.1). Against this background the simulations focus on two basic examples of divorces:

1. A divorce which occurs when youngest child is two; for a two-child family this is a marriage lasting 7 years.

2. A divorce which occurs when the youngest child is 12, after 17 years in the two-child case.

Applied to the different types of women, this means that, for example, in the case of Mrs Mid with two children an early divorce will occur when she is 32, and a late divorce when she is 42 (with four children, the ages of divorce would be 38 and 48). The model also allows for the possibility of remarriage, set to occur 10 years after an early divorce. The early divorce will help us to follow through a number of years of lone parenthood, while the late divorce types will be useful for examining the effects on women's pensions. For comparison, we also simulate a childless couple divorcing after a long and a short marriage. The characteristics of these hypothetical divorcees are summarised in Table 4.3.

Table 4.3: Age at which hypothetical individuals experience divorce

		Low	Mid	High
Divorce with 2 children	*Early divorce*	27	32	34
	Late divorce	37	42	44
Divorce with 4 children	*Early divorce*	33	38	40
	Late divorce	43	48	50
Remarriage	2 children	37	42	44
	4 children	43	48	50

(header: Skill level)

The early divorce type in the model falls in the most common age band for divorces, while the late type belongs to the third most common age band (representing 12% of divorces). It is also more likely that a woman divorcing later will not remarry, given that the decline in the rate of remarriage is more pronounced for women over the age of 35. Our case where Mrs Mid divorces at 32 is in line with the observation that the peak age band for women divorcing from first marriages was 30-34.[52] The remarriage assumption is in line with the finding by Ford et al. (1998: 32), that the exit from lone motherhood through repartnering tends to occur either early (particularly for young parents), or later when children are older (see Section 4.1 above).

Although there are many marriages of a shorter duration than those we simulate here, we have not found it interesting to examine them, particularly as typically they do not involve children. Where children are involved, available data suggest that if these divorced women remarry, they tend to do so quickly and while young, tending to have their second or third child in their early 30s.[53] There would be little advantage in simulating such a history, since it would be very similar to that of the average continuously married women. Also excluded from the modelling are women who are cohabiting (see section 4.1 above). This is because, analytically, these women are very similar to their married counterparts, the major difference being in pension splitting. We return to the question of pensions in Chapter 6.

4.4.2 The impact of divorce on labour market participation

The 'early' divorce is set to occur when the youngest child is aged two. For Mrs Mid, this is at age 32 if she has two children, or age 38 if she has four. Our simulations suggest that divorce slightly lowers the probability of labour market participation while there are dependent children, but that divorced women are relatively more likely to engage in full-time rather than part-time employment than their counterparts with unbroken marriages. The projected years of employment are summarised in Table 4.4. Considering the case of Mrs Mid, we see that, compared to the continuously married woman, the mid-skilled mother of two who divorces after a short marriage has four more years of full-time employment, but six fewer years of part-time employment. The mid-skilled mother of four would work 12 more years full-time after an early divorce than she would had she remained married – in that case she would have stayed part-time, although she would have spent two more years in employment. The women who have a 'late divorce', when the youngest child is 12, are projected to do almost the same amount of paid work as if they had remained married, except that, once again, the mother of four does more full-time work than if continuously married. Divorces have a similar impact on the participation of

---

[52] According to Table 4.4 in *Marriage, Divorce, and Adoption Statistics 1996*, spinster brides who divorced constituted 87% of women divorcing in that age group, which itself accounted for 17% of all divorcees.

[53] According to Table 3.3 in *Population Trends*, Spring 1999, the mean age of motherhood at birth within remarriage is 33.7. Rates (per thousands) of live births to remarried women aged 25-29, 30-34, and 35-39 were much lower than their counterparts, and were at 5.8, 13, and 9.5.

Mrs Low, with the changes being most noticeable for the mother of two. Our participation results are broadly consistent with evidence from the 1997 Labour Force Survey. The participation rates of divorced mothers are much lower than those of mothers in couples while there is a child under 10, but are nearly as high (and substantially higher for full-time employment) if the youngest child is 16-18 (Holtermann et al. 1999).

Table 4.4: Women's total years in employment and divorce

Number of children	Two			Four		
Type of marriage	Unbroken	Short	Long	Unbroken	Short	Long
Low-skilled						
Full-time years	13	20	20	0	6	7
Part-time years	20	10	13	25	13	18
Mid-skilled						
Full-time years	25	29	25	1	13	11
Part-time years	10	4	10	27	13	17
High-skilled						
Full-time years	34	34	34	30	30	30
Part-time years	1	1	1	5	5	5

Note: Years covered are from birth of first child until 65.

We have also simulated participation probabilities for women who remarry, concentrating for the moment on the case of Mrs Mid. The simulations for her can be found in Figure 4.5. She remarries at the age of 42, if she has two children, and at 48 if she has 4 children. For the mother of two, remarrying has no noticeable impact on the probabilities of participation, which are therefore identical to those of the divorced but un-remarried mother of two. The mother of four, on the other hand, exhibits spells of part-time work after remarriage, when her counterpart who had not remarried would have been more likely to be in full-time employment.

Figure 4.5: Participation probabilities of the mid-skilled mother: divorce with and without remarriage

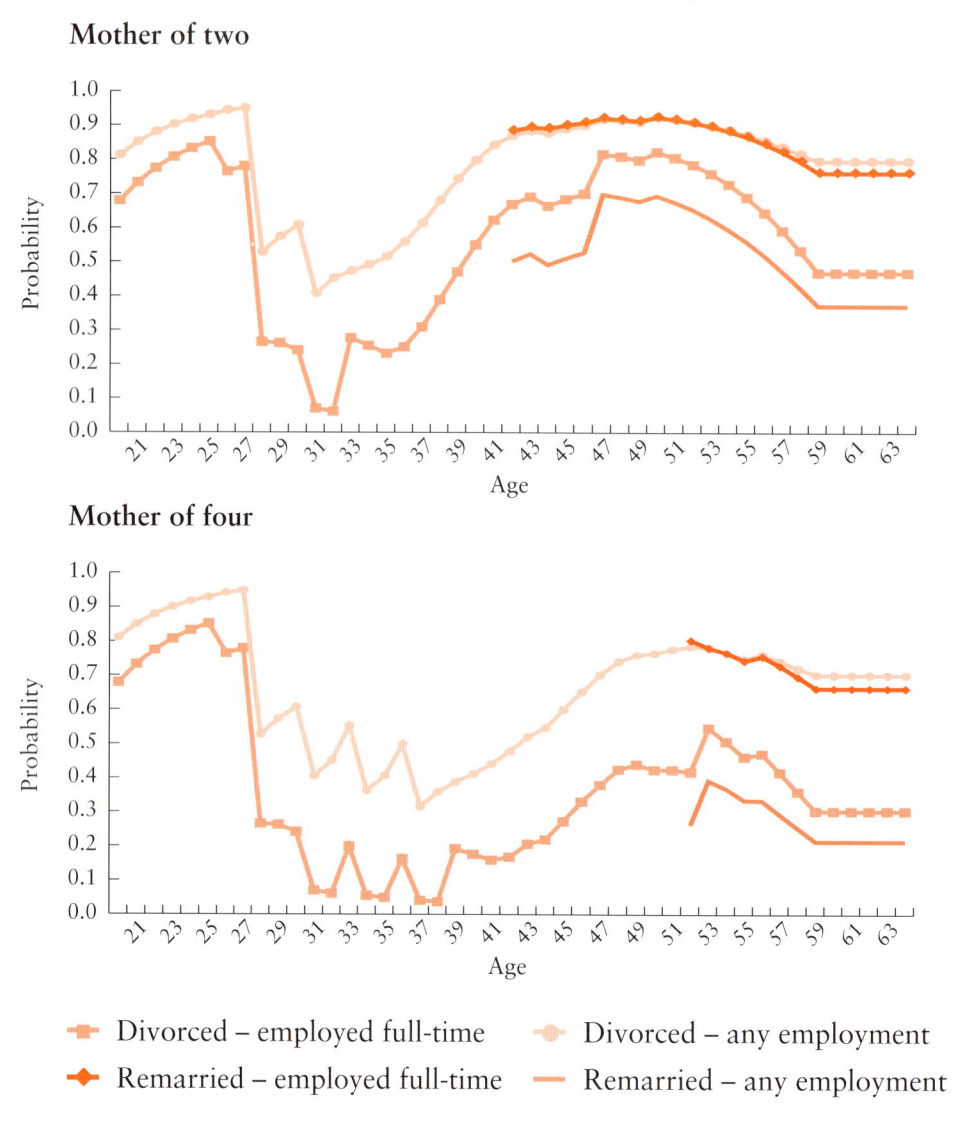

Mother of two

Mother of four

- ■ Divorced – employed full-time
- ○ Divorced – any employment
- ♦ Remarried – employed full-time
- — Remarried – any employment

4.4.3 Divorce and lifetime earnings

Table 4.5 summarises the total labour market income for the divorced mothers as well as those with unbroken marriages. These reflect the participation behaviour discussed above – in general, compared to married mothers, divorced lone mothers have higher earnings overall, with longer spells in full-time employment but also longer spells out of employment when children are young. Our simulated high-skilled mothers do not have their participation affected by divorce. By the time the mid-skilled mother of two who divorces after a long marriage gets her decree (at the age of 43) she is well established back on her career trajectory, and so her earnings are also unaffected by divorce.

Table 4.5: Women's lifetime labour market income[1] and divorce

Number of children	Two			Four		
Type of marriage	Unbroken	Short	Long	Unbroken	Short	Long
Low-skilled	226	277	288	62	107	135
Mid-skilled	446	474	446	161	290	267
High-skilled	1,336	1,336	1,336	1,270	1,270	1,270

Note: Years covered are from marriage.
[1] Labour market income equals gross earnings minus earnings-related pensions contributions plus earnings-related pension receipts.

The earnings profiles for married and divorced women appear in Figures 4.6 (low-skilled) and 4.7 (mid-skilled) with married women without children shown for comparison. Within each graph, the three women start out on the same trajectory. When childbirth and then divorce occur, the graph shows a new trajectory. In Figure 4.7, for Mrs Mid, early divorce brings her earnings profiles up, closer to that of her childless counterparts regardless of the number of children. The divorced mother of two earns much more than her married counterpart during her mid-thirties. The divorced mother of four makes the greatest gains from increased labour market participation. Her earnings reach a plateau of around £12,000 at the ages of 46 and 48 for early and late divorces respectively, compared to a peak of £8,000 or less for the continuously married woman. The story differs slightly for Mrs Low (Figure 4.6). For the mother of two, even early divorce does not make much difference to her total lifetime earnings, as she spends as many years with earnings above as below those of the continuously married Mrs Low. If Mrs Low with four children divorces early, she spends 6 more years earning nothing, which is below the trickle earned by her married counterpart. She does eventually take full-time work, but her earnings only reach a range of £6,000–£8,000 after the age of 48 for a period of 6 years, which is a noticeably shorter period than the mid-skilled woman in similar domestic circumstances.

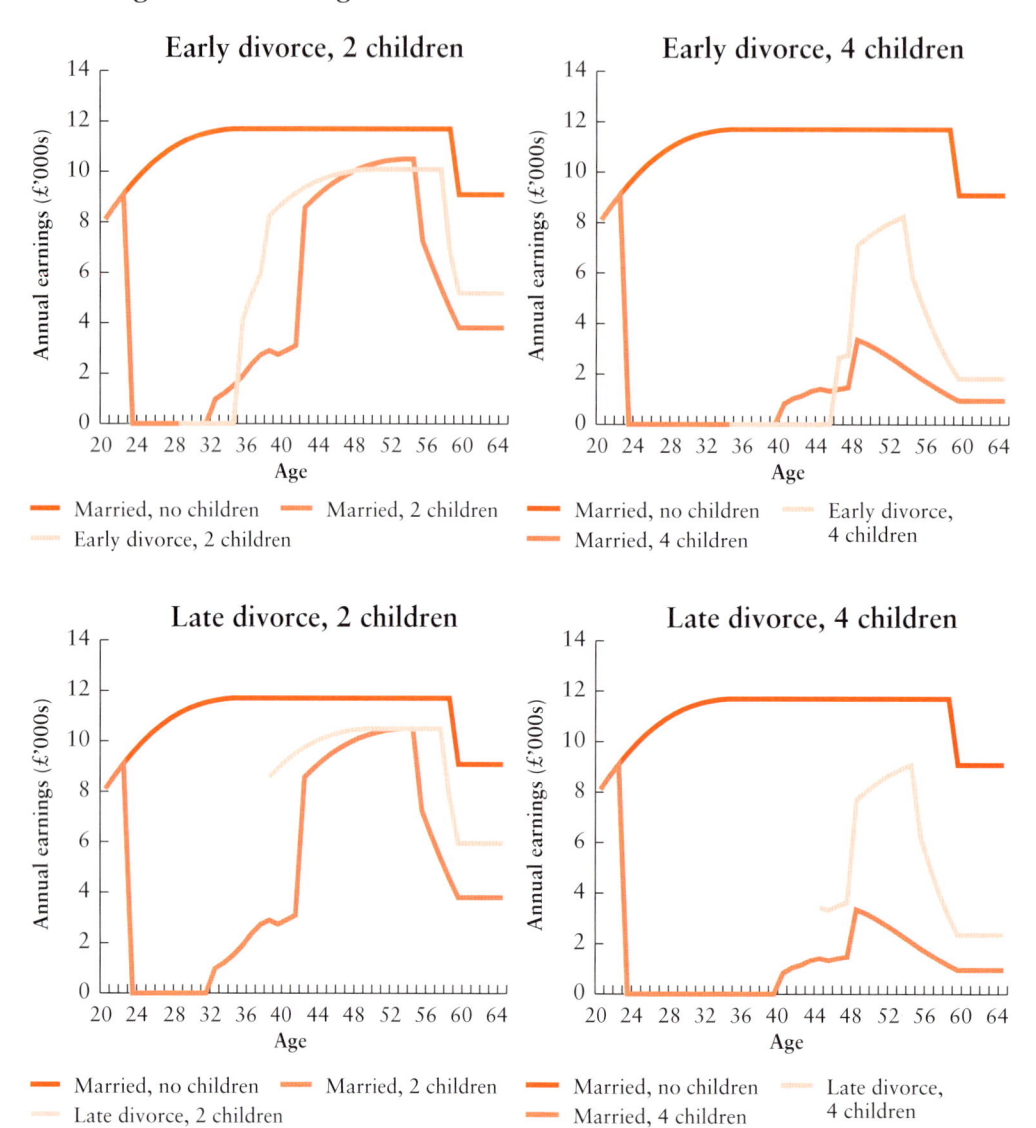

Figure 4.6: Earnings with and without divorce: low-skilled women

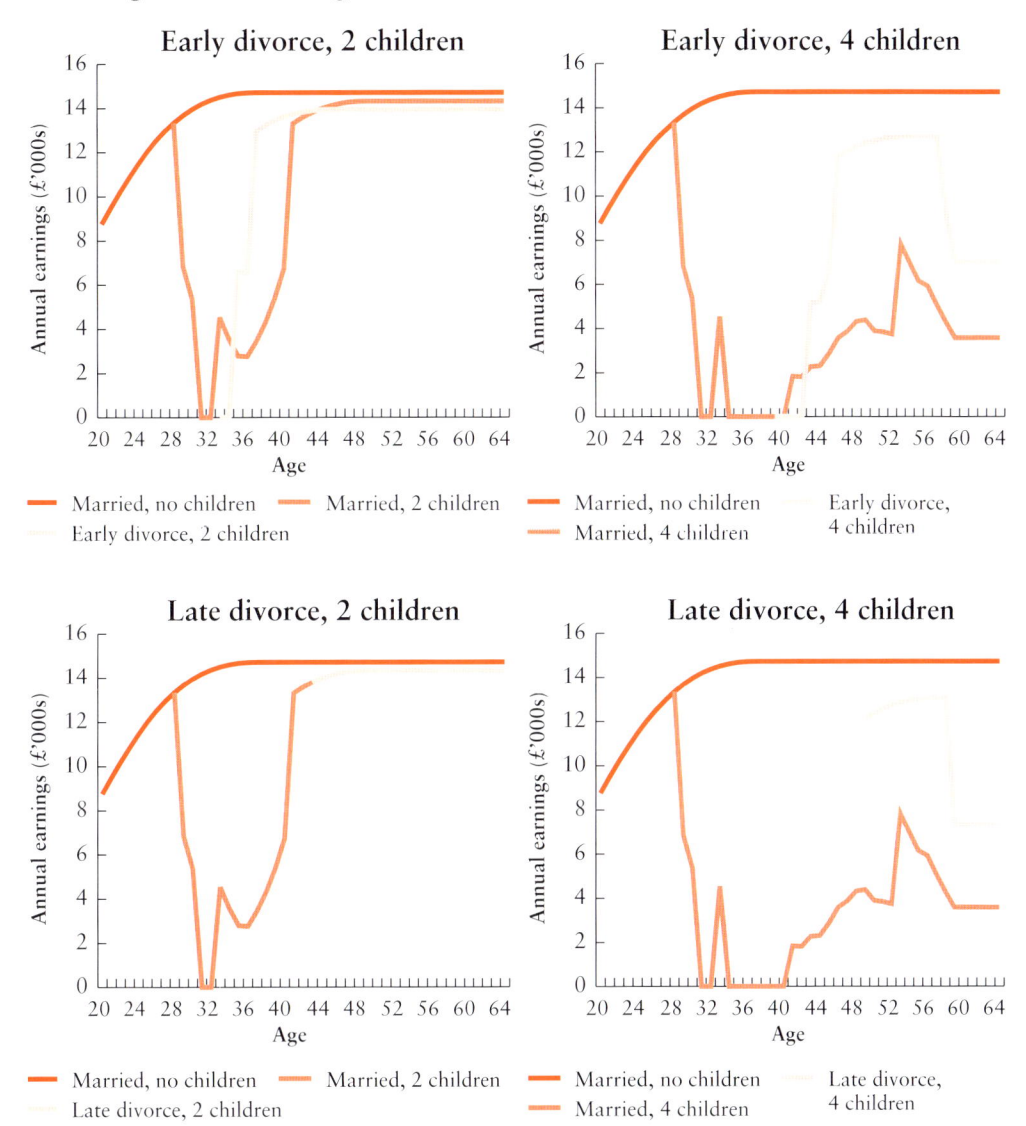

Figure 4.7: Earnings with and without divorce: mid-skilled women

Early divorce, 2 children

Early divorce, 4 children

Late divorce, 2 children

Late divorce, 4 children

Figure 4.8 plots the earnings profiles of Mrs Mid if she remarries 10 years after an early divorce[54]. Her earnings are lower than those of her divorced counterpart who does not remarry, as after the remarriage her profile is more like that of the continuously married woman. The lifetime difference in gross earnings between the remarried and un-remarried mothers is quite modest (about £20,000) if there are two children, but if there are four children it is about £90,000.

[54] The year of part-time earnings at age 33 in the four-child scenario occurs before the divorce.

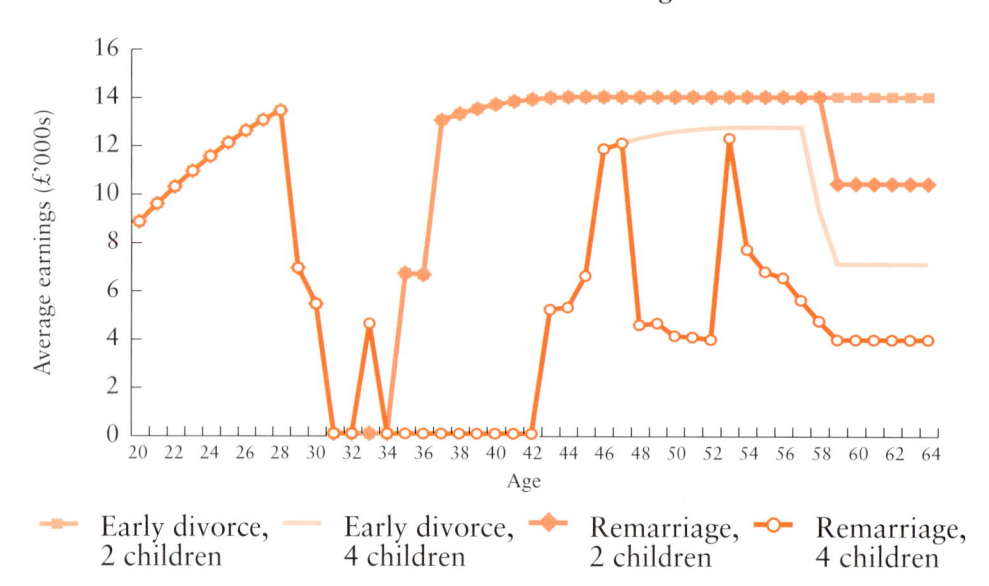

Figure 4.8: Earnings for divorced mid-skilled mother – with and without remarriage

4.4.4 Divorce: from earnings to income

The above discussion concerns labour market earnings only, and in the next section we consider other sources of income as well. Before continuing, we remind the reader that the responses of actual women (and men) to divorce are much more diverse than we have allowed for here in our descriptions of hypothetical biographies.

When a marriage breaks down, whatever income sharing went on in it is likely to end. We take the loss of the family transfer (and its posthumous component, the survivor's pension) as the loss from divorce. Although we do not know exactly how much income sharing takes place in any particular marriage, we assume that, as long as the marriage continues, income is shared equally.

In looking at the loss of purchasing power following divorce, we are not claiming to give an exhaustive account of the costs of divorce. We take no account of the transactions costs (legal fees, etc.) of the actual divorce, or of any emotional costs (or benefits) which the divorce brings. Although we explore the income consequences of divorce only in families with children, we do not consider the effect of the divorce on the children themselves.[55] We take no account of any extra costs of paid childcare following the divorce, nor of the loss of any domestic labour which the husband might have contributed. Although our

---

[55] This topic has been the subject of another research project which concludes that a major part of the fairly modest impact on children works through the low income of lone mother families (Joshi et al. 1999 a).

calculations assume that the dependent children stay with the mother after the divorce, we do not take any account of the fact that the upkeep of the children must be met entirely from her income, rather than being shared with their father. Studies which adjust for the expenditure costs of family size before and after divorce show that, measured in this way, women (and children) are worse off following divorce, than are men (Jarvis and Jenkins, 1999).

The loss of family transfer may be partly offset by payments from the ex-spouse. The extent to which men support families from which they have divorced is highly variable. Evidence suggests that only a minority of lone parents actually get any such contribution. Surveys of lone parents in 1991, 1993 and 1994 (after the introduction of the CSA) show that only 30% of lone parents receive maintenance. There is some evidence that divorced lone parents are, initially at least, somewhat more likely to be in receipt of maintenance than those who were separated from a cohabitation or were never-partnered. (Ford et al. 1998, Table 3.3)[56]

In our calculations, we heroically assume that all divorced fathers will contribute to their non-co-resident offspring at the rate prescribed in the recent White Paper on Child Support (DSS 1999b). Some may well be more generous, but we assume that all comply: this is in line with our general approach of assuming that everyone pays all the taxes they should and receives all the state benefits to which they are entitled. It is possible to see how much our results depend on this assumption as the amount of presumed child support is shown separately. The other mechanism for replacing part of the family transfer, currently being reformed, is the mechanism for pension sharing. We assume that this too is in place.

Table 4.6 shows the calculated initial income losses from divorce, the offsetting responses and the net outcome for our hypothetical cases. The initial income loss is calculated as the loss of the woman's portion (the income that a woman receives if the family transfer actually takes place) compared to that obtained by a similar woman who has an unbroken marriage. The capacity of a woman to respond to a loss of family transfer by increasing her own labour supply is a crucial determinant of her net income loss from divorce. The rather surprising result that the high-skilled mother of four who divorces after a long marriage loses more than the low-skilled woman in similar circumstances is due to the fact that the high-skilled woman who stays married is, by this stage of her life, back in full-time employment and has no scope to increase her earnings further, whereas the low-skilled woman can increase her labour supply to offset the initial loss from divorce.

[56] In Ford et al.'s sample, 44% of divorced lone parents received maintenance in 1991, but only 31% of them were receiving maintenance in 1995. Jarvis and Jenkins (1999) found that 24% of custodial parents in their sample from the BHPS received maintenance – their sample covered those from cohabitations as well as marriages which had ended.

Table 4.6: The incomes of divorced women compared to those with unbroken marriages

Income in £'000s Length of marriage Number of children	early divorce 2	late divorce	early divorce 4	late divorce	Remarriage, early divorce 2	Remarriage, early divorce 4
Low-skilled						
Initial loss from divorce	150	96	178	134	150	178
of which widow's pension	6	6	6	6	0	0
Offsetting income increases	115	73	124	119	147	170
From labour market	51	62	45	73	−15	−8
From child support	26	7	31	7	26	31
From pension share	2	5	4	7	2	4
From state tax-benefit system	36	−1	44	32	32	5
From 2nd husband					102	137
Net cost of divorce	35	23	53	15	3	8
Mid-skilled						
Initial loss from divorce	169	127	235	177	169	235
of which widow's pension	35	35	35	35	0	0
Offsetting income increases	144	86	264	181	222	314
From labour market	28	0	129	106	5	33
From child support	39	16	46	16	39	46
From pension share	35	57	49	71	35	49
From state tax-benefit system	42	13	41	−12	24	34
From 2nd husband					118	152
Net cost of divorce	25	41	−30	−5	−53	−79
High-skilled						
Initial loss from divorce	83	77	73	73	83	73
of which widow's pension	56	56	56	56	0	0
Offsetting income increases	91	48	111	54	131	144
From labour market	0	0	0	0	0	0
From child support	61	25	72	26	61	72
From pension share	7	1	10	8	7	10
From state tax-benefit system	23	23	29	20	0	6
From 2nd husband					63	56
Net cost of divorce	−9	29	−38	19	−48	−71

Child support payments are obviously more important for the women who have divorced when the children are younger (i.e. after a relatively short marriage). They are much larger where the father is a high-earner. Even with our assumption of full child support payments, Mrs Low with two children who divorces after a short marriage receives £26,000 in child support – under 20% of the loss we calculate she suffers from the divorce. For the parallel woman from the high-skilled partnership, the child support payments are estimated to be over twice as high, and compensate for nearly three-quarters of the estimated loss from the divorce.

The amount of help that a woman can expect from pension sharing, in contrast to that from child support, will be greater where the couple are older when they divorce. The amount a woman receives from pension sharing on divorce also depends on the absolute size of the pension gap between the spouses as evaluated at the time of the divorce. Thus, neither the women in the low-skilled couples, nor those in the high-skilled couples, gain much from pension sharing, the former because their ex-husbands had poor pension prospects, and the latter because both they and their husbands had good pension prospects. Some of the mid-skilled women are calculated to derive substantial sums from pension sharing: those experiencing a late divorce, in particular, are large beneficiaries from pension sharing.

Many of the low- and mid-skilled women are eligible for substantial sums in the way of Working Families' Tax Credit (WFTC). For example, the mothers of two who divorce after a short marriage are calculated to receive about £25,000 in WFTC (low-skilled mother) or £40,000 (mid-skilled mother). It must be emphasised that these calculations are based on experience of a world of benefit-traps. They make no allowance for the improved incentives and opportunities offered by the New Deals. The WFTC payments as well as the Income Tax and NICs on the change in earnings following divorce are included in the rows labelled 'From state tax-benefit system' in Table 4.6.

Our calculations show that some of our hypothetical women stand to gain in financial terms from divorce, the cases where the 'net cost of divorce' shown in Table 4.6 is negative. In view of the qualifications mentioned above regarding the scope of these calculations, it should be remembered that this increase in cash does not necessarily represent a higher standard of living. Nevertheless, when a couple divorce it is presumably because at least one of them expects to be (in some sense) better off in the divorced than in the married state. That this should sometimes be reflected in the rather narrow financial calculations presented here should not occasion great surprise. Given that we defined the loss from divorce in terms of the loss of 'family transfer', it is no surprise to find that re-marriage substantially reduces these loses. Thus, for example, the low-skilled mother of two who remarries is calculated to gain £102,000 worth of family transfer from her second husband, replacing two-thirds of the family transfer lost on divorce. Nevertheless, even with remarriage Mrs Low is a net loser from her divorce. The position of Mrs Low in this respect contrasts strongly to Mrs Mid and High – increases in their labour market activity while divorced, combined with the assumed transfer from the new husband, mean that they are net 'winners' from re-marriage. It should be remembered that these calculations assume that the second husband will share his income equally with the woman, even though some of this 'family transfer' is going to support children who are not his biologically.

4.5   CONCLUSIONS AND KEY FINDINGS

This chapter has looked both at the potential impact on women's income of partners' sharing of income and at the consequences of divorce for women's incomes. Women's experience of income sharing and of divorce is strongly differentiated by the educational level of the woman. Nevertheless, for all women, the experience of divorce has an important effect on their lifetime incomes. The findings to emerge from Chapter 4 are:

- *Potentially*, the family shares both domestic labour and income. Although the conventional assumption that families share income equally is debatable, we here show how important a transfer of income from husband to wife *might* be to women's lifetime incomes. For example, if we assume equal sharing of income, the family transfer accounts for over 30% of the lifetime incomes of the low- and mid-skilled mothers of two.

- The potential contribution of the family transfer is particularly important during childrearing years – over 60% of the income of the low-skilled mother of one or two during this period comes from the family transfer, suggesting that a high degree of financial dependency continues for some women within marriage.

- If current rates of divorce persist, two in five couples will ultimately divorce. It is, therefore, essential to look in detail at the economic consequences of divorce. We have estimated the consequences of divorce for a woman's earnings and income, but in line with the rest of the simulation, we do not take account of changes in expenditure and the fact that the upkeep of children following divorce may be met entirely from a woman's income, rather than being shared between spouses.

- The economic impact of divorce varies enormously according to the timing of the divorce, changes in labour market participation following divorce, whether remarriage occurs and the woman's educational level.

- We find that divorce means slightly fewer years in the labour market while there are dependent children, but a higher likelihood of engaging in full-time rather than part-time employment when in the labour market. The overall impact of this is, in general, to increase women's earnings – the mid-skilled mother is estimated to have £28,000 more earnings if she experiences an early divorce than either her un-divorced counterpart or the late divorcee.

- Taking into account the loss of the family transfer allows for an assessment of the overall cost of divorce – for the mid-skilled mother of two, the initial cost of divorce is estimated to be £169,000 where the marriage is short and £127,000 for a long marriage.

- Increase in women's labour supply, the tax-benefit system, pension sharing and child support payments may all play an important part in offsetting the initial income loss, of divorce. Assuming child support payments are made, and pensions are split equally, the income loss of divorce for the mid-skilled mother of two would be reduced to £25,000 for the short marriage (in this case, 32% of the reduction is accounted for by child support payments) and £41,000 for the long marriage (the assumed pension sharing makes up 66% of the reduction in this instance).

- The loss from divorce may be substantially reduced by re-marriage (assuming, of course, that income is shared in all partnerships). For example, the low-skilled mother of two who remarries is calculated to gain £102,000 worth of family transfer from her second husband, replacing two-thirds of the family transfer lost on divorce. Nevertheless, even with remarriage Mrs Low is a net 'loser' from her divorce. By contrast, the increases in labour market activity while divorced, combined with the assumed transfer from the new husband, mean that mid- and high-skilled women are net 'winners' from re-marriage.

5. PARENTING AND CARING FOR OTHERS

5: PARENTING AND CARING FOR OTHERS

This chapter takes as its main focus the impact of parenting on women's lifetime incomes, asking how women's incomes are affected by the experience of caring for children. We first examine the results from the simulation model that estimate the earnings that mothers of different skills levels forgo in bringing up children and how these, in turn, are affected by the timing of motherhood and the tax-benefit system (Section 5.1). In Section 5.2 we return to the question of the pay gap, and consider how the gender pay gap compares with the 'mother gap' and the 'parent gap'. The lifetime incomes of teenage mothers are considered in detail in Section 5.3, which looks at the earnings costs that such an experience brings, as well as effects into retirement. Section 5.4 then looks at the relationship between women's incomes and children from the opposite direction, and asks how women's incomes affect children's experiences, particularly the experience of childhood poverty. Lastly, while the majority of this chapter has considered parenting, we recognise that caring for older relatives and adult dependants will (increasingly) have an impact on women's lifetime earnings – this is considered in Section 5.5.

5.1   THE EARNINGS AND INCOME COST OF CHILDREN

We here consider the impact of having children on women's earnings and incomes. We consider the costs of children *only* in so far as children modify mothers' presence in the labour market and thereby reduce their earnings. Of course, this is only part of the cost of children. We are taking no account of the costs of expenditure on the children: we have not considered either the costs of feeding and clothing them (for example) or the costs of childcare (for reports that do so, see, among others, Finlayson et al. 1996, Middleton et al. 1999). Women who remain in full-time employment when their children are small, as do the high-skilled cases discussed here, might be expected to incur substantial childcare costs. We also look at the consequences of children for the state's expenditure on benefits and its receipt of taxes. State expenditure on goods and services for children – principally for education and health – is not considered here. The third omission is the cost of children in terms of their mother's leisure time and time contributed by other family members, fathers, grandparents, and other relatives and friends. The focus on the earnings and income cost of children is not to deny the value of children, nor the valuable unpaid work which goes into raising them. Women may forgo earnings in order to undertake unpaid caring work. This unpaid work is an indirect expenditure on children and forms part of the investment which parents are making in the human and social capital which will contribute to the national income and well-being in the future.

5.1.1 The impact of children on earnings

The profiles of women's lifetime earnings for the standard cases were first set out in Chapter 3 (Section 3.2.2) and the consequences of the different family scenarios for lifetime earnings are summarised in Table 5.1. The impact of skill level and number of children on gross lifetime earnings is illustrated graphically in Figure 5.1. The gaps in lifetime earnings between women with and without children measure the gross earnings cost of children. The income of the central (mid-skilled) case who stays in employment between her first and second births is £140,000, or 26%, below what would have been earned after the first birth if she had no children. The corresponding figures with four children are £414,000 and 77%. For the low-skilled woman, taking a traditional break from employment for childrearing, forgone earnings are £269,000 (58%) for two children and £426,000 (91%) for four. The high-skilled woman forgoes nothing if she only has one child (and receives maternity pay), £19,000 (2%) for two children and £90,000 (9%) for four. If Mrs Mid or Mrs Low has only one child the loss goes down but not quite *pro rata* to £86,000 (mid-skilled) or £185,000 (low-skilled). In general the higher the earning power, the less is lost, because of the great contrast in the employment participation attributed to the different women (see Figure 3.4).

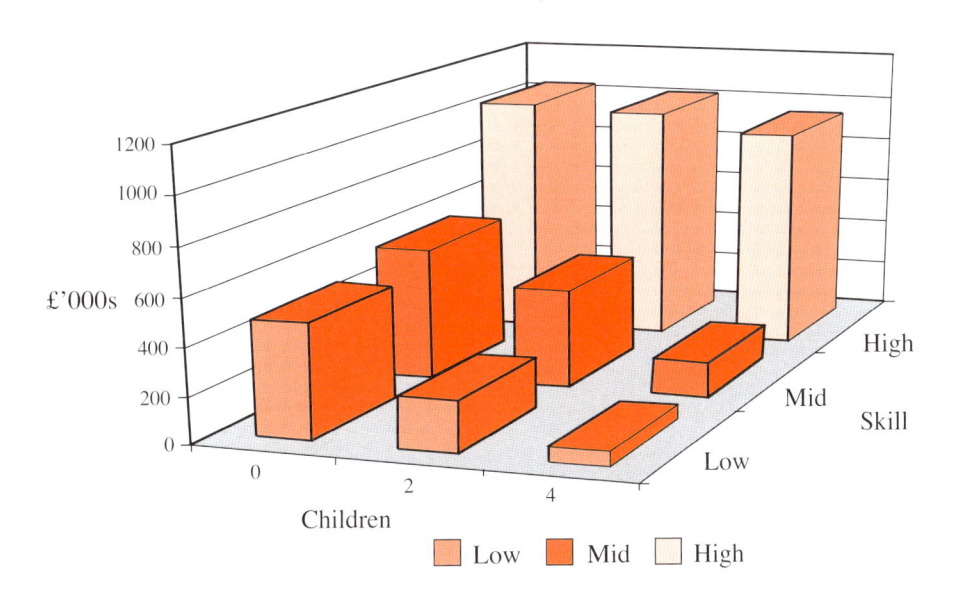

*Figure 5.1: Total gross lifetime earnings:
women in educationally matched couples*

Table 5.1: Forgone earnings costs of motherhood

	\multicolumn{3}{c}{Number of children}	
	One	Two	Four
Low-skilled mother			
Forgone earnings			
£'000s	185	269	426
As percent of potential earnings after 1st birth	40	58	91
Composition of loss – percentage due to:			
lost years	20	31	35
lost hours	48	37	33
lower pay	31	32	32
lower pay due to: lost experience	29	31	32
part-time penalty	2	1	0
Mid-skilled mother			
Forgone earnings			
£'000s	86	140	414
As percent of potential earnings after 1st birth	16	26	77
Composition of loss – percentage due to:			
lost years	0	19	28
lost hours	72	53	47
lower pay	28	27	25
lower pay due to: lost experience	11	18	19
part-time penalty	17	10	6
High-skilled mother			
Forgone earnings			
£'000s	0	19	90
As percent of potential earnings after 1st birth	0	2	9
Composition of loss – percentage due to:			
lost years	n/a	0	0
lost hours	n/a	55	54
lower pay	n/a	45	46
lower pay due to: lost experience	n/a	17	15
part-time penalty	n/a	29	32

Earlier work (see, for example, Joshi et al. 1996), has found that the extra earnings lost in having more children went down as the number of children increased. This indicated that there were economies of scale in raising children at home in their pre-school years. The younger children could 'free-ride' on the employment gap created by their siblings. With the present set of simulations, however, it is difficult to find clearly diminishing marginal costs in moving from smaller to larger numbers of children. It is now the case that, because of the increase in their labour market attachment, for both Mrs Mid and Mrs High, the marginal earnings costs of having children sharply increase with the number of children. The earnings lost by going from two to four children are around five times the change between one and two. It seems that the scale economies in this element of the costs of raising children are becoming more and more concentrated at the lower end of the social spectrum.

Figure 5.2 provides a breakdown of the four reasons contributing to these earnings shortfalls: fewer years in employment, shorter hours due to part-time jobs, and lost experience and the part-time penalty both of which contribute to lower pay per hour. 'Lost experience' reflects the legacy of having taken time out on subsequent earnings levels. This may work through loss of promotion prospects, but could also take the form of downward occupation mobility or depletion of skill on return after a gap. The 'part-time penalty' reflects the lower rates of pay offered to equally experienced workers in part-time jobs. This 'part-time penalty' operates in addition to the effect of fewer hours in paid work.

Figure 5.2: The earnings cost of two children: total and composition

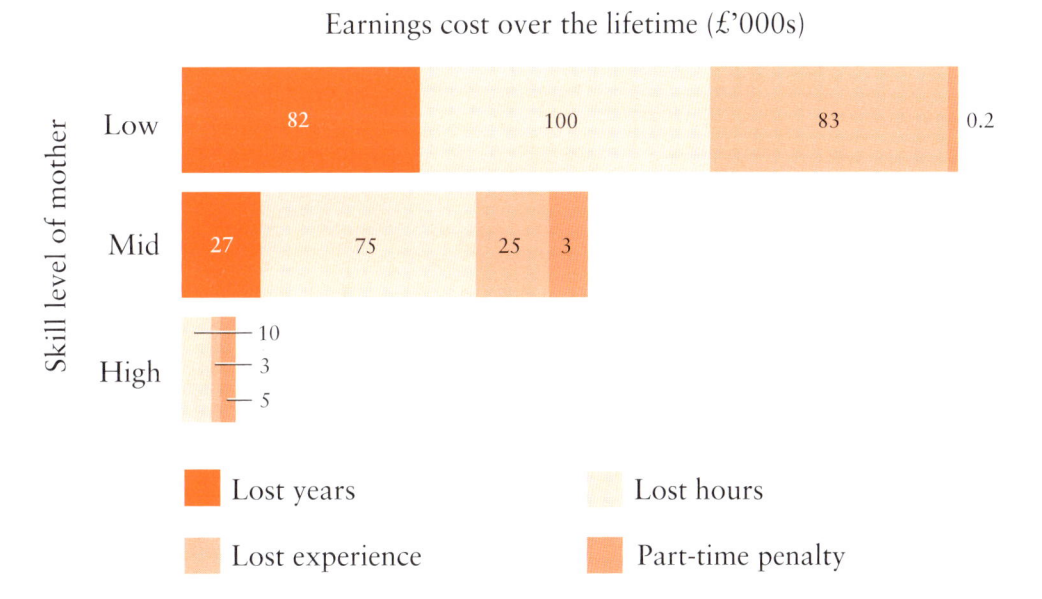

Earnings cost over the lifetime (£'000s)

Skill level of mother:
- Low: Lost years 82, Lost hours 100, Lost experience 83, Part-time penalty 0.2
- Mid: Lost years 27, Lost hours 75, Lost experience 25, Part-time penalty 3
- High: 10, 3, 5

Legend: Lost years, Lost hours, Lost experience, Part-time penalty

Mrs Low's lost earnings derive in roughly equal parts from lost years, lost hours and lower pay, with most of the pay effect arising from her loss of nine years of experience. Mrs Mid only drops out for two years, so lost earnings arise chiefly from lost hours, which in turn generates a more noticeable component from the part-time penalty. However, our current finding that 18% of Mrs Mid's lost pay is due to lost experience is well below the 31% found in the simulation based on 1980 data. It appears that the composition of forgone earnings of Mrs Mid and Mrs High are becoming more similar, and that Mrs Mid's long-term pay penalties of motherhood are diminishing. For Mrs High there is no lost years item and most of the little that is forgone reflects loss of hours and hourly pay while working part-time, with a small element of long-term pay reduction in full-time work. There is thus no one typical composition of lost earnings, just as there is no standard level of lost earnings.

The forgone earnings cost of motherhood reported here for the mid-skilled mother of two represents a sharp fall over previous estimates. In earlier work we estimated this cost at 55% of Mrs Typical's lifetime earnings (£230,000 at 1995 earnings levels). Why has this fallen to 26% (£140,000 at 1999 earnings levels)? Delayed childbirth seems to be responsible for lowering the cost.[57]

5.1.2 The timing of motherhood

We now explore the sensitivity of Mrs Mid's participation and earnings profiles to the age at which she starts her family. Figure 5.3 shows how our simulated participation probabilities vary with the age at which Mrs Mid has her first child. It shows the probability of part-time and full-time work in the period from the year before the birth until ten years afterwards. The height of the bars represents the probability of being in any paid employment, and if the bar cuts the horizontal line representing 0.5 probability, our model puts Mrs Mid into a paid job. The top set of bars represents the probabilities when the first birth takes place at 24. Her probability of employment remains over 0.4 after the birth and very nearly reaches 0.5 when the child is two, but then the birth of the second baby reduces the probability drastically. Our model suggests that nearly half of these women are likely to resume employment before their first child is 3. The model predicts that if Mrs Mid is a first-time mother at 24, she will be back in part-time market work (after a 7-year break) by the age of 31. The probability that she is in full-time employment hovers around 10% while she is in her late twenties and early thirties.

At the bottom of the figure, we show the probabilities corresponding to a first birth at age 30. In this case, the probability that a mid-skilled mother is employed in the year of the first birth is just over half (0.55) although the probability of full-time employment is only 0.29 (compared with 0.8 in the year before the birth). With the arrival of the second child, the probability of employment falls below 0.5, and that of full-time employment falls to under

---

[57] Alternatively one might say that the recognition of the savings afforded by postponing the first child have, themselves, led to the shift in fertility patterns.

0.10. The probability of part-time employment recovers rapidly and the chance of her being back at work is over 50% by the time the second child is two. Nevertheless, her chance of being in a full-time job remains low and is still under 30% when she is 40 (and her youngest child is seven).

Figure 5.3: Participation probabilities by age at first birth: mid-skilled women

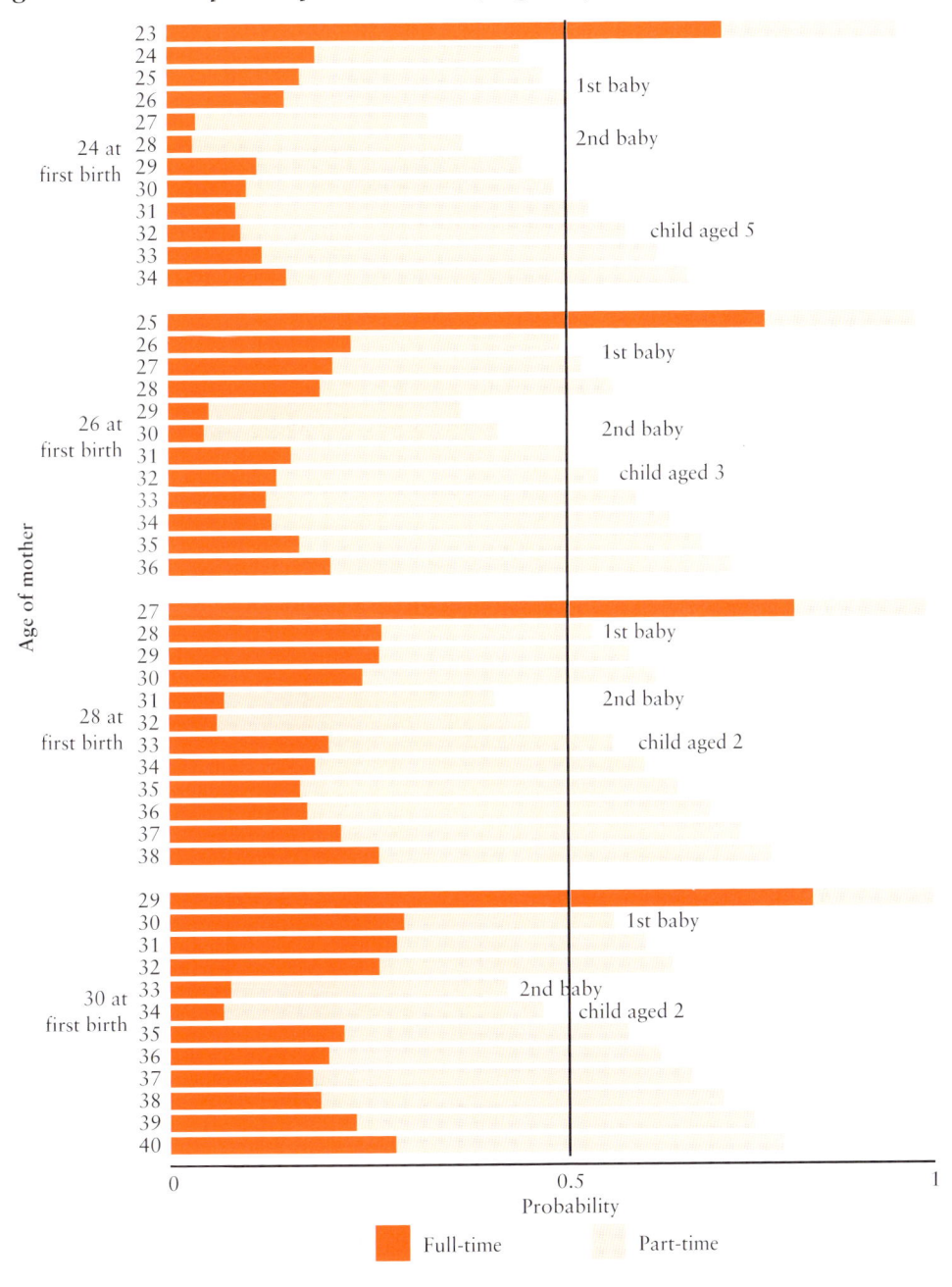

This analysis suggests that, for the mid-skilled women at least, the decision to return to work at the time of her first baby is very finely balanced, and is sensitive to the age at which the woman has her first child. If the first birth takes place while the woman is 24 or under, the representative woman captured in our simulations will leave employment when the baby arrives, but at age 27 (not shown) she is likely to carry on in part-time employment, and at age 28 she is (just) more likely to keep on a full-time job.

The relationship between employment and age at first birth can be explained in the following way. Employment experience increases potential wages, so that as Mrs Mid becomes older, the cost of quitting employment will rise, and her capacity to pay for childcare, if she should continue in paid work, increases. Thus, employment and age at first birth are related through potential earnings.

The dependence of Mrs Mid's labour force participation on the age at which she has her first child has implications for the forgone earnings cost of her children. These (and their composition) are shown in Figure 5.4. If Mrs Mid had the first of two births at age 24, and had a seven-year break from employment, her forgone earnings would be nearly £300,000 according to our model, with a similar mix of sources as Mrs Low (and earlier incarnations of Mrs Typical). Having a first child at the age of 30 nearly halves the amount of the forgone earnings compared to starting a family at the age of 26. Nevertheless, even if Mrs Mid delays her first child until the age of 30, her forgone earnings are seven times greater than total earnings forgone by a highly-skilled counterpart.

Although not illustrated here, the simulated late marriage and childbearing histories for the other two types of women indicate similar results although, in both cases, the amounts involved are much smaller. If Mrs Low has two children when she is 30 and 33 rather than when she is 23 and 26, she gains £43,000 in earnings. Mrs High, who tends to avoid losing any earnings at any age, would increase her forgone earnings to £50,000 if she had her first child at 23 compared to the £19,000 she forgoes when she has her first child at 30.

All this reminds us that the calculations presented here are for illustrative women. Although these women may be typical, the real world exhibits more variety than can be shown here.

Figure 5.4: Decomposition of forgone earnings cost of two children by age of mother at first birth: mid-skilled woman

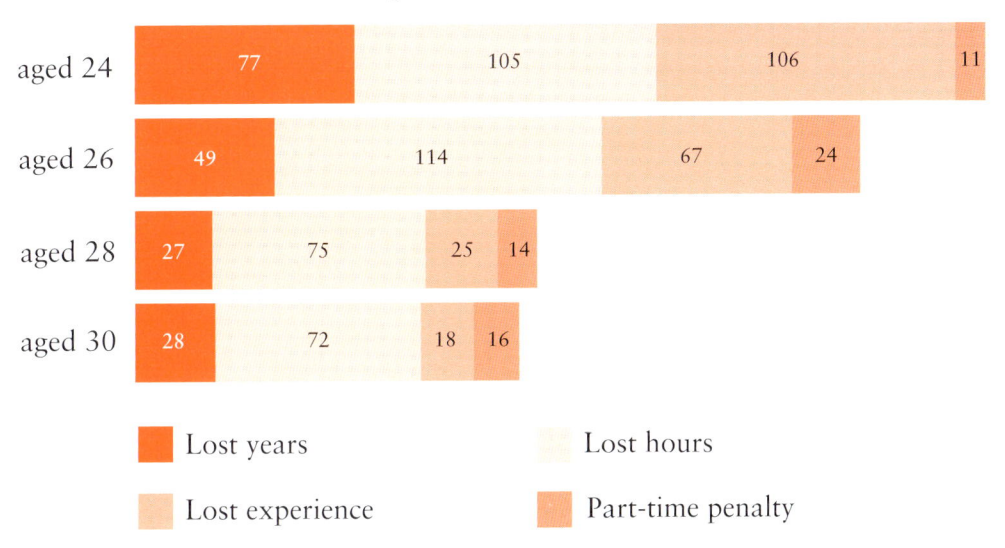

Earnings cost over the lifetime (£'000s)

Age	Lost years	Lost hours	Lost experience	Part-time penalty
aged 24	77	105	106	11
aged 26	49	114	67	24
aged 28	27	75	25	14
aged 30	28	72	18	16

■ Lost years   ▪ Lost hours
■ Lost experience   ■ Part-time penalty

5.1.3 The income costs of children

Thus far we have measured the cost of children as the earnings forgone as a result of the reduction in the woman's labour market activity.[58] The existence of pensions and of state taxes and benefits, however, means that a woman's forgone gross earnings from motherhood do not measure her net income costs. Table 5.2 shows the steps involved in going from the woman's forgone earnings to her net income costs. It also shows an additional complication – the effect on her husband's income. Although our model assumes that a man's earnings are not affected by whether he is married or whether he has children,[59] the operation of the tax-benefit system means that his net income may be affected. We discuss this in detail below.

The relationship between the gross earnings cost of children and the net income cost is shown in detail in Table 5.2.

Consider the case of Mrs Mid with two children (in boldface in the table). She earns £140,000 less than a woman who is identical in all respects, but is childless. These lower earnings have an effect on her earnings-related pension. Over her lifetime, she pays £2,000 less in pension contributions, but then in retirement she receives a total of £7,000 less in pension payments. When we have taken account of these factors, the mother receives £145,000 less over her

---

[58] This approximately measures the economic output forgone. Strictly speaking, the employers' NI Contribution should be included to get a complete measure of forgone output.

[59] We have not attempted to model the increases in hours sometimes found for fathers of young families.

lifetime than her childless counterpart. Since we are treating earnings-related pensions as deferred earnings, we call this the "labour market cost" (gross earnings adjusted for pensions). We next take account of the role of taxes and benefits. Lower earnings mean lower Income Tax and NICs. Motherhood brings with it Child Benefit (and possibly other cash benefits). These reduce the effect of the gross income loss – in this case by £65,000. Overall her gross earnings cost from two children is reduced from £140,000 to a net income cost of £80,000.

The table also gives the total effect of children on the husband's income. The tax-benefit system may result in a father having higher net income than a childless man with the same gross income. One source of change to the husband's income is the state basic pension.[60] This (rather small) amount affects the husbands of the low-skilled mothers of four only and increases the husband's income by about £4,100 over the lifetime. The second source of change is Income Tax.[61] The total effect on the man's lifetime Income Tax is shown in the table – the effect is largest for the man in the mid-skill couple with four children, when it reaches £11,000.

The third way in which husband's net income may be affected is through the operation of Working Families' Tax Credit (WFTC). It will be for each couple entitled to WFTC to decide who should receive the payment. The calculations shown here assume that the couple elect to have the payment made to the woman in the case of the low-skilled couple with four children. In other cases, our assumption is that the man will receive the WFTC unless his wife is employed for over sixteen hours per week. The calculations underlying Table 5.2 include WFTC,[62] but the amounts of WFTC and the person to whom they are assumed to be paid are shown explicitly in Table A.2 in the Appendix. Although WFTC might be very useful to the families concerned at the time it is paid, it does not greatly affect the incomes of the couples examined here over the whole lifetime. Therefore, varying the assumption about who receives the WFTC would have only a small effect on the woman's net income cost of children.

---

[60] The impact arises because, in our simulations, we assume that wives are two years younger than their husbands. This, coupled with our assumption of equal state pension age, means that when the a man reaches 65, he may be eligible for a dependency addition to his state basic pension if his wife is not earning. As the standard childless women are simulated to be in employment during this period, while some of the mothers are not, this is one way in which parenthood can affect a man's income.

[61] The existence of Children's Tax Credit (CTC) (to be introduced in 2001, but modelled in our simulations) means that fathers will pay less tax than childless men with the same income. We assume that (where permitted) a couple will generally split the CTC between them, but that where the woman is not employed (or does not earn enough to exhaust her share of CTC) the man receives the entire tax credit. The tax position is (sometimes) further complicated by the fact that the dependency addition for basic pension is taxable.

[62] As part of the man's net income adjustment where it is paid to the man and as part of the calculation of 'state benefits, net of taxes' where it is paid to the woman.

Table 5.2: Gross earnings and net income costs of children to women and couples

	Number of children		
	One	Two	Four
	(Lifetime totals in £'000s, 1999 prices)		
Low-skilled couple			
Woman's income			
Gross forgone earnings	185	269	426
Less: Saving on pension contributions	3	4	5
Plus: Forgone pension	7	10	19
Labour market cost	190	275	440
Less: taxes saved plus extra benefits	55	80	142
Net income cost to woman	134	195	298
Less: net income increase for man	9	17	14
of which: higher basic pension	0	0	4
lower Income Tax	7	8	10
Net income cost to couple	125	178	284
Mid-skilled couple			
Woman's income			
Gross forgone earnings	86	140	414
Less: Saving on pension contributions	1	2	6
Plus: Forgone pension	5	7	22
Labour market cost	89	145	429
Less: taxes saved plus extra benefits	42	65	152
Net income cost to woman	47	80	277
Less: net income increase for man	5	7	23
of which: higher basic pension	0	0	0
lower Income Tax	5	7	11
Net income cost to couple	42	73	254
High-skilled couple			
Woman's income			
Gross forgone earnings	0	19	90
Less: Saving on pension contributions	0	1	7
Plus: Forgone pension	0	0	0
Labour market cost	0	17	83
Less: taxes saved plus extra benefits	18	34	74
Net income cost to woman	-18	-17	9
Less: net income increase for man	4	5	6
of which: higher basic pension	0	0	0
lower Income Tax	4	5	6
Net income cost to couple	-22	-21	3

These increases in the man's income reduce the income cost of children for the couple considered together, and we now take them into account. These factors have a relatively small effect on our hypothetical couples – the 4-child couples are most affected – to the tune of about £23,000 over the lifetime if the couple is mid-skilled.

5.1.4 How do the earnings and income costs of children compare?

Given that the tax-benefit system can compensate for the gross earnings cost of children, it is useful to compare this with the net income cost that pertains after the tax-benefit system has been taken into account. This reveals that for Mrs Low, the net income costs of children are about 70%–85% of the gross earnings cost but for Mrs Mid, the net costs are only about half of the gross costs (two-thirds if she has four children). This is a reflection of two factors. The mid-skilled women reduce their labour supply much less than the low-skilled women, producing a lower earnings cost. One of the main ways in which the tax-benefit system can compensate for the gross earnings cost of children is through Child Benefit. Given that Child Benefit is a flat-rate benefit it makes up a larger fraction of the smaller income difference for the mid-skilled. Additionally, we assume that Child Benefit is paid to Mrs Mid until her children are 18 (we assume that they stay on at school for A levels or equivalent). By contrast, the children of low-skilled couple are assumed to leave school at age 16 at which point Child Benefit payment ceases.

The net effects of the smaller reduction in labour supply at higher levels of skill, together with the flat-rate effect of Child Benefit, mean that the picture for the high-skilled women looks very different from that for the others. Table 5.2 shows that our hypothetical high-skilled women experience a *gain* in net income as a result of having one or two children (shown by a negative sign in the table). This is because they gain Child Benefit and CTCs, but reduce their labour market participation only a little, if at all, below the level of their childless counterpart. As we discussed in Chapter 3, by no means all the highly educated women will behave in this way. The probabilities depicted in Figure 3.4 indicate that no more than two-thirds of them may be expected to maintain continuous full-time employment, with the others reducing their labour supply much more substantially. For those mothers who do take a break, it is likely that they will experience job downgrading on return. Therefore, their earning profiles will follow closely those displayed by Mrs Mid. As noted above, the mothers who have continuous (or near-continuous) labour market participation are likely to incur substantial childcare costs, which we have not accounted for here and these costs may well exceed the net income gains we have calculated.

5.1.5 How are the costs of children divided?

We have so far discussed the cost of children in terms of a mother's forgone earnings and her net income. We have also looked at the effect on her husband's net income of the operation of the tax-benefit system. With all these components accounted for, we can now consider how the income costs of children are divided between wife, husband and the state.

The state bears part of the forgone earnings cost of children. The mother receives benefits not paid to childless women (principally Child Benefit) and also pays less into the public purse, especially if she earns less.[63] The notion of the family transfer raises the possibility that another part of the cost of children is borne by the husband. Table 5.3 shows the impact of the costs of any reduction in the woman's labour market income associated with children. It is calculated on the assumption that income is shared equally within the marriage. It shows that for most cases involving the low-skilled woman the costs of children are almost equally split between the wife, the husband and the state. This is a reflection of fact that the state loses about one-third of the marginal pound of earnings (in Income Tax plus NICs), and that the remainder is split equally between husband and wife. Despite the assumption of equal sharing of income, husband and wife do not bear exactly equal shares of the cost of children, because they live for different lengths of time.[64] When we turn to the mid- and high-skilled women, the picture looks rather different. In the case of the mid-skilled mother, the state bears a higher fraction of the cost (about half if there are one or two children).[65] This is because, with the smaller reduction in the mother's labour income, the payment of Child Benefit (not related to income) is a larger fraction of the state's contribution. This in turn makes the average contribution of the state (shown in the table) much larger than its marginal contribution (which reflects the marginal rate of Income Tax plus NICs). For the high-skilled mother of two who reduces her labour market participation very little, having children leads to a net gain in income which comes entirely from the state, and is split equally between husband and wife.[66]

---

[63] Even if her earnings are unaffected, a mother will pay lower tax once the new CTCs are introduced, as we assume here. In addition to Child Benefit, a mother could receive WFTC, but see the discussion above and in Chapter 2.

[64] The woman's earnings-linked pension may be lower as a result of having children. Her husband does not share the part of this cost incurred after his death.

[65] The state's absolute contribution depends on the balance between the (mainly) flat-rate expenditures and the revenue loss. Comparing the cases of the mid-skilled and low-skilled couple, if there are two children the state's contribution is £98,000 in the low-skilled case and £72,000 in the high-skilled case, but if there are four children the figures are £156,000 and £175,000 respectively.

[66] Our simulation also allows for a calculation of how the costs of children are shared where there is a divorce. Constraints of space mean that these are not shown in detail here. In general, the simulated increases in labour market participation of women following divorce shown in Chapter 4, mean that the costs of children are reduced by divorce. However, except for Mrs High, the state always pays more towards the cost of children through Income Support and/or Working Families' Tax Credit. Not surprisingly, the fathers usually contribute less where there is divorce, especially early divorce.

Table 5.3: Who pays the cost of children?

Percentage contributions to the cost of children	Number of children		
	One	Two	Four
Low-skilled couple			
Mother	34	33	33
Father	32	32	32
State	34	35	35
Mid-skilled couple			
Mother	24	26	30
Father	23	25	29
State	53	49	41
High-skilled couple			
Mother	n/a	-61	2
Father	n/a	-61	2
State	n/a	223	97

5.2 MOTHERHOOD, PARENTHOOD AND THE PAY GAP

In Chapter 3 (Section 3.4) we considered the impact of the gender pay gap over the lifetime. Using a similar analysis we can look at the lifetime gender pay gap (reproduced from Table 3.5) alongside the earnings gap between mothers of two and childless unmarried women.[67] This provides us with an estimate of the relative size of the pay gap that women experience because of their sex, and that they experience in addition if they choose to become mothers. In addition, comparing the lifetime earnings of mothers and fathers allows us to estimate the size of the parental pay gap.

Recall the case of the childless mid-skilled woman who experienced a lifetime gender pay gap of £241,000 or 37% of her lifetime earnings. The effect of having two children is to reduce the mid-skilled woman's earnings by an additional £140,000 (27% of the mother's lifetime earnings) (Table 5.4). Looking across the skill levels in the middle panel of the table, we find further evidence of polarisation between mothers of different skill levels. The motherhood earnings gap is 114% of the low-skilled mother's lifetime earnings, but only 2% of the high-skilled mother's. Although most of the gap for the low-skilled arises because the mothers are employed for fewer hours than the

---

[67] In our simulations, there turns out to be no difference between the earnings of childless married and unmarried women – except for an £16,000 (3%) difference for the low-skilled.

childless women, a sizeable chunk arises from the difference in wages, and part of this is, in turn, a result of the gap between part- and full-time wages.

The variation shown here in the size of the hourly pay penalty for motherhood by skill level is consistent with the analysis by Joshi and Paci (1998). They established that the pay penalty to motherhood in the 1958 Cohort Study predominantly affects those women who do not preserve employment continuity. From Table 5.4 we see that where the hours gap between the mother and the childless woman is larger, so is the pay penalty. Hence the loss of earning power associated with motherhood (including effects on experience and hours) is absolutely, and relatively larger for the low-skilled, but smaller for the mid-, and especially high-skilled. This does not sit well with the assertion sometimes made that as gender pay gap narrows, the only pay differences remaining between men and women will be those due to motherhood – assuming hours at work are the same. What we see from the simulation is that the pay penalty of motherhood is low for those with high levels of labour force attachment, but there remains a strong pay penalty to motherhood in the cases where having children disrupts labour market attachment.

Table 5.4: Gender, mother and parent gaps in lifetime earnings

	Skill level		
	Low	Mid	High
Man-woman (gender gap)			
Lifetime earnings in £'000s:			
man	731	891	1,333
childless woman	534	650	1,190
Difference (absolute)	197	241	143
Difference as %			
relative to woman	37	37	12
Difference in hours	24	16	5
Difference in rates of pay	11	18	7
Interaction	3	3	0
Mother – childless unmarried woman (mother gap)			
Lifetime earnings in £'000s:			
childless woman	534	650	1,190
mother of two	249	510	1,171
Difference (absolute)	285	140	19
Difference as %			
relative to mother	114	27	2
Difference in hours	77	19	1
Difference in rates of pay	21	7	1
Interaction	16	1	0
Man-mother of 2 (parent gap)			
Lifetime earnings in £'000s:			
man	731	891	1,333
mother of two	249	510	1,171
Difference (absolute)	482	381	161
Difference as %			
relative to mother	194	75	14
Difference in hours	120	37	6
Difference in rates of pay	34	27	7
Interaction	40	10	0

Source: Calculations from simulation model

The bottom panel of Table 5.4 takes the preceding two stages in one step. Since the men's wages in our simulations do not change if they become fathers, the earnings gap between the man and the mother can be regarded as a 'parent gap' and provides a further indication of possible economic inequalities within marriage. Here again, the variation in this gap by level of qualifications is striking. The low-skilled mother has lifetime earnings nearly a half a million pounds below her husband's (nearly twice her own lifetime earnings), while the high-skilled mother earns just £161,000 less than her husband (14% of her lifetime earnings). The bulk of the gap experienced by the low-skilled mother arises from her lower hours, but lower wages account for about one-third of the difference in earnings between both the low- and mid-skilled parents.[68] The difference in rates of pay corresponds conceptually almost exactly to the estimates made by Joshi and Paci (1998, Chapter 6) of the percentage by which mothers' pay would rise if they were paid at the same rates as men. Joshi and Paci's estimates of 34% for the average 32 year old mother in 1978 and 22% for 33 year olds in 1991, correspond reasonably closely to the estimates provided here of 34% for the low-skilled mother averaged over her lifetime and 27% for the mid-skilled mother. Thus we have confirmation from independent evidence that our simulations bear some resemblance to actual experience so far.

5.3 THE LIFETIME INCOMES OF TEENAGE MOTHERS

In Section 5.1 above we identified the sensitivity of lifetime earnings to the timing of motherhood. In this section we explore this further by looking at how a birth during the mother's teenage years may affect lifetime incomes. In addition, we look at the lifetime impact of partnership on women who have this early experience of motherhood.

5.3.1 A profile of teenage mothers

Before looking at the simulation model of teenage motherhood, it is necessary to establish an accurate picture of teenage motherhood in contemporary Britain.

- In 1997, there were 44,000 live births to teenage mothers in Britain. Of these, about 5,000 were registered inside marriage, and another 12,000 were registered jointly. Thus, at best, only 39% of teenage mothers were living with partners (Social Exclusion Unit 1999b, p.6, p.12.).

---

[68] The very large size of the interaction effect for the low-skilled case is because the gap in *both* hours *and* rates of pay are so large.

- Contrary to what catches newspaper headlines, teenage motherhood occurs most frequently in the late teens. Data from the 1970 British Cohort Study shows that 101 of the 206 teenage mothers were aged 19, and only 41 under 18. Mothers under 18 represented under 1% of all women in the study.

- While teenage pregnancy is seen across socio-economic classes, evidence suggests that a significant proportion, if not a majority, of such mothers either come from or end up in very difficult circumstances (Ford 1996, Social Exclusion Unit 1999b, Shouls et al. 1999).

- Data from both the 1958 and 1970 Birth Cohort Studies show that the social origins of women who became teenage mothers were relatively disadvantaged. The odds of becoming a lone parent were significantly raised for the daughters of men in RG classes IV and V (semi and unskilled) and for the daughters of parents who had left school at the minimum age (Bynner et al. 1999). Together with the data on births to mothers under 20 years old, this confirms that teenage single motherhood remains a socially differentiated phenomenon.

- Existing studies point out that teenage mothers typically have poor educational attainment. Data from the 1970 British Cohort Study shows that of all women born in 1970, 4.5% had become mothers by age 20. Among those with no qualifications the percentage was 29.6%, and 62% of all women who had had a teenage birth had qualifications no higher than GCSE.

- Likewise, the DSS/PSI Lone Parent Cohort study (1991-1998) shows that 46% of all lone mothers sampled in 1991 had no qualifications, while only 6% had higher qualifications.[69]

Teenage mothers and lone motherhood

It should be noted that:

- teenage mothers are not always single (i.e. never-married) lone mothers, and even if they are outside a partnership at the time of birth, they may not necessarily remain so (see below);

---

[69] Unpublished tabulations kindly supplied to the authors by Alan Marsh, PSI.

- those teenage mothers who are lone mothers form only one part of the lone mother population. Thus, the report has already considered the case of divorced mothers, as divorcees have long been a sizeable section of the lone parent population. It should be noted, however, that as the number of births outside marriage has grown, never-married lone mothers have become the fastest growing group of lone parents.[70] Never-married lone mothers grew as a proportion of all lone mothers from 36% to 42% between 1990 and 1997 (Holtermann et al. 1999).

While teenage motherhood and lone motherhood should not be confounded, a high percentage of young mothers have, nevertheless, never been married. In the 1997 LFS sample, 88% of lone mothers aged under 25 were never-married (Holtermann et al. 1999). Similarly, Haskey (1998a, p.10) shows that the peak age for never-married lone mothers is early twenties, with more than a third aged under 25 at the date of the count.

In the same way as all lone mothers, those who have had a teenage birth may, of course, form partnerships. Recent research confirms that never-married lone motherhood (of which teenage lone mothers form a part) takes on a diversity of forms. For example, Ford (1996) gives examples of lone mothers who had partnered young, had children as teenagers, divorced quickly, and of those who remained unmarried. Among all women who gave birth outside marriage, those who jointly registered the birth with the father and gave the same address (and were therefore presumably cohabiting with the father) had a 30% chance of marrying – twice the chance for women who were sole registrants (Haskey 1999c, p.9). While younger lone mothers are more likely to exit through repartnering, those who do not "have the potential to remain lone parents the longest" (Ford et al. 1998, p.22). Among those teenage mothers who do have partners, there are higher rates of breakdowns and of unstable relationships, according to both the GHS[71] and *The Teenage Pregnancy Report* (Social Exclusion Unit 1999b, p. 24 and p.65).

5.3.2 Modelling teenage motherhood

As the data above demonstrates, no less than any other group, women who become teenage mothers exhibit a wide variety of behaviour. Although we think it is worth using our model to explore a range of cases in an attempt

---

[70] Note, however, that even those classified as never-married have partnership histories which include broken cohabitations (Haskey 1998c, p.19).

[71] According to *Living in Britain* 1996 (ONS 1998b:.201 and 200), teenage mothers are more likely to divorce: 19% of first marriages between 1985-89 ended within 3 years and 32% within 5 years. For all women marrying under the age of 30, the proportion of marriages ending within 3-5 years rose since the 1960s, but only to 12-18%.

to quantify the long-term effects of becoming a mother when a teenager, these simulations are necessarily more speculative than those for our standard cases. The labour market behaviour of lone parents is subject to rather different constraints than that of married women, partly because of the benefit system, and partly because there is only one parent in the home. In interpreting the simulation results, it is also important to bear in mind that our evidence is based on the behaviour of women before the New Deals had been introduced. Our calculations allow for the tax-benefit structure in 1999 as it affects income, given labour force participation behaviour, but they do not allow for the improved incentive effects of the reform of the benefit structure, and increased childcare provision.

The simulations allow for two basic types of teenage lone mothers (summarised in Table 5.5). In both cases the woman has her first child when she is 19 and unpartnered (a 'typical' teenage motherhood scenario as the evidence presented above implies). In the first case, the woman never marries (or cohabits) and she has a second child when she is 22. She is assumed to seek (and obtain) employment in accordance with the predictions of our labour supply model. In the second case, the woman enters an enduring marriage when she is 21 and has her second child at the age of 24 (or 28 if mid-skilled). To highlight the situation of women who bring up children without the support of a partner, we have assumed in these cases that the fathers of the children born outside wedlock are unemployed or on very low wages, so that they contribute only minimal child support. In the case of the teen mother who gets married, we assume that the husband is not the father of the child, and is continuously employed. In this case, the teenage birth might be expected to have a relatively small effect on the woman's lifetime income, compared to a scenario with early marriage but no teenage motherhood. This 'teenage bride' scenario is also simulated and used to compare the two basic types, in particular when highlighting the effects of having a child while young and without the support of a partner. Our teenage bride thus marries at 19 but does not have children until aged 21 and 24.

Table 5.5: Hypothetical teenage mothers: assumed ages at first and second births

		Skill level	
Scenario	Birth	Low	Mid
Never married	1st	19	19
	2nd	22	22
Marries at 21	1st	19	19
	2nd	24	28
Teen bride	1st	21	21
	2nd	24	24

In line with evidence about the educational attainments of the majority of teenage mothers, our simulations of teenage mothers do not include any cases of highly educated women.

5.3.3 Projected participation probabilities of teenage mothers

Figures 5.5 and 5.6 show the participation probabilities projected for low and mid-skilled teenage mothers. For comparison, we include the childless never-married woman, as well as the teenage bride. For women with either mid or low skill levels, we see that teenage birth depresses the probabilities of participation. In both cases, the trajectories of any employment for the never-married mother and the teenage mother who marries at 21 are below that of a childless unmarried woman. They are also below the trajectories of a woman marrying at 19 and having her first child at 21 (the 'teen bride'). For the mid-skilled women in Figure 5.7, consider the simulated teen mother who never marries and who re-enters the labour market. She does this when her children are teenagers, but our calculations suggest that about 25% of these women are likely to take employment (almost all part-time) once the youngest child is of primary school age. Over 40% are likely to be employed once the youngest child is in secondary school, and about a third of these are likely to be in full-time paid work. By contrast, the participation probabilities of the teenage mother who gets married at 21 fall below those of the never-married mother by the late twenties, and her full-time participation rates are well below 30% throughout. The same patterns apply if (as is more likely) the women are of low skill.

Figure 5.5: Probabilities of participation of teenage mothers and a teen bride: low-skilled women

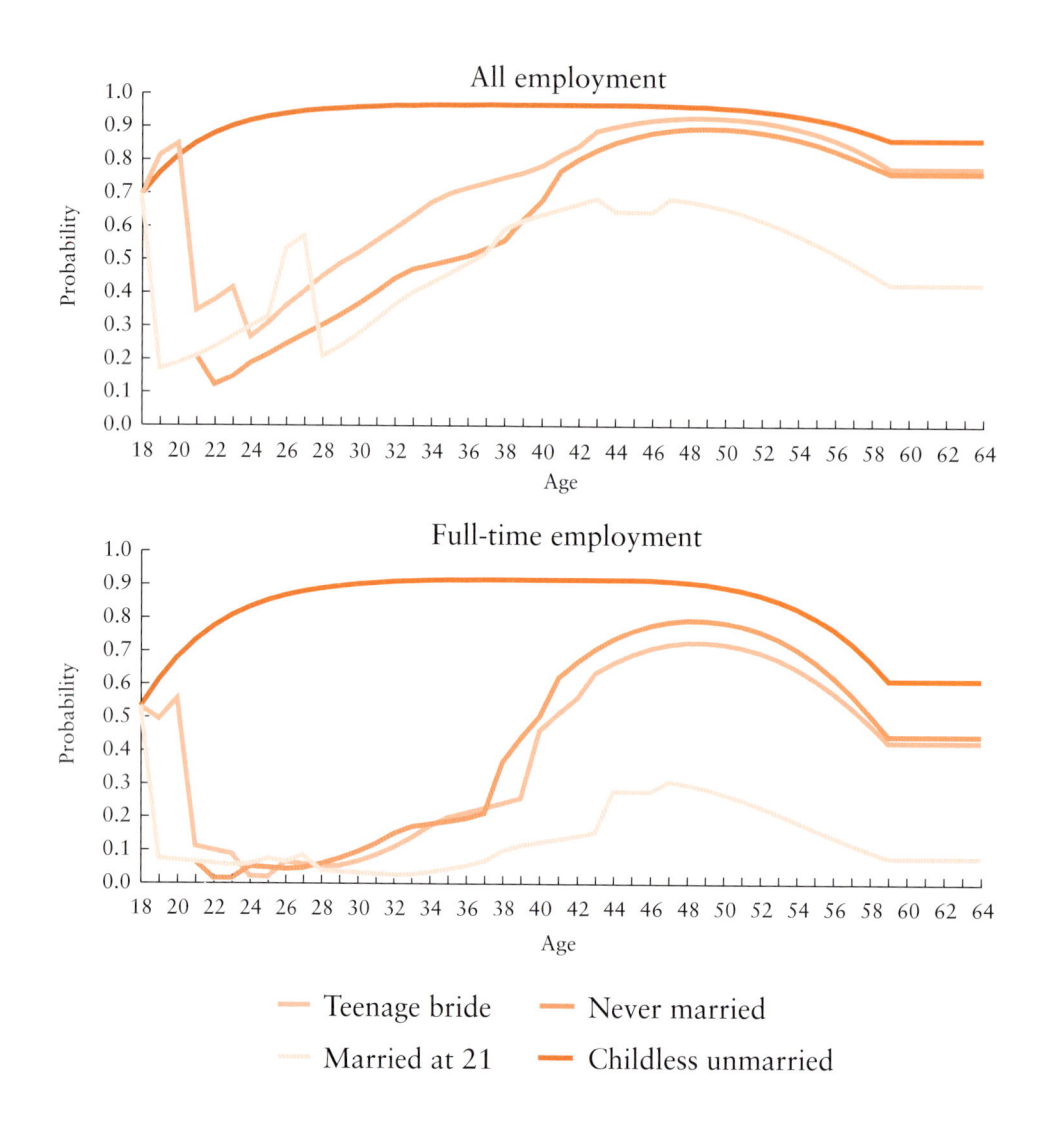

Note: In all scenarios, mothers have their first birth at the age of 19, except in the case of the teen bride, who marries at 19 but has her first baby at 21.

Figure 5.6: Probabilities of participation of teenage mothers and a teen bride: mid-skilled women

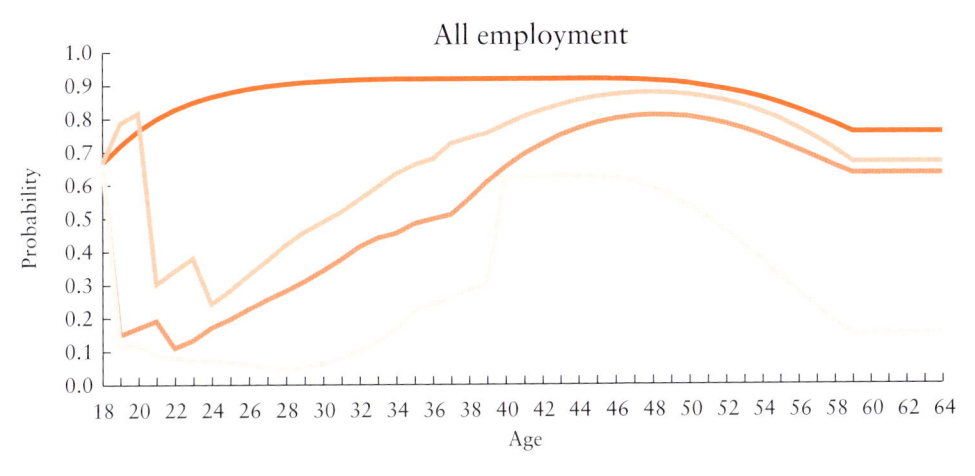

Note: In all scenarios, mothers have their first birth at the age of 19, except in the case of the teen bride, who marries at 19 but has her first baby at 21.

Does having the first birth and marriage in reverse order make a difference? The two year delay in childbearing permits high employment (predominantly full-time) at ages 19 and 20, when the young mothers have a very low chance of employment. The woman who delayed childbearing till 21 has higher chances of being employed at most subsequent ages than those who become mothers at 19. When the probability of full-time work is considered the teenage mother who never marries overtakes the teenage bride who defers childbearing.

How do our simulated participation probabilities compare to what we know from current data on lone mothers? Never married lone mothers are consistently less likely to be employed than other lone mothers. For example, analysis of the 1997 Labour Force Survey reveals that 32% of never married lone mothers were employed, compared with 56% of divorced lone mothers and 45% of all lone mothers (Holtermann et al. 1999).[72] Data from the DSS/PSI Lone Parent Cohort study support the model's simulation of low employment among lone mothers. However, the data also show a good proportion of lone mothers maintaining full-time participation (with, in a similar way to all mothers, rates affected by the age of the youngest child).[73]

5.3.4 The lifetime earnings of teenage mothers

Figure 5.6 plots earnings profiles for women who become teenage mothers and compares them with our standard case of married mothers of two who appear in the bottom two panels. These graphs show that all selected types of teenage mothers earn less than the continuously married Mrs Low or Mrs Mid. Since the shortfall between their profiles and that of a childless woman is bigger over a longer period, they have higher gross earnings costs of motherhood. Although she forgoes less than our women who become unmarried teenage mothers, our teenage bride (who has her first child at 21) earns less than the standard married mother of two, throughout her twenties, especially if she is mid-skilled. Hence, although in her forties her profile is similar to that of our Mrs Low and Mrs Mid, the maximum annual amounts that she can expect are still some £2,000–£3,000 lower. Her lower earnings represent the continued legacy of early childbearing. Our teenage mother who never marries follows her path closely, but re-enters the labour market some 6–7 years later, implying that at

---

[72] The study also showed considerable difference by ethnic origin in the labour market participation rates.

[73] In 1998 the non-employment rate among all lone mothers was 42%. For mothers with a youngest child under 5, 43% were out of work, while over 15% worked over 24 hours (tabulations provided by Alan Marsh). It should be noted that the poor labour market participation levels of teenage mothers reflects the lower educational levels they typically attain.

the later stages of her life, her maximum annual earnings will be another £1,000 or so lower than the teenage bride.

Our teenage mother who has the baby first and marries later has a very different profile. As her labour market participation is not projected to recover significantly after childbearing, even when her children are older, her annual earnings never exceed £4,000. This is almost half of the amounts potentially earned by the other teenage mothers, and is similar to those earned by a married mother of four. Partnering and the labour market are not, in these cases, equivalent routes out of welfare dependency.

The totals of the earnings graphed in Figure 5.7 are given in Table 5.6.

Table 5.6: Lifetime gross earnings of teenage mothers and others

| | | Teenage mother of 2 ||| Standard ||
		Teenage bride	Never Married	Marries at 21	Childless unmarried	Two children
Low skilled	Lifetime gross earnings	266	234	96	534	249
	of which: Earnings after birth	247	216	77		197
Mid skilled	Lifetime gross earnings	354	304	76	650	510
	of which: Earnings after birth	340	290	62		400

Note:
Teenage mother has first birth at 19. Teeenage bride has first birth at 21.
Standard mother of 2 has first bith at 23 (low-skilled) or 28 (mid-skilled)

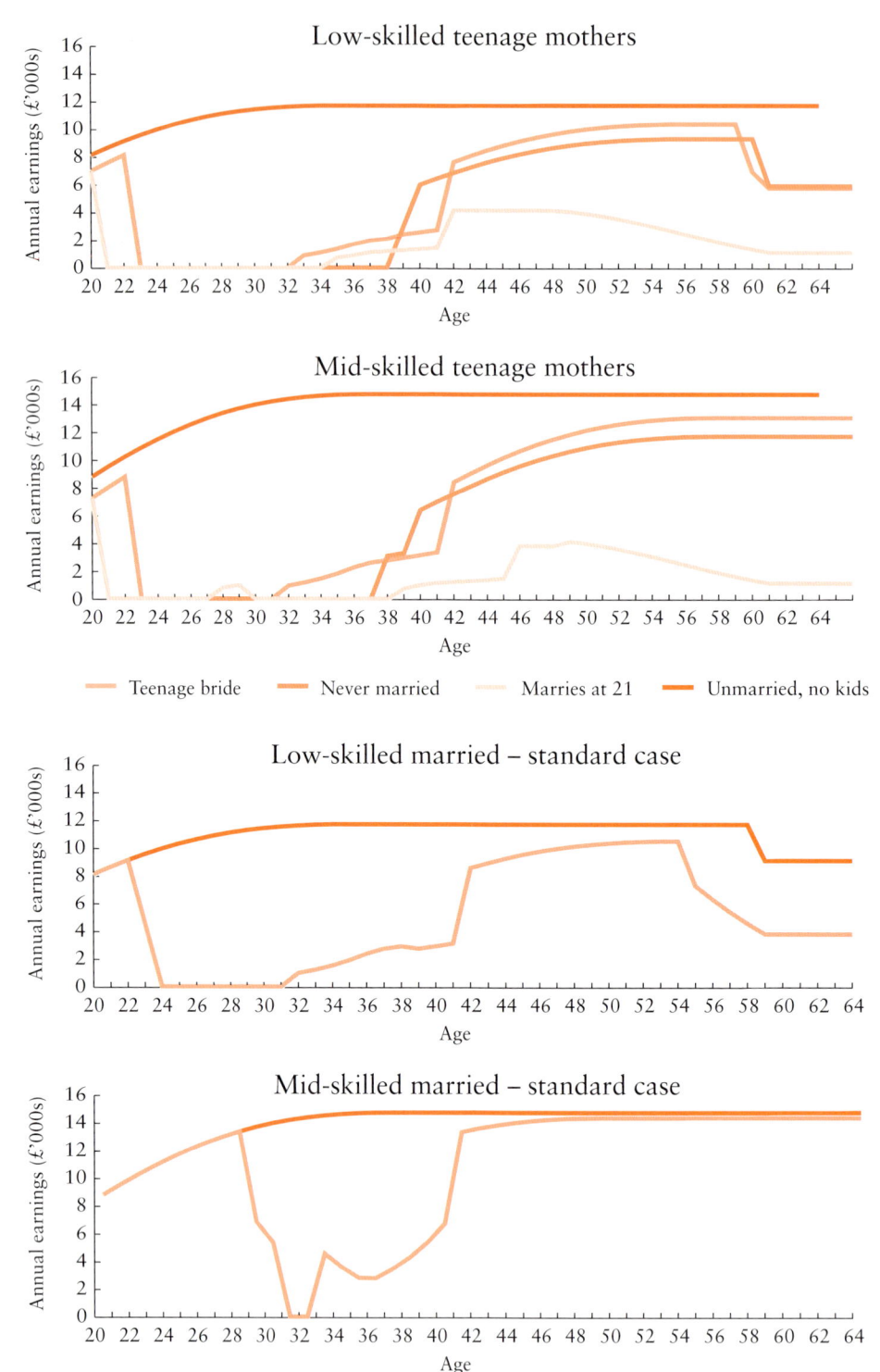

Figure 5.7: Earning profiles of teenage mothers and a teen bride

Low-skilled teenage mothers

Mid-skilled teenage mothers

— Teenage bride — Never married — Marries at 21 — Unmarried, no kids

Low-skilled married – standard case

Mid-skilled married – standard case

— No children — 2 children

5.3.5 Sources of income of teenage mothers

In this section we highlight the long-term effect of living with no partner by comparing examples of never-married teenage mothers with partnered women. Table 5.7 shows the components of lifetime income for our simulated teenage mothers (here 'lifetime' is defined to be the period since the birth of the first child). The results for the teenage mothers are in the two central columns, while the bordering columns are shown for comparison. The leftmost column shows the results for a woman who never marries and has no children. She is the direct comparator for computing the forgone earnings cost of children according to our standard method. Comparing the two leftmost columns shows that the hypothetical never married teenage mother of two children forgoes £300,000 in gross earnings, if she has low skills – 58% of her counterpart's lifetime earnings. If she has mid-level skills, the hypothetical teenage mother loses slightly more in earnings – but a slightly lower fraction (54%) of her counterpart's earnings. In terms of net income, the costs to the teenage mother are only about half of the gross earnings cost – amounting to 28% and 25% respectively of the low- and mid-skilled counterpart's net incomes. We assume that the father of the teenage mother's children does not give her much cash help – he is assumed to be unemployed or on very low wages so that, although he complies with the impending child support legislation, he contributes only the minimum amount (£5 per week). The narrowing of the gap between the gross earnings of the teenage mother and her childless counterpart is therefore due to the operation of the tax-benefit system. The teenage mothers depicted in column two each get about £70,000 in Income Support, whether they are low- or mid-skilled. The low-skilled woman gets about £4,000 in WFTC, while the mid-skilled woman, with her rather higher rate of labour force participation, gets about £20,000 in WFTC over her lifetime.

The third column of Table 5.7 illustrates another possibility – the teenage mother who forms an enduring marriage a couple of years after the birth of her first child. She can be contrasted not only with the unmarried woman to the left, but also with a continuously married woman represented in the last column. The 'teenage bride' marries earlier than the 'standard' married woman we have discussed above. She marries at 19, and has her first child at 21 – making these important lifecourse transitions at the same ages, but in the opposite order to the teenage mother. As discussed above, the hypothetical later-marrying teenage mothers do not participate very much in the labour market.

Table 5.7: Teenage mothers vs. others: components of lifetime income

Income totalled over a lifetime, £'000s, in 1999 prices

	Unmarried, childless	Teen mother at 19 Never married	Teen mother at 19 Marries at 21	Teen bride (marries at 19, birth at 21)
Number of children	0	2	2	2
Low-skilled woman				
Gross earnings	516	216	77	247
Earnings-related pension	24	14	2	16
Labour market income	534	228	79	261
Widow's pension	0	0	6	6
Child support	0	5	4	0
State benefits, net of taxes	-36	127	77	45
Net income	498	359	162	311
Family transfer	0	0	242	173
Woman's portion	**498**	**359**	**403**	**484**
Mid-skilled woman				
Gross earnings	637	290	62	340
Earnings-related pension	32	21	1	25
Labour market income	661	308	63	361
Widow's pension	0	0	35	35
Child support	0	5	5	0
State benefits, net of taxes	-73	125	81	17
Net income	588	439	184	413
Family transfer	0	0	320	234
Woman's portion	**588**	**439**	**503**	**647**

Notes
Labour market income is gross earnings less earnings-related pension contributions, plus earnings-related pension receipts.
Woman's portion is net income plus family transfer.
Lifetime: period after age at which mother has first child.

Our calculations show that, for these simulated cases, the lifetime net incomes of the never-married teenage mothers who participate in the labour market are slightly higher than those of their continuously married counterparts. The teenage mothers who find a husband later, paradoxically, have the lowest net incomes of all.

This, however, is only part of the story: after all what distinguishes our teenage mothers from the continuously married counterpart is the absence of a partner. If there is almost any degree of income sharing within partnerships, the continuously married mother will be substantially better-off. The next two rows of Table 5.7 show the effects of the conventional assumption of equal sharing of income within marriage. On this assumption, all our hypothetical teenage mothers are very substantially worse off than teenage brides. The low-skilled never married teenage mother is £125,000 worse off than if she had acquired a husband rather than a baby at age 19. Of our hypothetical teenage mothers, the ones who appear to do best in terms of lifetime incomes are those who find a partner and form an enduring union within which adults share their incomes equally. Although married for a shorter period, these women benefit from the sharing of income within marriage (the family transfer) more than their counterpart who married at 19: this is because their earnings are lower than those of the continuously married women (the husbands are assumed to have identical earnings). This happens, in turn, partly because the different ages at which the women give birth (together with the absence of a husband in the early years) mean that the teenage mother loses work experience in her late teens/early twenties which lowers her potential wage later on. The components of lifetime income are illustrated in Figure 5.8.

Figure 5.8: Teenage mothers and others: components of lifetime income

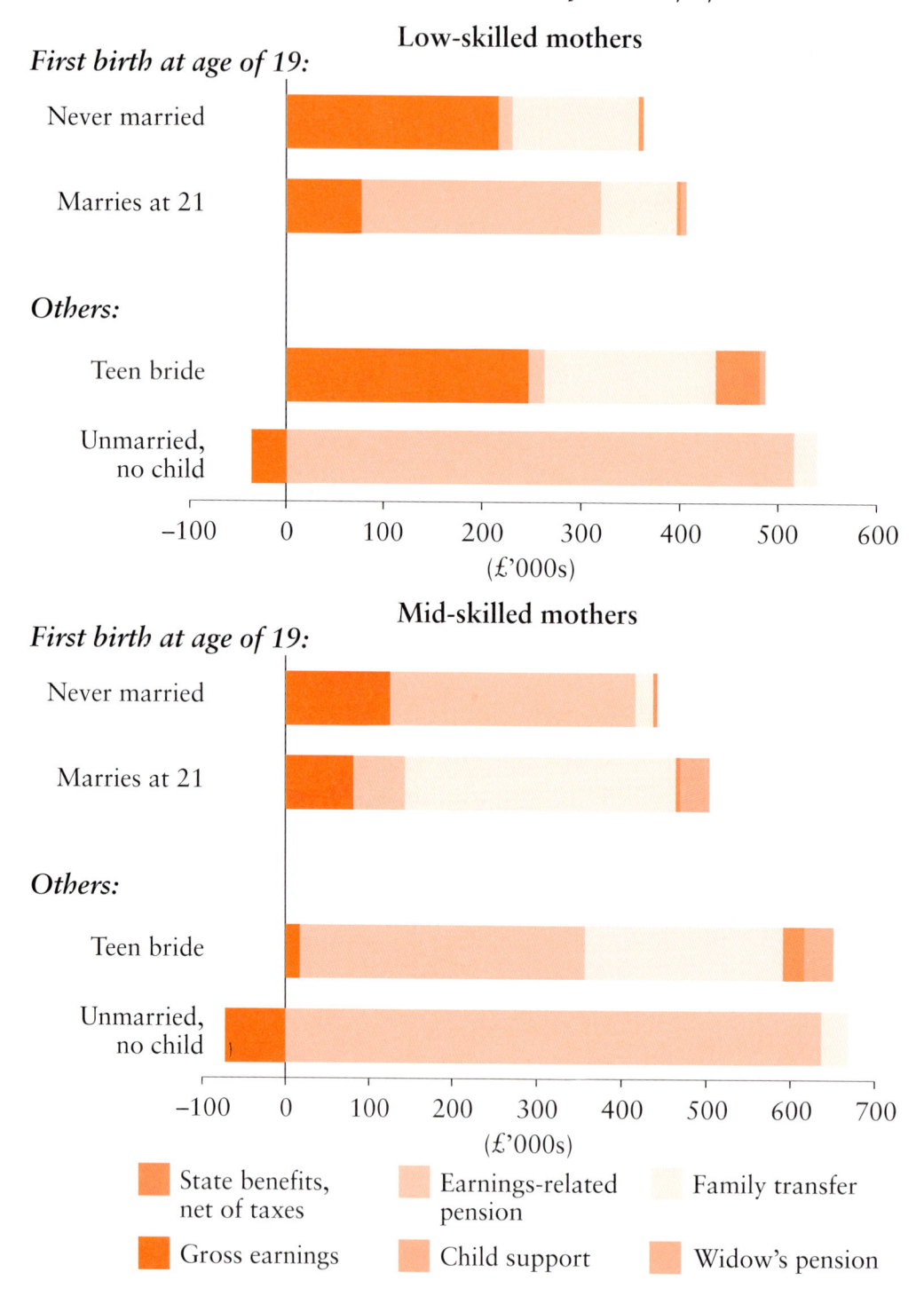

Low-skilled mothers

First birth at age of 19:
- Never married
- Marries at 21

Others:
- Teen bride
- Unmarried, no child

(£'000s)

Mid-skilled mothers

First birth at age of 19:
- Never married
- Marries at 21

Others:
- Teen bride
- Unmarried, no child

(£'000s)

- State benefits, net of taxes
- Gross earnings
- Earnings-related pension
- Child support
- Family transfer
- Widow's pension

5.3.6 How do teenage mothers fare in retirement?

Figure 5.9 shows retirement income of teenage mothers in comparison with those of some of their peers. In the case of the married women, we are assuming that their husbands share income with them equally. Figure 5.9 shows that the teenage mother is scarcely worse-off than the low- or mid-skilled unmarried woman who never has children. Among the women depicted here, what makes a big difference is marriage to a man with mid-level skills (and access to a good pension scheme). The mid-skilled teenage mother who marries later (at 21) has much more income in retirement than the teenage mother who remains unmarried, though she only gets about 85% of the retirement income that the teenage bride might expect, reflecting her early loss of employment experience.

Figure 5.9: Woman's portion in retirement for teenage bride and teenage mothers

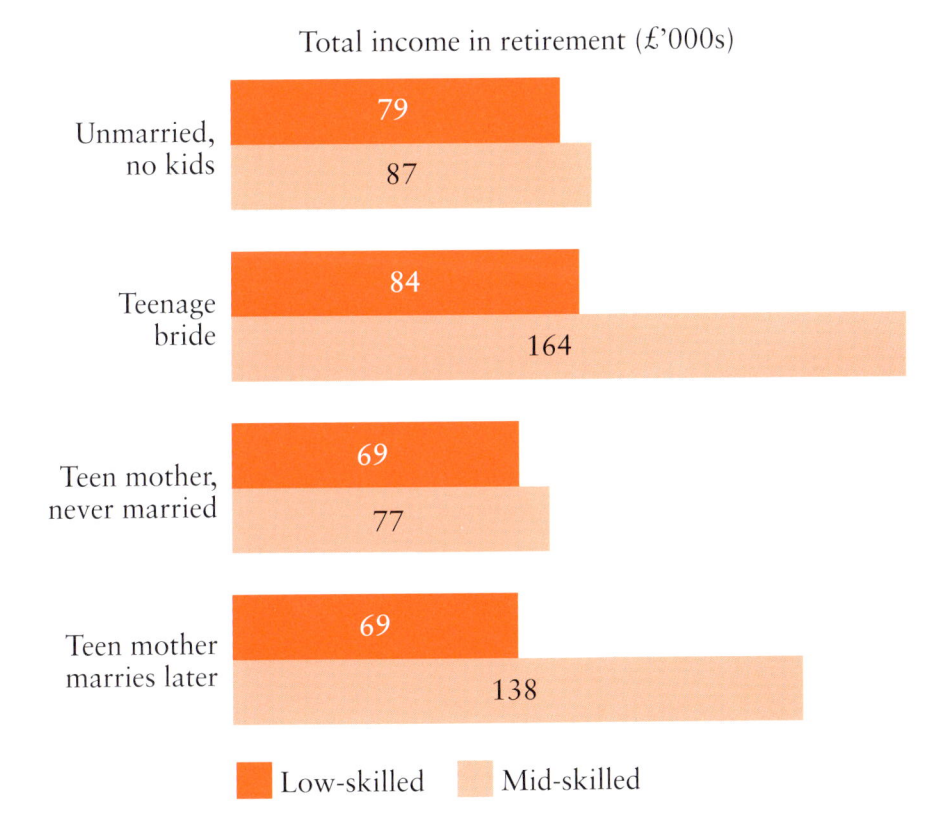

Total income in retirement (£'000s)

	Low-skilled	Mid-skilled
Unmarried, no kids	79	87
Teenage bride	84	164
Teen mother, never married	69	77
Teen mother marries later	69	138

5.4 WOMEN'S INCOMES AND CHILDHOOD POVERTY

We have examined the impact of having children on mothers' incomes. The relationship between women's incomes and children can also be viewed from the perspective of the child to see how mothers' incomes affect the risk of childhood poverty, An additional, and essential, feature of parenting from a child's point of view is the value of parental inputs of time into their care. This is outside the main scope of this report.

Establishing the connection between mothers' incomes and childhood poverty is given a particular impetus by the large increase in the numbers of children living in poverty over the last 20 years – estimates suggest that around 4.3 million or one in three children were in poverty in 1995/6 compared to 1.4 million or one in ten children in 1968 (Gregg et al. 1999: 164). This growth of childhood poverty has occurred alongside growing income in equality and a growing polarisation between 'work rich' and 'work poor' families (Gregg and Wadsworth 1996).[74] A third of children in poverty are estimated to be in lone parent families not in paid employment and a further fifth in couple families where neither partner is in the labour market. But childhood poverty is not all about households without paid work – 37% of children in poverty live in a couple family where at least one parent is in paid work and a further 9% in a lone parent household where the lone parent is in paid work (Gregg et al. 1999: Table 1).

Turning our attention first to households without paid work, by comparison to other European countries, the UK has one of the lowest rates of labour market participation among lone parents: around 40% of lone parents are in paid work compared to 60% in the US, 70% in Sweden and over 80 per cent in France (Bradshaw et al 1996).[75, 76] Children in poverty are increasingly concentrated in lone parent households – in 1968 around a fifth of all children in poverty lived in lone parent households, compared to more than two-fifths in 1995/6. It should be noted that the percentage of *poor* children living in lone parent families has grown more rapidly (by about 24%) than the percentage of all children living in lone parent families (which has grew by about 16% from 1968-1995/6) suggesting that lone parent households have become increasingly vulnerable to poverty over the past 20 years. Lone parents are less likely to move out of low income than couples with children, and the persistence of low income is therefore a distinct feature of lone parenthood. Analysis of the BHPS

---

[74] Gregg, Harkness and Machin (1999).

[75] It should be noted that these figures refer to the period prior to New Deal schemes, specifically the New Deal for Lone Parents that is aimed at addressing this issue.

[76] Calculated from the Labour Force Survey, Spring 1999, ONS.

suggests that 63% of lone mothers have incomes in the bottom 30% of the income distribution in at least four years out of seven, more than twice the proportion of the population as a whole (DSS 1999d). Given that 90% of lone parents are women,[18] there is a clear link between the incomes of lone mothers and childhood poverty (see also sections 4.4 and 5.5 of this report) and as analysis earlier in this chapter suggests the risks of childhood poverty may be particularly high for children of teenage mothers.

The percentage of children in poverty living in couple households where there are no adults in paid employment has also increased over the past 20 years (by about 5%), although the increase is much less marked than that among lone parent households. The association between having a household member unemployed and experiencing low income is clearly seen in Table 5.8 – 74% of households with children where no adult is paid employment fall within the bottom fifth, and 93% in the bottom two-fifths of the distribution. Given the high rates of male and female unemployment among some ethnic minority groups, it is not surprising that children from minority ethnic groups are over-represented at the bottom of the income distribution. For example, while 25% of White children had incomes[77] in the bottom fifth of the income distribution, 65% of Pakistani and Bangladeshi children were among the poorest fifth of the population as were 41% of all Black children (DSS 1999c, Table 4.7).

As Table 5.8 also demonstrates, having one adult in work may not be enough to protect children against poverty – 56% of children from households with one adult in the labour market are in the bottom two-fifths of the income distribution, compared to just 21% of households where both adults are in paid employment. Analysis of the distribution of family income up to 1990 found more evidence of women's earnings raising families above the poverty line than propelling them into the top reaches of incomes (Davies and Joshi 1998). Harkness et al. (1996) also report that the net effect of increased female employment between 1979 and 1991 has been to reduce income inequality among couples and to keep many families out of poverty. They estimate that in 1991 the poverty rate among couples would have been "up to 50 per cent higher if it had not been for women's earnings".[78] The proportion of non-elderly couples with two earners is rising – from 56% in 1977 to 64% in

---

[77] Incomes are net equivalised household income measured before housing costs.

[78] See Harkness et al. (1996, p.178). They use data from the GHS on women aged 24-55 and define 'poverty' as below half equivalised mean income, Davies and Joshi (1997) use the bottom quintile of a differently equivalized income distribution, over all adult ages from the FES.

1990.[79] Census data on the rise of both dual- and zero-earner couples is shown in Table 5.9. Around 1980 only about half of married women were in paid work at any one time, by the 1991 census, 60% of couples had two earners.

Table 5.8: Percentage distribution of income for children by the economic status of the family

	Bottom quintile	Second quintile	Third quintile	Fourth quintile	Top quintile	All children (millions)
Children in couple families						
with a full-time worker	10	20	27	24	19	6.8
with a part-time worker only	61	17	10	7	5	0.5
with two working adults	5	16	29	28	22	4.6
with one working adult	29	26	21	14	11	2.7
with no working adult	74	19	5	1	0	1
All in couple families	**21**	**20**	**23**	**20**	**16**	**8.3**
Children in single parent families						
with a full-time worker	8	20	34	24	14	0.4
with a part-time worker	26	47	18	6	3	0.6
with one working parent	19	36	24	13	8	1
with no working parent	61	30	7	1	1	1.8
All in single parent families	**46**	**32**	**13**	**6**	**3**	**2.9**

Source: DSS 1999c, Table 4.3.
Note: Net equivalised disposable household income before housing costs. The self-employed and children living in pensioner households are excluded.

---

[79] FES data, Davies and Joshi (1998). FES counts anyone as an earner who received pay in the past three months, whereas the reference period for the census (Table 5.9) is one week. Another reason for the higher proportion of earners in 1990 than 1991 is the employment recession at that time.

Table 5.9: Couples of working age at three censuses by number of earners (1971, 1981 and 1991)

	Percentages		
	1971	1981	1991
No earner	3	7	9
One earner	51	42	31
Two earners	46	51	60
of whom:			
woman earns part-time*	21	26	28
woman earns full-time	24	25	32
Sample numbers	*93,850*	*95,219*	*96,333*

Notes:

* Man aged 16-64 in a couple where the woman aged 16-59
* Couples are self-declared co-resident married couples in 1971; include also some inferred defacto couples in 1981 and self-declared cohabitations in 1991
* Part-time status is self-declared in 1981 and 1991, in 1971 it is based on hours <31 (or 25 for teachers), and includes hours unknown.

Source: Davies, Joshi and Peronaci (1998), data from ONS Longitudinal Study for England and Wales

5.5 CARING FOR OTHERS, EMPLOYMENT AND INCOME

So far this chapter has focused on the impact that caring for children has on women's lifetime incomes. Further types of caring activity, and their economic consequences, now provide the focus of discussion. We have not explicitly simulated an employment scenario perturbed by caring duties. Given the diversity of caring duties, there is no one pattern that seems particularly realistic. However, a caring responsibility might have generated scenarios similar to those labelled 'early retirement' or 'unemployment' in the next chapter. We here review statistical data to establish the extent of caring duties and how they impact on employment and income.

In 1995/6 the General Household Survey found that 14% of women and 11% of men over 16 were providing care to other adults. From these figures it is calculated that 3.3 million women and 2.4 million men are engaged in some sort of caring activity. Table 5.10 shows the age profile of carers, showing that for both women and men caring activity is most common for those aged 45–64, with a slightly greater percentage of men in the 65 plus age group involved in care.

Table 5.10: Percentage of adults who were carers: by age (1995–96)

Great Britain	Percentages Women	Men
16-29	6	5
30-44	13	8
45-64	22	17
65 and over	11	14
All aged 16 and over	14	11

Source: ONS 1998b (derived from General Household Survey).

From Table 5.11 we can see that the older profile of male carers is partly explained by the fact that they are more likely to be caring for their (elderly) spouse, while women are more likely to be caring for relatives of a previous generation. Further, while similar numbers of women and men were caring for someone in their own home, one and a half times as many women as men were caring for people outside their own homes.

Table 5.11: Dependant's relationship to carer by gender of carer (1995–96)

Great Britain	Percentages of carers Women	Men
Dependants		
Parent	37	28
Spouse	16	23
Friend/neighbour	15	13
Other relative	15	14
Parent-in-law	8	12
Child under 16	5	4
Child aged 16 and over	4	4
Other		1
All	100	100

Source: ONS 1998b (derived from General Household Survey).

Over time, the intensity of care appears to have changed slightly – in 1985 of all female carers a quarter were engaged in care for more than 20 hours, while in 1995 that had risen to just under a third (Table 5.12). In the same period, men experienced a similar rise, but intensive caring remains a female domain – in 1995/6, of all those who spent 20 hours or more caring, three-fifths were women (ONS 1998a: 58).

Table 5.12: Hours spent caring per week by carers (1985–95/96)

	\multicolumn{6}{c}{Percentages}
	Women			Men		
Great Britain	1985	1990-91	1995-96	1985	1990-91	1995-96
Hours						
0 – 4	35	30	23	41	38	31
5 – 9	19	25	23	21	23	20
10 – 19	20	21	22	16	17	19
20 – 49	11	12	17	9	12	17
50 or more	14	12	15	13	9	14
All carers	100	100	100	100	100	100

Source: ONS 1998b (derived from General Household Survey).

In a similar way to caring for children, providing care for other adults may have both direct and indirect consequences for an individual's lifetime income. There are a number of costs directly associated with caring (for example, the cost of having an extra individual living in the household).[80] Indirect costs may also be borne if accommodating caring activity into one's daily life requires a concomitant change in labour market activity. This will have short term consequences – e.g. the immediate loss of earnings associated with reduced hours or total withdrawal from the labour market – and longer-term consequences for employability, the earnings that can be commanded while caring or on re-entering the labour market. As with caring for children, an assessment of the cost of caring must look both at the immediate consequences on earnings and income and on the lifetime consequences for employability, earning power, pension rights and income in old age.

As with our assessment of the earnings cost of children, caution needs to be exercised when looking at the impact of caring on labour market activity. Without the necessary longitudinal data, it is very difficult to assess the line of causality between care and employment status – thus while care may lead to an individual cutting down their hours or withdrawing from the labour market, employment status may itself affect an individual's propensity to care. Furthermore, in assessing the economic consequences of providing care, quantitative analysis suggests that it is crucial to distinguish different types

---

[80] As with all types of caring, caring for other adults also has consequences for time-use, with lost leisure being one of the hidden costs of caring.

of caring and carers (Evandrou 1995). Caring for other adults takes an enormous variety of forms, each of which will have a distinct impact on employment and, hence, lifetime income. The caring experience will differ according to the intensity of caring (in terms of hours and the type of care provided), the context in which care takes place (within or outside household), whether or not the caring is shared, and the relationship between care-giver and receiver. The characteristics of the carers themselves also vary, and age, gender, own health and employment status will all influence the economic consequences that follow from caring. Some forms of caring may be combined with employment while others constrain participation in the labour market, and further, for some, caring activity begins when a household member falls ill – in such circumstances the carer may have to meet caring duties and replace the loss of household income by taking up paid work.

Diversity among carers and caring activities may explain why, especially for women, there is no clear relationship between caring and employment. For example, analysis of the British Household Panel Study found that for women there was no clear effect of caring on employment status or income. By contrast, men in the panel who were unemployed when the caring period started were twice as likely to remain unemployed, while men who cared for someone within their own household were slightly more likely to leave the labour market after the caring period began (London Economics 1998). Similarly, analysis of the 1985 General Household Survey revealed a more marked impact of caring on men's labour market participation than women's (Parker and Lawton 1994). This indicates that for men, caring duties reach a particular threshold beyond which, in the absence of part-time work options, they withdraw from the labour market. While women may also experience a negative impact of caring on labour market experience, they are more likely to respond to their caring duties by reducing their hours of work (Evandrou 1995: 22).

Not surprisingly, research reveals that the greatest impact on employment and income comes from care that is provided to a member of the same household and is of a high intensity. For example, Evandrou's analysis of the 1990 General Household Survey suggests that women caring for someone within the household are only half as likely to be in full-time employment as non-carers with similar characteristics and also experience reduced chances of being in part-time work. By contrast, caring for someone outside the home reduces the probability of being full-time employed by 29% and increases the probability of part-time working by 30%. Evandrou's analysis also suggests that for women there is a negative association between hours of care and probability of being in full-time work. The probability of full-time employment for women caring for fewer than 10 hours a week is 25% less than non-carers, while those caring for 50 hours are 80% less likely to be in full-time employment than non-carers with similar characteristics. In addition, she shows that both male and female carers receive lower rates of hourly pay than non-carers, suggesting that, in a similar way as parents, they may suffer a wage penalty by entering flexible, part-time employment that fits with their caring duties.

5.6　CONCLUSIONS AND KEY FINDINGS

In recognition that the link between children and women's incomes runs in two directions, we first presented evidence of the impact of parenting on women's earnings and lifetime incomes. Our analysis revealed that the timing of motherhood was an important determinant of the income cost of children. In order to explore this further, we looked at teenage motherhood to examine the specific effects an early birth has on women's lifetime incomes. Looking then from another perspective (how women's incomes affect childhood poverty) we found evidence of a strong link between women's incomes and children's risk of experiencing poverty. Finally, we provided a brief review of the diverse impact on earnings and incomes of caring for older relatives and other dependants.

Some key findings from this chapter are:

- The amount of earnings forgone by mothers increases with the number of children, but most importantly, decreases with the skill level of the mother. The low-skilled mother of two is calculated to forgo earnings of over a quarter of a million pounds (almost 60% of her potential earnings after childbirth), compared to the high-skilled mother of two who forgoes under £20,000 (just 2% of her potential earnings after childbirth).

- Comparisons between this simulation (based on data from the mid 1990s) and a previous one (modelled on data from 1980) show a dramatic drop in the 'cost of motherhood' for the mid-skilled mother (the forgone earnings of the mother of two having fallen from £230,000 to £140,000). Further investigation reveals that the timing of motherhood has an important impact on lost earnings – the mid-skilled mother of two who starts her family at 24 forgoes more than twice the amount of earnings forgone by the mother first birth is at age 30.

- The tax-benefit system relieves women of some of the gross earnings cost of children – for example, the mid-skilled mother of two children receives £65,000 more from the tax-benefit system (both because she pays less tax and receives more benefit) than her childless counterpart, and this reduces her net income loss to £80,000.

- The possibility of sharing income with a partner can also relieve women of some of the gross earnings cost of their children. If husband and wife share their incomes equally, then the mid-skilled mother of two will have her net income loss approximately halved – to about £40,000.

- Because women of different skill levels have such different employment patterns, the relative impact of the state varies by skill level. Thus, mid-skilled women reduce their labour supply much less than low-skilled women, yet both receive flat-rate Child Benefit. Child benefit provides a relatively greater compensation to the mid-skilled woman, with her relatively low earnings cost of children, than it does to the low-skilled mother.

- The simulation allows for a calculation of the 'mother earnings gap' over the lifetime (calculated by comparing the lifetime earnings of mothers of two with childless women) and to compare this with the 'gender earnings gap' explored in Chapter 3. The mid-skilled childless woman is estimated to experience a lifetime gender earnings gap of £241,000. The mid-skilled mother of two experiences an additional earnings penalty of £140,000 (or 27% of her lifetime earnings after childbearing).

- Thus, for the mid-skilled woman the lifetime earnings cost of motherhood is smaller in absolute, and relative terms, than the cost of being a woman. This is not the case for women of all skill levels – the mother gap is £285,000 for the low-skilled mother (114% of the mother of two's lifetime earnings) compared to a gender earnings gap of £197,000.

- The parent gap – the difference between mothers and fathers of two children – has a big impact on mothers across the skills spectrum. The low-skilled mother of two is estimated to earn over her lifetime just under half a million pounds less than her low-skilled husband (for mid-skilled the equivalent figure is £380,000).

- It is noticeable that the impact of gender and of motherhood on the earnings of high-skilled women is considerably less. The high-skilled mother of two is estimated to 'lose' only 2% of her earnings (or £19,000) through motherhood while she experiences a gender earnings gap of £143,000. As a result, the gap between the lifetime earnings of the high-skilled couple is relatively low (£161,000, or 14% of the mother's lifetime earnings).

- Teenage motherhood is estimated to have a negative impact on lifetime incomes both because of the reduced probability of employment and loss of shared income from a partner.

- Teenage mothers forgo more earnings than those who postpone their first birth – the low-skilled never married teenage mother of two children, for example, forgoes £300,000 in gross earnings (just under 60% of the lifetime earnings after the age of childbearing of the equivalently skilled childless woman).

- This loss is substantially, although not completely, compensated for by the tax-benefit system – the state contributes approximately £127,000 to the low-skilled teenage mother of two which represents about 42% of her forgone earnings.

- Women's incomes are key in determining whether or not a household is defined as poor in both lone parent and two parent households. 90% of lone parent households are headed by a woman. Around two-fifths of all children in poverty live with lone parents. This proportion doubled in the period 1968-1995/6. While the number of lone parents grew dramatically in this period, evidence suggests that lone parent households were more vulnerable to poverty in 1995/6 than they were twenty years earlier.

- 56% of children from households with one earner were in the bottom two-fifths of the income distribution compared to 21% of children from households with two earners. In the light of this, and the growth in two-earner families over the past 30 years, women's incomes are an important factor in protecting children from poverty.

6. LATER LIFE

6. LATER LIFE

This chapter focuses on later life and, first, considers evidence from quantitative surveys about the distribution of income of those currently over pension age. Patterns of pension scheme membership and the holding of other financial assets are also examined (Section 6.1). In Section 6.2, the incomes in later life of the hypothetical individuals are discussed. This is followed by an analysis in Section 6.3 of the pension consequences of earlier lifetime events – in particular having children, and experiencing divorce. Lastly in Section 6.4, the simulation model is used to look at two types of interrupted labour market behaviour – unemployment and early retirement – both occurring in later life. The impact of these episodes on retirement income and on sources of individual income is examined.

6.1 ECONOMIC RESOURCES IN LATER LIFE

6.1.1 Income in later life

Women's greater longevity, and hence their greater likelihood of experiencing widowhood and solo living, puts them in a distinct position from men in later life. Life expectancy for the average woman aged 60 is currently 22.4 years, compared to 18.5 years for a man; 20 years ago, life expectancy at the same age was 2 years shorter for a woman and 3 years shorter for a man (ONS 1999: Table 5.1). Greater longevity means, for the majority, an extension of the time spent in retirement, reliant on pensions, investment income or state benefits rather than earnings. This means that, for women in particular, the adequacy of pensions, investment income or state benefits is key.

Care needs to be exercised when comparing the incomes of men and women and looking at differences among women in later life. Overall in the UK, income is more equally distributed among the older population – the flat-rate state pension has an equalising effect on incomes, and the extremes of the earnings distribution are not yet reflected in other pension benefits. Along with lower inequality overall, differences in income between women and men are less pronounced in later life. In looking at incomes in later life we need to be careful that concern with gender equality does not blind us to the experience of low income among the older population. After all, gender equality that is a result of women's incomes being 'levelled up' to a comparable level with men's is a qualitatively different situation to one in which it has resulted from men's incomes being 'levelled down' as is the case for many when in old age. As with other stages of the lifecycle, a further complication arises when looking at differences between individual and household income. Widowhood may bring with it entitlement to individual income – rights to SERPS or an occupational pension may be inherited or a claim to Income Support may be made in the widow's own name. Thus, for many women who previously had little or no entitlement to income in their own right, widowhood will coincide with an increase in individual income, even if household income falls simultaneously. This reminds the reader that different measures of income tell us of different aspects of the distribution of economic resources, and should not be confused with measures of welfare or well-being. A further cautionary note needs to be sounded. The cross-sectional evidence we present in this section tells us of the situation of older people today which, while a vital indicator of the economic position of women of that generation, will not capture the many changes that have occurred in the patterns of labour market participation of younger generations. The model allows us to do this, and to explore how the trend towards polarisation among women affects women's incomes in old age.

Figure 6.1: Women and men pensioners: percentage distribution of weekly gross individual income in £100 bands (1996/97)

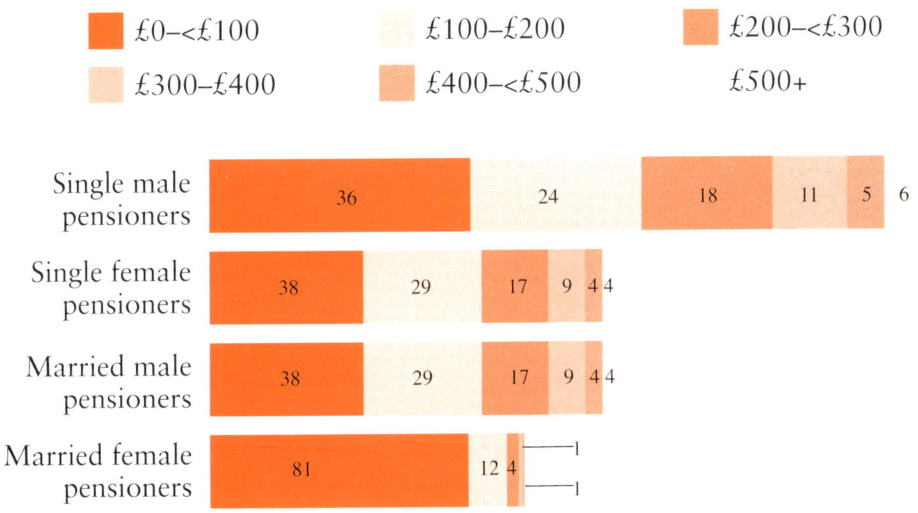

	£0–<£100	£100–£200	£200–<£300	£300–£400	£400–<£500	£500+
Single male pensioners	36	24	18	11	5	6
Single female pensioners	38	29	17	9	4	4
Married male pensioners	38	29	17	9	4	4
Married female pensioners	81	12	4	1	1	

Source: Women's Unit 1999.

Looking first at the distribution of individual income, Figure 6.1 shows that similar proportions of single male and female pensioners[81] and male pensioners in couples have individual incomes of less than £100 per week, with around

[81] We here use the category single as a label for those living alone. This category includes a mix of marital statuses, both the never-married and the widowed or divorced and separated.

40% of each group falling in this income band, although male pensioners are more likely to reach higher income levels than their female counterparts. The position of pensioner couples is distinct: over 80% of women pensioners in couples have an individual income of less than £100, more than double the proportion of men in couples. Around 5% of men, and just 1% of women, in pensioner couples have individual incomes of over £500 per week.

Table 6.1: Distribution of income of single male and female pensioners by age (1996–8)[1]

Single female pensioners	Bottom quintile	Second quintile	Third quintile	Fourth quintile	Top quintile	Total grossed numbers (millions) (=100%)
70 and under	21	34	22	15	9	1
71 to 75	28	35	19	11	6	0.7
76 to 80	31	33	20	10	6	0.6
Over 80	30	32	20	13	5	0.9
All individuals	27	33	20	13	7	3.2
Single male pensioners						
70 and under	16	32	26	15	11	0.3
71 to 75	16	38	21	15	9	0.2
76 to 80	24	33	19	15	9	0.2
Over 80	24	31	22	15	8	0.2
All individuals	20	34	22	15	9	0.9

1 Income is net equivalised household income before housing costs. The self-employed are excluded from this table.
Source: DSS 1999d. Analysis of two years (1996/7 and 1997/8) of the Family Resources Survey.

Using household income as the measure we find that *all* pensioner households are disproportionately represented at the bottom of the income distribution. Of all pensioner households, those made up of a single female are most likely to be found at the bottom of the income distribution (in 1997/8, 60% fell within the bottom two-fifths of the income distribution and 7% within the richest fifth) followed by single male pensioners and then pensioner couples. (DSS 1999c: Table 2.5).[82] Alongside lower incomes overall, pensioners, and especially single female pensioners, have a high risk of experiencing persistently low incomes. Of single female pensioners, 28% were in the bottom three deciles for seven consecutive years from 1991–97 while 45% had incomes in

[82] These figures refer to a measure of net equivalised household income before housing costs. See DSS 1999c for a full discussion.

the bottom three deciles for four of the seven years (DSS 1999d). Of all family types within the population, only lone parents experience similar levels of persistently low income (DSS 1999c, Table 6.6 and 1999d, see also Jarvis and Jenkins 1998). As Table 6.1 reveals, the proportion of single pensioners experiencing low incomes increases with age for women and men. For example, the percentage of women in the bottom fifth of the income distribution rises from 21% for pensioners aged 70 and under, to 30% among those over 80, while for men the equivalent figures stand at 16% and 24%.

6.1.2 Women and pensions

In the light of the increase in prosperity enjoyed by some pensioners as a result of better coverage and payments from occupational and personal pensions, gender differences in pension scheme membership will increasingly be an important source of income inequality among the older population. An analysis of the sources of income in retirement shows that occupational and personal pensions are a major source of difference in women's and men's incomes in later life, particularly among pensioner couples. Women pensioners in couples receive an average of just £12 per week from occupational pensions,[83] compared to £75 received by men in pensioner couples. The position of single female pensioners appears to be better – they receive an average of £27 per week from occupational pensions (compared to £45 received on average by single men pensioners) (Women's Unit 1999, Tables 2.4 and 2.7). However, these occupational pensions may be inherited as well as earned directly – while some single women have been single throughout their lifetime and are therefore more likely to have an occupational pension in their own right, many more are widows who may have inherited a portion of their partner's pension. Analysis of the pension income of widows reveals the importance of inherited rights to a pension – in 1994, 52% of widows received a pension inherited from their spouse which was worth on average £27 per week, while less than half that proportion (23%) received a pension in their own right, worth an average of £7 per week (Disney et al. 1997 Table 5.22). Data from the Retirement Survey show that over 30% of women aged 60–74 in 1994 who had joined an occupational pension will never draw a pension from it, compared to 14% of men. This is mainly because almost 40% of the women who had been a member of an occupational scheme at some point during their working lives had cashed in their entitlements sometime before retirement (Disney et al. 1997 Table 5.4 and 5.5). This option is not, however, available any longer.

[83] Income from occupational pensions is defined to include any annuities purchased from a personal pension. We here consider income from occupational and personal pensions together. Personal pension scheme membership was relatively rare for the current generation of pensioners and hence income from such a source is likely to be limited. We consider current patterns of personal pension membership below.

The incomes of today's elderly population, and the lower levels of occupational pensions among women pensioners, reflect patterns of labour market participation that prevailed in previous decades. Nevertheless, figures on current occupational and personal pension scheme membership show continuing differences in women's and men's membership patterns. Table 6.2 shows that for the 1994–96 period 54% of women working full-time and 23% of those working part-time were members of an occupational pension, rates of membership being 59% for men working full-time. For both women and men overall rates of membership of personal pensions are lower and follow similar patterns of membership as occupational pensions. Differentials among women are also apparent, with membership rates markedly lower among women in manual occupations, with a particularly marked gradient for those women working part-time – 67% of professionals working part-time were members of an occupational or personal pension, while fewer than a quarter of women employed part-time in semi/unskilled manual occupations had some pension scheme coverage.

Table 6.2: Employees who are members of pension schemes: by socio-economic group (1994–96)[1]

Great Britain	Occupational pension			Personal pension			Any pension		
	Women Full-time	Women Part-time	Men Full-time	Women Full-time	Women Part-time	Men Full-time	Women Full-time	Women Part-time	Men Full-time
Professional	66	51	75	24	24	27	79	67	89
Employers and managers	63	43	68	24	24	33	78	59	88
Intermediate non-manual	68	41	72	20	16	21	80	53	85
Junior non-manual	51	25	62	19	11	21	65	34	75
Skilled manual[2]	41	17	48	21	13	32	56	30	72
Semi-skilled manual	30	16	46	17	8	23	46	23	64
Unskilled manual	28	11	39	12	5	20	39	16	54
All socio-economic groups	54	23	59	20	10	10	67	33	77

1 Combined years 1994–95 and 1995–96
2 Includes own account non-professional
Source: General Household Survey, Office for National Statistics.

What explains these differences in membership rates? Looking first at occupational pensions, differences in membership reflect differences in where women and men are located in the labour market. The high concentration of female employment in small firms and in the service sector means that women are more likely to work in companies that do not offer occupational provision. Given the higher rates of job segregation for part-time workers, this problem is particularly acute for women working part-time. In addition, even in firms that offer occupational pension coverage, part-timers may have experienced exclusion from the pension scheme – this practice is now contrary to the Part-Time Work Directive which is due to be implemented by April 2000. Further, women's greater discontinuity of employment (see Chapter 2) means they are less likely to meet any years of service requirement placed on membership of an occupational pension. For personal pensions, differences in women's and men's membership rates are explained by slightly different factors. Personal pension schemes are, in principle, open to all in employment or self-employment. Nevertheless, women's lower earnings will often make personal pensions less affordable – where a proportion of management fees for the personal pension is fixed, those able to pay only small contributions will end up paying a relatively large portion of their contributions in charges. Further, the practice of front-loading[84] management fees penalises those who terminate their membership after a short period of time. Women's lower personal pension scheme membership may, therefore, be driven either by their lower earnings, and/or by a calculation that such schemes offer lower value for money than the State Earnings Related Pension (SERPS) in their particular circumstances.

It should be noted that the cross-sectional figures on pension scheme membership given in Table 6.2 may underplay the differences between women's and men's ultimate pension entitlement. An employee who has an interrupted employment history or who changes employer is likely to suffer some loss in the value of pension rights. Standard methods for valuing preserved pension rights for those who leave before retirement do not match the increases that accrue to those who stay in the scheme (see Blake and Orszaug 1997). Women's employment patterns mean that they are more likely than men to suffer from such losses.

While differences in occupational pension coverage partially explain women's lower incomes from occupational pensions, lower lifetime earnings also contribute substantially to reduced pension income in old age. This is explored below (Sections 6.2–6.4) by using the simulation model to examine the impact of childbearing and lifetime earnings on income in old age.

6.1.3 Wealth, savings and financial planning

Differential accumulation of wealth is an important marker of economic inequality throughout the lifetime. Of course, wealth may be held in a variety

---

[84] Management fees on the personal pension fund are front-loaded where the majority of the fees are payable in the early years of pension scheme membership.

of forms – housing, pensions and investments, all of which vary in their accessibility and liquidity. While all these forms of wealth are important to individual and household well-being, our focus on income means that our previous discussion of pension income is followed here by consideration of incomes drawn directly from investments.[85] One reason for reserving our discussion of investment income until this chapter is the fact that income from investments provides an important income stream for some in later life and makes up, on average, a larger proportion of the total income of pensioners than non-pensioners. The 1996/7 Family Resources Survey reveals that almost two thirds of single pensioners have some income from investment. The amount received is, however, very small. For those in receipt of income from investment, the median amount is slightly lower for single female pensioners – £3 a week, compared to £5 for single male pensioners, while the means stand at £20 and £30 (the difference between the two reflecting the skewed distribution of investment income) (DSS 1999e).

Although pensions and home ownership remain the principal vehicles through which individuals save for retirement, financial provision above and beyond this may also be made through savings accounts, insurance or endowment policies. Saving behaviour is, not surprisingly, closely correlated to income (Banks and Tanner 1999; Banks, Dilnot and Low 1994; Rowlingson, Whyley and Warren 1999). This, in part, explains the gender differentials in saving for retirement, although differentials may also arise independently of income if women are more likely to depend upon their spouse to make savings on their behalf. A survey of 60–75 year olds in 1994 found that 62% of men compared to 38% of women had ever made any financial provision for old age. The survey found that, regardless of marital status, men were more likely to have made some savings, but the difference between women and men was particularly marked among those married – in just over a quarter of all married couples men had made some financial provision for old age while women had not (Disney et al. 1997: 200–201 and Table 6.3).

What existing cross-sectional data does not reveal is how far women's lower pension scheme membership and lower amounts of investment and savings incomes are purely a result of their lower lifetime earnings. It may be that, in addition, women feel less confident in the financial services industry and/or less convinced of their need to make independent financial plans, especially for retirement.

---

[85] Although an important component of wealth, housing wealth does not enter into our analysis because individuals rarely draw income directly from their housing wealth.

6.2 SIMULATED INCOME IN LATER LIFE

We first consider our standard hypothetical individuals in order to analyse their simulated income in old age. For our standard illustrative cases of married women, retirement is divided into two periods: a period of 11 years while both they and their husbands are alive is followed by 5 years of widowhood. As usual with our calculations, it must be borne in mind that they only provide illustrations – variations in age at death will lead to much more diverse outcomes than we consider here. These variations in death rates are not purely random: those in the higher income classes have higher life expectancy than those from lower income classes. These differences would give the high-skilled woman about two more years of life and the low-skilled about two years less than the central case. For men the differences are about three years either way (see Hattersley 1997). To simplify, our model takes no account of this social gradient. We do take account of the different life expectancies of men and women on average, but we ignore the significant number of cases where women die before their husbands.

The incomes that people are calculated to enjoy during retirement will also depend on their pension arrangements. Our assumptions are that men are members of final-salary pension schemes unless they are low-skilled, while women are only members of final-salary schemes if they are high-skilled. People who are not in final-salary schemes are assumed to be in the State Earnings Related Pension Scheme (SERPS). Additionally, we calculate entitlement to state Basic Pension, and also test for eligibility to Income Support in retirement.

6.2.1 Individual income in retirement

Figure 6.2 shows, for each of the 'standard' women, the total of their own net income throughout their years of retirement – for the married women this consists of 11 years while their husband survives and a further five years of widowhood. As this deals with their individual entitlements, it includes their survivor's pension, but excludes any transfer from a husband during his lifetime. A rough idea of the (net) value of the survivor's pension can be obtained by comparing the childless married woman's entitlement with that of her unmarried counterpart.

The overwhelming impression given by Figure 6.2 is that differences between women with different fertility are swamped by differences due to skill level. These are a consequence of both the very different earnings histories of the women, and the assumed differences in their pension scheme membership. Remember we are assuming that the mid-skilled women are in SERPS, but a substantial number of these women may be in final-salary pension schemes. Those who are can expect very much better pensions than indicated by Figure 6.2. To give an indication of this difference, we have calculated the gross pension to which a mid-skilled woman would be entitled were she in a final-salary scheme rather than SERPS. Mrs Mid with two children has SERPS entitlement of £1,570 per annum. Had she been in a final-salary scheme throughout her working life, her pension would be £9,420 per annum. This confirms our suggestion above that membership – or not – of an occupational pension scheme will be an ever more important source of income inequality among women.

Figure 6.2: Women's own net income in retirement by skill level and number of children

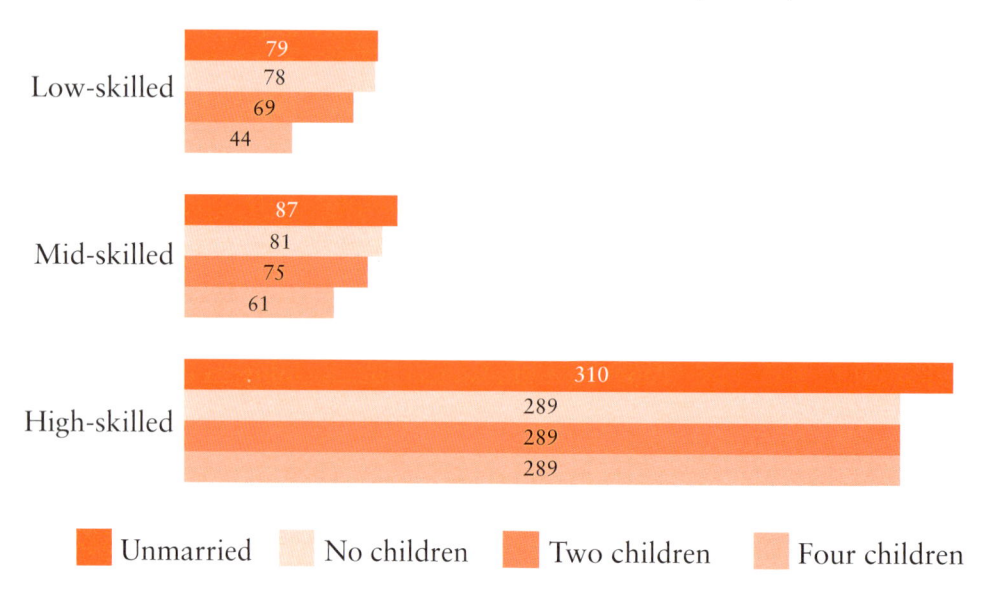

Total own net income in retirement (£'000s)

Low-skilled
- Unmarried: 79
- No children: 78
- Two children: 69
- Four children: 44

Mid-skilled
- Unmarried: 87
- No children: 81
- Two children: 75
- Four children: 61

High-skilled
- Unmarried: 310
- No children: 289
- Two children: 289
- Four children: 289

■ Unmarried   ■ No children   ■ Two children   ■ Four children

6.2.2 The family as a source of income in retirement

Figure 6.3 shows the total incomes of our standard cases over their retirement years, again adding together both phases. The income concept used here is once again the 'woman's portion' – that is, it includes the family transfer which would occur during the period of marriage if a couple shared their income equally, as well as the survivor's pension. Income is measured after state taxes and benefits.

Figure 6.3 brings out how far earnings differences by number of children are carried on into old age by the pension system. The biggest differences between the incomes shown in the figure are those between the women in the low-skilled, mid-skilled and high-skilled couples. Alongside the married women in these categories, we also show the income of an unmarried woman. The net income of the high-skilled unmarried woman in retirement is nearly four times that of the low-skilled unmarried woman, but this is small relative to the 14-fold difference in their gross earnings-related pension.

Figure 6.3: Retirement income by skill level and number of children

Total 'woman's portion' in retirement (£'000s)

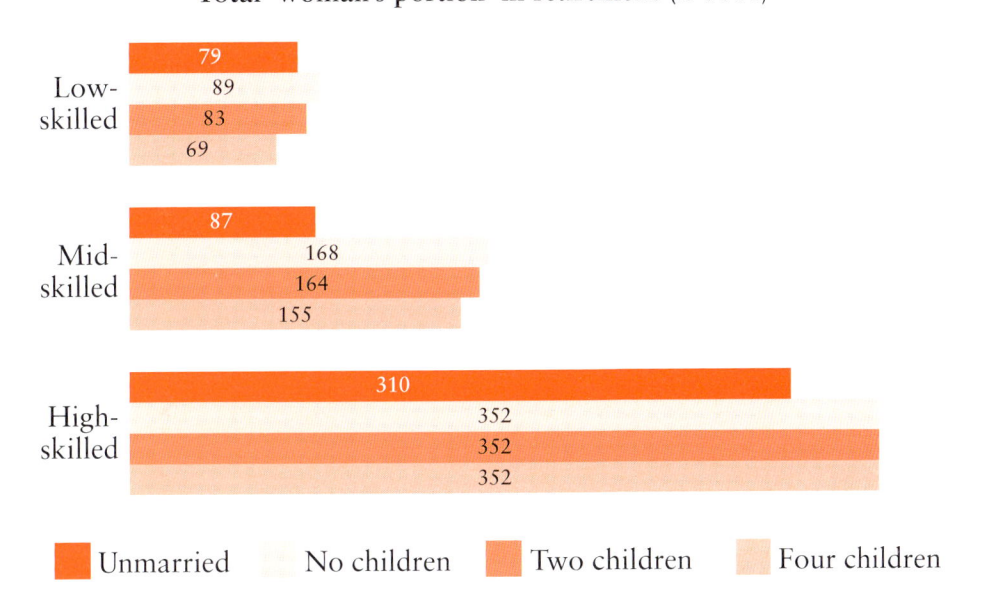

Skill	Unmarried	No children	Two children	Four children
Low-skilled	79	89	83	69
Mid-skilled	87	168	164	155
High-skilled	310	352	352	352

■ Unmarried   □ No children   ■ Two children   □ Four children

The difference between the income of the unmarried woman and her adjacent married (but childless) counterpart gives an indication of the benefits that a marriage where the couple share their incomes can give in old age. The greatest retirement income benefit from marriage accrues to the women in the mid-skilled couple. The childless mid-skilled married woman (on the assumption of income sharing) has a total retirement net income almost twice that of the unmarried mid-skilled woman, whose income in retirement totals £87,000.

6.2.3 Sources of income in retirement

The composition of the woman's portion during the two stages of retirement is shown in Table 6.3.

As Table 6.3 shows, in retirement, most of our hypothetical women are net beneficiaries from the state. The low percentage contribution of the state towards the incomes of the low-skilled mothers of four is because their earnings record is not sufficient to earn them a full Basic Pension. Only the high-skilled women pay more in tax than they get in benefits (principally the Basic Pension).[86] The family transfer is important for the mid-skilled couple. This is a reflection of our assumptions about pension provision. The low-skilled couple are heavily reliant on the Basic Pension (with a small supplement from SERPS) and therefore have relatively equal incomes in retirement and so the family transfer plays only a small part. The mid-skilled women are assumed to be in SERPS but their husbands have a better pension as they are in a final-salary scheme – thus the family transfer potentially plays a big part in these women's standard of living.

The importance of a widow's pension, even for the high-skilled women, emerges from the right-hand panel of Table 6.3. The low-skilled widows of low-skilled men are heavily reliant on state benefits, the SERPS survivor's pension left by their husbands only accounting for about 20% of their income. Only the widows from the high-skilled couples are net taxpayers during this phase of their life.

Table 6.3: Sources of women's retirement income by stages of lifecycle as percentage of woman's portion

	\multicolumn{5}{c	}{While retired (not widowed)}	\multicolumn{4}{c	}{While widowed}
	Unmarried	\multicolumn{4}{c	}{Married}	\multicolumn{4}{c	}{Married}
Number of children	0	0	1	2	4	0	1	2	4
Low-skilled	\multicolumn{5}{c	}{(in percent)}	\multicolumn{4}{c	}{(in percent)}
Labour market	30	27	20	16	6	24	18	15	5
State	70	65	68	69	52	57	62	64	72
Family transfer	0	8	13	15	43	19	20	21	24
Woman's portion ('000s)	£79	£59	£56	£55	£44	£30	£28	£27	£24
Mid-skilled									
Labour market	36	19	17	16	7	18	16	14	6
State	64	34	35	35	37	20	21	22	25
Family transfer	0	46	49	50	57	62	63	64	69
Woman's portion ('000s)	£87	£112	£111	£110	£105	£56	£55	£54	£51
High-skilled									
Labour market	106	102	102	102	102	78	78	78	78
State	-6	-6	-6	-6	-6	-21	-21	-21	-21
Family transfer	0	3	3	3	3	43	43	43	43
Woman's portion ('000s)	£310	£220	£220	£220	£220	£132	£132	£132	£132

[86] Recall that we count SERPS and final salary pensions as labour-market income.

6.3 LIFE EVENTS AND INCOME IN LATER LIFE

In this section we look at the impact of key life events on income in retirement. We focus on the pension consequences of children and at the pension consequences of divorce, and the extent to which the recent legislative reforms seem likely to compensate for these. The impact of a late spell of unemployment and early retirement on income during the working life and in later life is examined in Section 6.4.

6.3.1 The pension consequences of children

Figure 6.3 suggests that there is relatively little difference between the retirement income of women according to the number of children they have had. This, however, shows the net outcome after the effects of both the family transfer (both the presumptive transfer *inter vivos* and the survivor's pension) and the state tax-benefit system (including the Basic Pension). If we look at the earnings-related (or occupational) part of the pension system as one measure of the pension consequences of children, then we find evidence of the impact of children on income in retirement.

Table 6.4 shows two measures of the pension consequences of children. The upper panel shows the loss of the mother's total own pension (i.e. state Basic Pension plus SERPS or final-salary pension). The lower panel shows a parallel set of calculations, confined to the earnings-related pension (e.g. SERPS or final-salary pension) only. In both cases, the pension lost is shown as a percentage of the corresponding amount for the childless woman'.[87] The figures demonstrate that the key determinant of the pension loss is loss of earnings. Looking first at total own pension, we see that the mothers of two suffer only modest losses. With four children, however, the pension losses for all except the high-skilled women are at least 25%.

The figures for loss of earnings-related pension give a slightly different picture. They show that the mothers of four children lose most of the earnings-related pension they would have earned had they remained childless, unless they are high-skilled. Thus, the low-skilled mother of four loses 84% of her earnings-related pension while the mid-skilled mother of four loses 69%. Similarly, the low-skilled mother of two loses 42% of her earnings-related pension. By contrast, the near-continuous employment histories simulated for our high-skilled women mean that they do not suffer any pension loss.

---

[87] These calculations relate to the whole period after the woman retires.

Table 6.4: Pension consequences of children

(a) Entire pension

Loss of mother's own pension as a percentage of childless married woman's total own pension

Number of children	2	4
Low-skilled	12	44
Mid-skilled	8	25
High-skilled	0	0

(b) Earnings-related pension

Loss of mother's earnings-related pension as a percentage of childless married woman's earnings-related pension

Number of children	2	4
Low-skilled	42	84
Mid-skilled	21	69
High-skilled	0	0

Comparing the two panels of Table 6.4 reveals the much lower 'loss' incurred if we look at the total pension than when we focus on the earnings-related pension. This reflects the important role paid by the flat-rate State Basic pension in ameliorating the pension consequences of motherhood. Some countries offer a positive bonus in pension rights to those who bring up children. As the table demonstrates, in the UK, Home Responsibilities Protection offers considerable compensation for motherhood by offering credits to the Basic Pension, and a very small amount of protection for SERPS. However, the contrast between the two panels of Table 6.2 also indicates that, if the Basic Pension becomes smaller relative to the earnings-related pension achieved by those with continuous employment records, then the usefulness of this protection will diminish over time.

6.3.2 The pension consequences of divorce

Table 6.5 shows the retirement income consequences of divorce in some detail. For example, look at the case of the mid-skilled couple with two children who divorce after a 'short' marriage (in boldface in table). As compared to a similar woman who did not divorce, the divorced woman loses £89,000 family transfer (nearly half of the portion she would enjoy if she did not divorce). This consists of two parts (not shown separately in the table) – the transfer deriving from the husband on the assumption that the couple share their income equally, and the survivor's pension which she would have received in widowhood. There may be offsetting changes in other components of the woman's income and these appear in the following rows. As discussed in Chapter 4, divorce is likely to be followed by a change in labour market participation, and hence in the woman's earnings-related pension – in this particular case, this amounts to £2,000 over all the years the woman spends in retirement. Under the new legislation, the woman may also gain a share in her ex-husband's pension, and the calculated pension transfer is shown next – it amounts to £35,000 in this case. There may also be a change in the net state benefits the woman receives – in this case the divorced woman's net receipts from the State are £3,000 more than those of her counterpart with an unbroken marriage. When we take account of all these offsetting income increases, the woman ends up with £49,000 less income than she would have received had she continued in the marriage. In this case, therefore, the offsetting items make up for almost half the initial loss of the family transfer.

Table 6.5: Retirement income: consequences of divorce

Income (£'000s) totalled over retirement

Type of marriage	Two children Short	Long	Remarries	Four children Short	Long	Remarries
Low-skilled couple						
Woman's portion if no divorce	83	83	83	69	69	69
Change in family transfer	-14	-14	0	-25	-25	0
Offsetting effects						
Change in own pension	2	4	-2	4	4	0
Share of ex-spouse pension	2	5	2	4	7	4
Change in net state benefits	0	0	0	13	15	-7
Net change in income	-10	-5	0	-4	2	-4
Mid-skilled couple						
Woman's portion if no divorce	164	164	164	155	155	155
Change in family transfer	-89	-89	-11	-94	-94	-17
Offsetting effects						
Change in own pension	2	0	1	10	9	2
Share of ex-spouse pension	35	57	35	49	71	49
Change in net state benefits	3	-1	-4	1	-4	-5
Net change in income	-49	-33	20	-35	-18	29
High-skilled couple						
Woman's portion if no divorce	352	352	352	352	352	352
Change in family transfer	-64	-64	-2	-64	-64	-2
Offsetting effects						
Change in own pension	0	0	0	0	0	0
Share of ex-spouse pension	7	1	7	10	8	10
Change in net state benefits	19	21	-2	18	19	-4
Net change in income	-37	-42	3	-35	-37	4

In most respects, the position of a woman following the break-up of partnership may be expected to be rather similar whether the partnership is a cohabitation or a marriage. The two situations will, however, be different in respect of pensions. Pension schemes do not normally pay a survivor's benefit to cohabitees. Furthermore, the law provides no mechanism for a formerly cohabiting couple to share their pensions after they split up.

Figure 6.4: Pensions and divorce: share of ex-spouse's pension as a fraction of lost family transfer by number of children and length of marriage

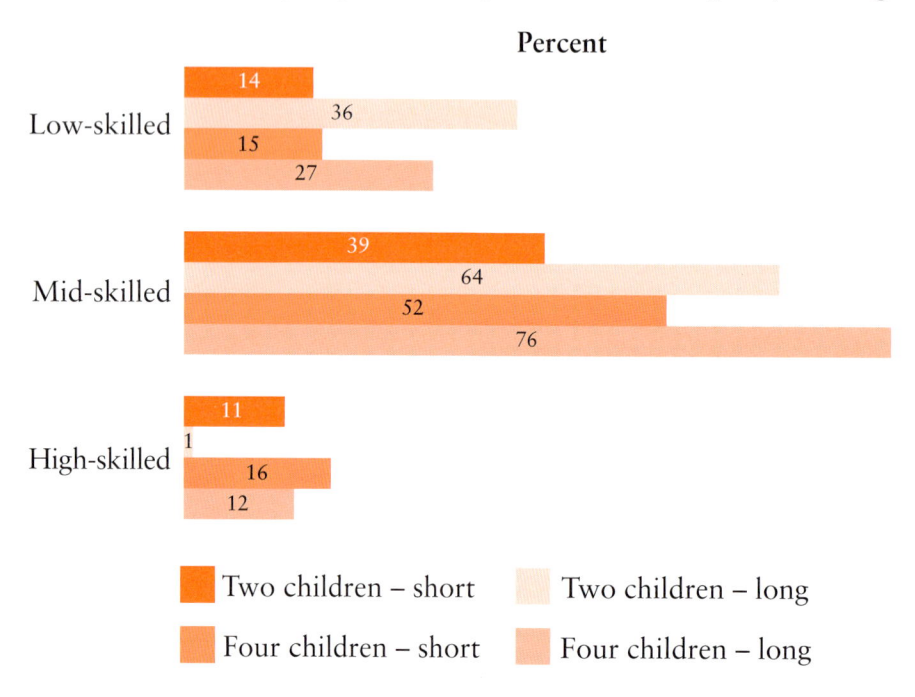

Percent

Low-skilled
- Two children – short: 14
- Two children – long: 36
- Four children – short: 15
- Four children – long: 27

Mid-skilled
- Two children – short: 39
- Two children – long: 64
- Four children – short: 52
- Four children – long: 76

High-skilled
- Two children – short: 11
- Two children – long: 1
- Four children – short: 16
- Four children – long: 12

■ Two children – short   ▫ Two children – long
■ Four children – short   ▫ Four children – long

The biggest transfer losses are experienced by the women from the mid-skilled couples. This is true both in absolute sums of money and relative to the income of the women with an unbroken marriage. As pointed out above, in these cases the man and woman are quite unequally pensioned – wage differences are intensified by the generosity of their assumed pension schemes. In these cases also, the share of the ex-spouse's pension could provide a substantial compensation for the family transfer which the woman might have expected to enjoy had her marriage endured. Figure 6.4 shows how far the pension share compensates for the lost family transfer. As expected, the pension share provides greater compensation where the marriage has lasted for longer. For example, the simulated pension share received by the mid-skilled mother of two who divorces after a long marriage (17 years) is worth 64% of the loss of family transfer. By contrast, the pension share received by the low-skilled mother of two after a short marriage is worth only 14% of lost family transfer. Where the woman remarries, the calculations shown in Table 6.5 suggest that (unless low-skilled) her retirement income will be higher if she divorces. For the sake of clarity, these cases are omitted from Figure 6.4. (They would introduce bars over 100%.)

It should be noted that the legislation on pension sharing is enabling rather than prescriptive. The results shown here are calculated on the assumption that the divorce settlement will provide for equal sharing of the partners' pensions. What actually happens will depend on the details of the divorce negotiations. These calculations do, however, give an indication of the possibilities of the legislation, and somewhat similar calculations will surely form part of divorce negotiations – at least in cases where substantial sums are involved.

6.4 INTERRUPTIONS TO EMPLOYMENT IN LATER LIFE

In previous analysis, our simulated people have enjoyed very full employment histories. Motherhood has been the only reason for interruptions to employment. We now look at other interruptions to employment. In 1997, 58% of men aged 55-65 were in paid employment compared to 81% of all men. 20% of men aged 55-65 (compared to 13% of all men) were classed as 'economically inactive' (Labour Force Survey data quoted in Campbell 1999). We therefore simulate a late spell of unemployment and early retirement. Employment may also be curtailed for other reasons – notably caring for older relatives or perhaps education. These spells have not been explicitly modelled here, but in so far as their effect is similar to spells of unemployment and early retirement they will have a comparable impact on lifetime incomes.

6.4.1 Unemployment and lifetime incomes

Unemployment may occur at any age in the working life, and may be of short or long duration. Some people have repeated spells of unemployment throughout the working life. Of many possible unemployment scenarios, we have chosen to investigate one where the husband becomes unemployed when he is 45, and never finds another job. We also assume that the wife is unemployed when her husband is. We have deliberately chosen a very long spell of unemployment to provide a sharp contrast with the 'extreme' of full employment on which we have concentrated up till now. As Campbell (1999) has shown, long spells of unemployment have become increasingly common in the 1990s for men in late middle age. The assumption that both partners are unemployed is also extreme, but it is realistic. Although the reasons are not fully understood, empirical work consistently finds that women are much less likely to be employed in households where the man is unemployed. These couples we simulate here are examples of 'work poor' households (Gregg and Wadsworth 1996), contrasting with the (mainly) 'work-rich' households we have discussed so far. Longitudinal evidence shows that once a couple has no earners it is quite likely to stay in the same state, particularly where the man is over forty and has a low level of education (Davies et al. 1998a).

The composition of lifetime income for the women in the unemployed couples is shown in Table 6.6. The right-hand panel of the table also shows the difference from the standard, employed case. The unemployment scenario cuts the women's labour market income by over half in most cases. The drop is proportionately largest for the women who have taken time out of the labour force or have done long spells of part-time work while their children were young, but who then return to full-time work. For example, the mid-skilled mother of two earns only £120,000 from the labour market if she experiences a late spell of unemployment, £326,000 less over the lifetime than her counterpart who does not experience unemployment – a loss of 73% of her lifetime income from the labour market. The reason for this dramatic drop in labour market income is that these women earn a large fraction of their lifetime labour income after the age of 45. Where motherhood has led to absence from the labour market or part-time work, a disproportionate fraction of full-time employment is undertaken during the latter stage of their life (the time when we have simulated the spell of unemployment).

Not surprisingly, unemployment is accompanied by an increase in the state's net contribution. This is almost entirely due to reduction in Income Tax and NICs paid on earnings. The model reflects the operation of the benefit system, and so Income Support paid to the unemployed is paid to the man.[88] The increase in the family transfer observed in many cases reflects this. Where the family transfer was small because the couple had a small earnings gap (as in the case of the highly-skilled couple) then it becomes larger (though out of a smaller income). For example, the high-skilled mother of two experiencing unemployment 'gains' £38,000 more from the family transfer, or, to put it another way, becomes potentially more dependent upon the family transfer that her husband may make. Where the transfer was already large then it becomes smaller – reflecting the drop in the husband's income. This applies to the case of the mid-skilled mother of four who is calculated to receive £72,000 less from the family transfer.

---

[88] Given our focus on lifetime incomes, we simplify the benefit system by ignoring the (relatively) short period of entitlement to Job-Seeker's Allowance.

Table 6.6: Unemployment: lifetime incomes of married women.

Income totalled over the lifetime (£'000s)

	Unemployed cases			Difference from employed cases		
Number of children	0	2	4	0	2	4
Low-skilled						
Labour market	252	52	24	-250	-175	-38
State	3	57	113	32	6	0
Family transfer	103	183	169	26	2	-61
Woman's portion	357	292	305	-192	-167	-99
Mid-skilled						
Labour market	254	120	70	-336	-326	-91
State	-8	57	87	59	59	1
Family transfer	154	199	227	3	5	-72
Woman's portion	401	377	384	-274	-261	-162
High-skilled						
Labour market	559	533	463	-793	-802	-807
State	-88	-49	-3	205	210	215
Family transfer	134	138	163	28	38	50
Woman's portion	606	623	623	-561	-554	-542

Notes: Woman's portion is calculated on the assumption of equal sharing between husband and wife. Sums of money are undiscounted totals at 1999 prices. Lifetime is here defined as the period from the age of marriage until death. The family transfer includes its posthumous component, the survivor's pension.

Compensation from changes in income from the family transfer and from the tax-benefit system means that the decrease in the woman's portion following unemployment is generally smaller than the drop in labour income. The women who suffered most (proportionately) – the mothers of two from the low- and mid-skilled couples – find that their portion falls by 35%–40% rather than the 75% by which their gross labour income fell.

These results assume that the family transfer indeed takes place. They quantify the way in which wives in 'work-poor' families are more reliant on their husbands for financial support than are wives in families where market work is abundant. This is, in fact, a consequence of the benefit system treating the couple as an entity.

6.4.2 Unemployment and the earnings cost of children

Table 6.7 shows the forgone earnings cost of children for the mothers in these unemployed couples. These costs are calculated as the difference in earnings of the mothers from those of childless women in families subject to identical spells of unemployment. For women of low- or mid-skill, the forgone earnings costs for the unemployed are less than those for standard cases of fully-employed families in Chapter 2. From 45 onwards, neither mothers nor the childless women earn anything so there is no difference between their earnings. In cases where women are in high-skilled couples, unemployment does not have much effect on the small forgone earnings. In cases where there had been a big difference (mothers of four) unemployment has a big effect – substantially reducing the forgone earnings cost of motherhood. In percentage terms, for both Mrs Low and Mrs Mid, the forgone earnings cost of children in this unemployment scenario is roughly half what it was in the standard cases. This demonstrates that our standard estimates of the earnings cost of children will tend to be reduced in any scenario which cuts the earnings of childless women more than those of mothers.

Table 6.7: Unemployed: forgone earnings cost of children

Forgone earnings cost of children	Mother of 2	Mother of 4
Amounts – £'000s		
Low-skilled	194	222
Mid-skilled	130	183
High-skilled	17	81
Percentage change from standard cases		
Low-skilled	-28	-48
Mid-skilled	-7	-56
High-skilled	-8	-10

6.4.3 Unemployment and retirement income

The retirement income of the unmarried women and the wives from same-skill couples who have experienced unemployment is depicted in Figure 6.5, expressed in terms of the woman's portion of joint income where there is a husband. Just as in the cases not subject to unemployment, it is noticeable that the differences by type of family are small relative to those by skill level. The inclusion of unmarried women gives an indication of the gains obtainable from marriage. The figure shows that, in these simulations, it is the women from the mid-skilled couples who gain most from marriage in terms of retirement income. This reflects what is by now a familiar pattern: the low-skilled women gain little from being married to a low-skilled (and therefore poorly pensioned man); the high-skilled women have good pensions in their own right and gain relatively little from their husbands. These calculations show that this familiar pattern persists even with prolonged unemployment in the second half of the working life.

Figure 6.5: Woman's portion in retirement with experience of unemployment

Total 'woman's portion' in retirement (£'000s)

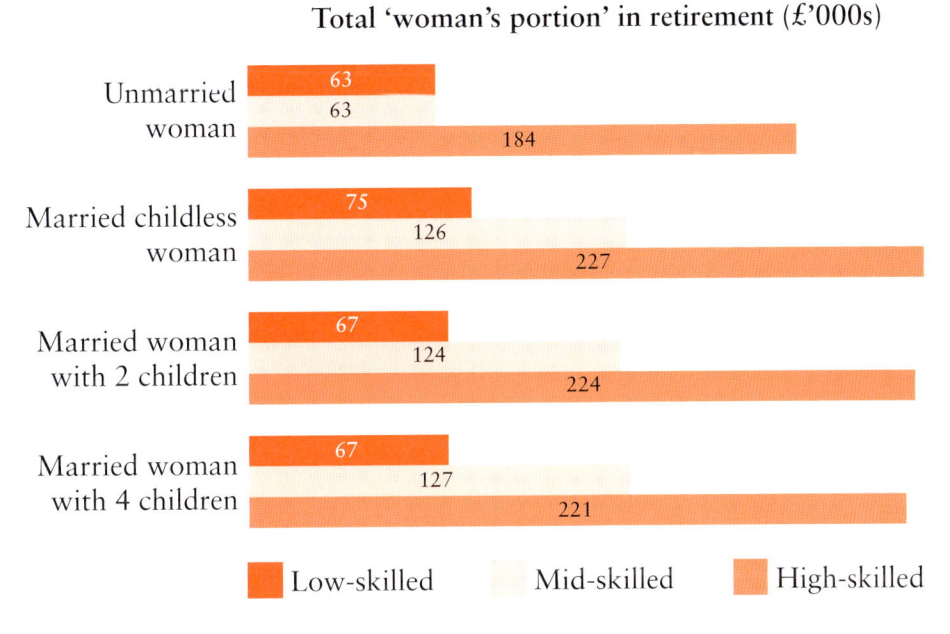

	Low-skilled	Mid-skilled	High-skilled
Unmarried woman	63	63	184
Married childless woman	75	126	227
Married woman with 2 children	67	124	224
Married woman with 4 children	67	127	221

Table 6.8 shows retirement income (again defined as the woman's portion) for those affected by unemployment as a percentage of the income they would enjoy if they had experienced the standard employment histories predicted by the model. The most striking feature is that the experience of unemployment results in a lower relative income loss for the low-skilled than for the more highly skilled. This reflects the relative importance of the Basic Pension to the low-skilled, and the low levels of SERPS which are paid to these couples, even if they do not have unemployment. The low-skilled women with the shortest employment records (the mothers of four) apparently suffer hardly any retirement income loss from the experience of unemployment. This is because the women not subject to unemployment do not earn a lot more than those who are, and also that unemployment brings about a rather small drop in the (low) retirement income of their husbands.

Table 6.8: Women experiencing unemployment: Retirement income as a percent of that of fully-employed counterpart

	Unmarried	Childless	Mother of two	Mother of four
Low-skilled	80	84	81	97
Mid-skilled	73	75	76	82
High-skilled	59	64	64	63

These results are only illustrative. If we had selected a period of unemployment earlier in life – say during the couple's twenties or thirties – the results would have been different. Spells of unemployment at those ages are much more likely to be of shorter duration, and therefore to have less effect on lifetime incomes (though there is some long-term effect on subsequent pay). The effect on forgone earnings cost will vary. Where the standard forgone earnings cost is large, it is likely to be reduced by unemployment during the child-caring years. In the unemployment scenario, both the women we compare to estimate the earnings cost of children will have their earnings reduced, thus the difference between them will be smaller than in the standard scenario. This is not to deny that unemployment at earlier ages will have a big effect on any children in the family and that it is likely to cause child poverty. This, however, is a cost that unemployment inflicts on children, rather than an effect of unemployment on the earnings cost of children.

6.4.4 Early retirement and lifetime incomes

Another way in which lifetime earnings are reduced is through early retirement. Our assumptions are that the men are given early retirement at age 52 (when their wives are fifty). We assume that wives retire at the same time as their husbands. These assumptions may seem fairly extreme, but they are again chosen to contrast sharply with the fully-employed couples who take up most of our story. We assume that early retirees who are in final-salary pensions schemes have been offered a deal by their employers such that they get their pension as soon as they retire – but they do not get any 'added years'. Members of SERPS, however, do not get any early retirement package – the situation for them is just as if they were unemployed (as discussed before). For that reason, the low-skilled couple, both of whom are assumed to be in SERPS, is excluded from this analysis. Our early retirement scenario does not model any disability or incapacity benefits.

Figure 6.6 shows the effect of the early retirement assumption on the income of the woman – measured by shared income of the couple, i.e. on the assumption that the family transfer takes place. This graph emphasises how much better off the high-skilled couple are than the others. Even with early retirement, the high-skilled women have higher incomes during their working lives than almost all the other women achieve.

Figure 6.6: Early retirement: woman's portion

Total 'woman's portion' in retirement (£'000s)

Category	Standard cases	Early retirement
Mid-skilled, no children	507	391
Mid-skilled, 2 children	474	360
Mid-skilled, 4 children	390	328
High-skilled, no children	814	677
High-skilled, 2 children	824	682
High-skilled, 4 children	813	666

■ Standard cases   ▫ Early retirement

6.4.5 Early retirement and the earnings cost of children

Table 6.9 shows the effect of early retirement on the gross earnings cost of children. Just as in the case of unemployment, we measure the earnings cost by comparing the mother with a childless woman with the same employment history. Again, and for similar reasons, early retirement tends to reduce the gross earnings cost of children. Figure 6.6 demonstrated that, in terms of the woman's portion, the early retirement scenarios modelled here tend to reduce the differential between the mothers and childless women very substantially.

Table 6.9: Early retirement: earnings cost of children

Forgone earnings cost of children	Mother of 2	Mother of 4
Amounts – thousands of pounds	£'000s	
Mid-skilled	134	262
High-skilled	18	86
Percentage change from standard case	in percent	
Mid-skilled	-4	-37
High-skilled	-2	-4

We have not specified why early retirement takes place. Ill-health is one possibility, although we have not simulated the payment of any disability benefits. Nevertheless, the ill-health of one of the partners, with a need for care from the other, is one reason why both partners might take early retirement at the same time. Where a woman gives up paid work in order to care for a parent or older relative, this may often happen when she is in her fifties, as in the examples here. In such cases, however, it is not especially likely that both partners will retire at the same time. The calculations reported here might be thought of as an upper bound for such cases.

6.4.6 Early retirement and retirement income

Figure 6.7 shows the retirement income in cases where the women (and their husbands) have taken early retirement. By retirement income here, we mean the woman's portion accruing after the state pension age (i.e. 65). These calculations therefore relate to the same number of years as those for the other groups considered in this chapter. We do not consider early retirement for the low-skilled couple, assuming that for them early retirement would be indistinguishable from unemployment. As the assumption is that early retirement takes place when the men are 52 (and the women are 50), these lifetimes have more years of pensionable service than those of the unemployed, whose earnings stop at 45. This results in higher retirement incomes than in the cases of unemployment just considered. Otherwise, the pattern of results for the retirement incomes of the early retired looks very similar to that of the unemployed. In particular, the women from high-skilled couples are relatively well-off in retirement and retain around 80% of the income they would have achieved had they (and their husbands) not taken early retirement.

Figure 6.7: 'Woman's portion' in retirement with experience of early retirement

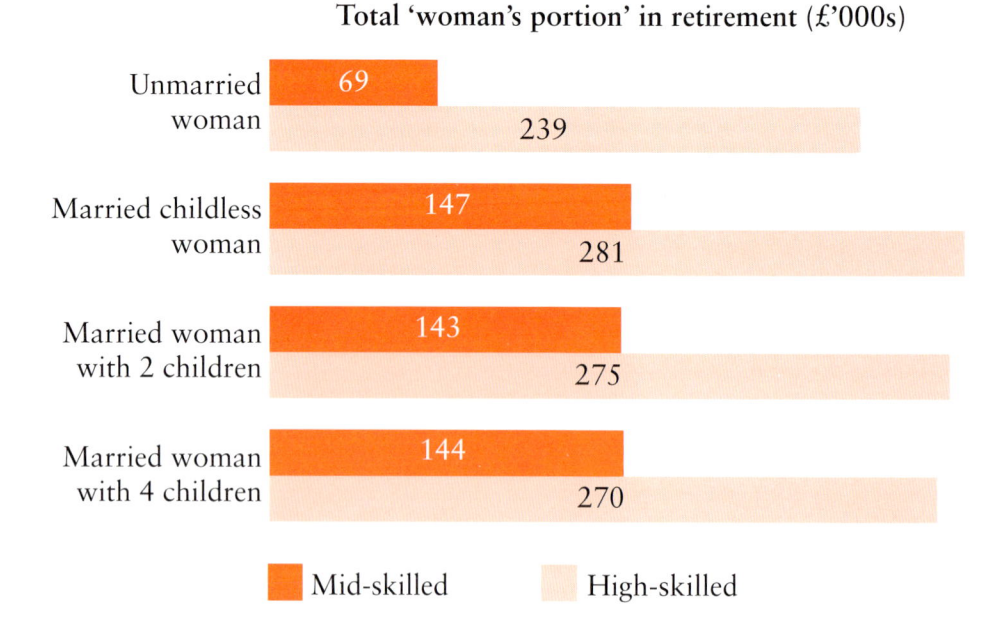

Total 'woman's portion' in retirement (£'000s)

	Mid-skilled	High-skilled
Unmarried woman	69	239
Married childless woman	147	281
Married woman with 2 children	143	275
Married woman with 4 children	144	270

[178

6.5 CONCLUSIONS AND KEY FINDINGS

This chapter has shown considerable variation between the incomes of the various simulated women in later life. Our simulations do not allow for all the sources of diversity which might be encountered in the real world, and are therefore likely to understate the variety in the incomes that older women experience. The results reported here demonstrate that the polarisation in employment and earnings between the high-skilled women and the rest carries on into retirement. The women who, according to our model, have relatively high incomes in old age are mainly those who have had high earnings during their working lives.

The pension cost of children is low for those mothers who have preserved employment continuity. For most mothers of two, the Home Responsibilities Protection in the Basic Pension, together with the flat-rate nature of this pension softens the pension cost of motherhood.

Our results also point to the cases where sharing a husband's pension, and entitlement to a survivor's pension, are of most importance. The husband's pension is not very much help if he is himself low paid and poorly pensioned. Where both parties are well-pensioned high earners, then the net effect of income sharing while both are alive will be small, but the survivor's pension has considerable value. Where the couple are both mid-skilled, however, then the husband's pension (if shared with his wife) and the survivor's pension constitute a large portion of the woman's income. In the case of the mid-skilled couple, the lifetime earnings gap between husband and wife is reinforced by relative generosity of the pensions schemes to which they are each (plausibly) assumed to belong. Where mid-skilled women are in final-salary pensions schemes they will be less reliant on their husband's pension than the mid-skilled woman we have simulated here.

We have looked at the effect of the new legislation enabling partners to agree to share pensions after divorce. Our results show that, if a couple were to agree on equal pension sharing, this could be worth quite a lot where the man has a good pension and the marriage has lasted for quite a long time. Where, however, the husband's pension is low, as is likely to be the case for many women whose own pensions are low, the benefit from pension sharing after divorce will be small (see Joshi and Davies, 1991).

The examples we have considered of disruptions to the employment history in the form of early retirement or unemployment result in lower pensions to those affected, but do not much alter the pattern of relativities in retirement income.

The key findings of this chapter are:

- Pensioner households are disproportionately represented at the bottom of the income distribution, but the risk of being at the bottom of the income distribution is higher for single female households (in 1997/8, 60% fell within the bottom two-fifths of the income distribution) and, in common with lone parents, single female pensioners experience high levels of persistent poverty.

- Our picture of labour market change presented in Chapter 2 would lead us to believe that the incomes of future generations of female pensioners are set to increase. While this may be true for some, figures on current occupational pension membership reveal continuing disparities among women and men in their membership of occupational pension schemes – in 1994-6, only 23% of women working part-time and 54% of women working full-time were members of an occupational pension scheme compared to 59% of men working full-time.

- Looking at the income estimated by our model of lifetime incomes shows a large degree of variation among women according to their skill level and type of pension scheme membership. The graduate mother of two received a total income in retirement of £289,000 compared to the £69,000 received by the low-skilled mother. In widowhood, especially, low skilled mothers are heavily reliant on the Basic Pension.

- The model allows for a calculation of the pension consequences of children. For high-skilled women these are zero. By contrast, low-skilled mothers of two lose 42% of their earnings-related pension (rising to 84% for mothers of four), while the mid-skilled lose 21% if they have two children and 69% if they have four.

- If the whole of pension income is taken into account, a much lower cost is borne by mothers – this testifies for the importance of the credits that the state Basic Pension gives to those caring for their children.

- The income costs of divorce extend into retirement – the net loss incurred by the mid-skilled mother of two who divorces after seven years is £49,000, even after we take into account the value of the pension shared on divorce (worth £35,000 in this case). For longer marriages, the value of the shared pension is higher – in the same case, a woman with a marriage of 17 years is estimated to derive £57,000 from the pension split on divorce.

- A prolonged late spell of unemployment (experienced by both husband and wife) reduces women's income by around a third or more in all but one of the cases simulated here. The payment of income support to male head of household means that women in these 'work-poor' families are particularly reliant on the financial support of their husbands.

- Early retirement has similar effects on income as unemployment according to our simulation. The differences between women of different skill levels were greater than the differences by employment history – even with early retirement, the graduate mother of two had a retirement income double that of her mid-skilled counterpart.

APPENDIX I
GENDER WAGE DIFFERENTIALS

APPENDIX I
GENDER WAGE DIFFERENTIALS

This Appendix provides a more detailed treatment of the decomposition of the gender pay gap. After an explanation of the leading method of decomposing the gap, there follows a summary of recent results on the gender pay gap in Britain.

The most widely used technique for decomposing wage differences between men and women into components due to differences in their attributes and differences in the rates at which these attributes are rewarded is the Oaxaca decomposition (Oaxaca, 1973).

The approach starts from separate equations for the wages of men and women, as follows:

$w^m = X^m \beta^m + u^m$

$w^f = X^f \beta^f + u^f$

where superscripts m and f denote male and female respectively, and, for $i=m, f$:

N_i denotes the number of observations in category i.

w^i is an N_i vector of natural logarithms of hourly wages

X^i is a $N_i \times k$ matrix or regressors

β^i is a $k \times 1$ vector of coefficients

u^i is an $N_i \times 1$ vector of disturbances

The regressors typically include human capital variables such as education and employment experience, though other variables may be included as well. The regression coefficients may be interpreted as the rate at which these attributes are rewarded. For example, the coefficient of years of employment experience measures the effect of an extra year's employment on the log of the hourly wage[89]. In this framework, differences between the coefficients for men and women (i.e. differences in the rates at which attributes are rewarded) are

---

[89] Assuming that the wage equation contains only a linear term in experience.

interpreted as discriminatory. If the coefficient vectors were identical for men and women, then both sexes would be rewarded at the same rate for their experience, education and so on. Any systematic differences in the wages of men and women would then be attributable differences in their characteristics (e.g. levels of education or experience). The Oaxaca decomposition is a method for breaking down an observed wage gap into part due to differences in characteristics and part due to differences in rewards (discrimination).

After fitting the above wage equations, the method proceeds as follows:

using bars to denote sample means and carets to denote fitted values, we have:

$$\bar{w}^m = \hat{\beta}^m \bar{X}^m \quad \text{and} \quad \bar{w}^f = \hat{\beta}^f \bar{X}^f$$

Hence

$$\bar{w}^m - \bar{w}^f = \hat{\beta}^m C \bar{X}^m - \bar{X}^f h + e\hat{\beta}^m - \hat{\beta}^f j \bar{X}^f$$

The first term on the right-hand side represents the difference in characteristics evaluated at the men's coefficients. The second term gives the difference between the valuation of the attributes of the woman with average women's characteristics at the rates paid to males and to females. This second term provides the basis for the most widely used measure of wage discrimination. Remembering that the dependent variable is in logarithms, we have:

$$D_f = \exp[e\hat{\beta}^m - \hat{\beta}^f j \bar{X}^f] - 1$$

This discrimination index may be interpreted as the percentage increase in the hourly wage which would be obtained by a woman on average full-time wages if she were paid like a man.

Neither the above decomposition, nor the index based on it, are unique. Analogous methods may be used to decompose the differential between full-time and part-time workers.

For a more extensive treatment of the measurement of wage discrimination, see Joshi and Paci (1998).

Table A1: Summary of recent empirical results on decomposing gender wage differentials in Britain

	1978	1991	1980	1994	1994
	Cohort Studies		Women and Employment Survey	British Household Panel Survey	
	age 32	age 32	Married	partnered	all
Average woman's wage as % man's[a]	61.2%	73.1%	67.8%	71.0%	74.8%
Difference in Wage offers (logarithms)[b]	0.491	0.313	0.388	0.343	0.291
Attributable to differences in: (logarithms)					
Human capital of men and women In full-time jobs	0.091	0.011	0.09	0.101	0.075
Human capital of women in Full-and part-time jobs[c]	0.079	0.064	0.041	0.029	0.025
Remuneration of women in Full-and part-time jobs[c]	0.107	0.082	0.085	0.130	0.108
Remuneration of men and women In full-time jobs	0.214	0.156	0.172	0.082	0.083
Percentage of women part-time	56	37	55	43	36

Notes:
a) evaluated at the geometric mean of samples including women in both full-and part-time jobs, and men full-timers only
b) the estimates from the Women and Employment Survey and the BHPS were adjusted For sample selection
c) the entries in these rows have been weighted by the percentage of women part-timers, shown in the last row
d) parameter differences are weighted by the characteristics of women full-timers

Sources:
Cohort Studies: Joshi and Paci (1998).
   Sample contains workers of the specified ages only
Women and Employment Survey: Ermisch and Wright (1992).
   Sample of married women under 60 and their spouses
British Household Panel Study: Davies et al (1997)
   Sample covers all working ages, and not just those with partners.

APPENDIX II
THE SIMULATED
TAX-BENEFIT SYSTEM

APPENDIX II
THE SIMULATED TAX-BENEFIT SYSTEM

Children's Tax Credit (CTC)

From April 2001, the married couple's allowance (MCA) and its related allowances (such as the Additional Personal Allowance) will be replaced by Children's Tax Credit (CTC). In our simulations, we have assumed that these changes have taken effect. We use the rates already announced, but other elements of the Income Tax system are set at their April 1999 values. Most couples will be able to split the CTC equally, just as they currently may split the MCA. We assume that, when permitted, a couple will split the married couple's allowance equally, unless by doing so they would not be able to use the full value of the CTC. When a couple includes higher-rate taxpayers, the model applies the taper to the higher income, as the Inland Revenue envisages.

The Working Families' Tax Credit (WFTC)

Our model simulates Working Families' Tax Credit, introduced in the Autumn of 1999. WFTC, like its predecessor Family Credit, is assessed on the joint income of a couple. A couple who are entitled to WFTC will be able to choose which of them will receive the credit. As the possibility of receiving WFTC through the pay packet will not be introduced until the spring of 2000, no-one knows how couples will choose to receive any credit to which they are entitled. We have assumed that the couple will choose to have the credit paid to the man, except in cases where the woman has a substantial involvement in the labour market (i.e. where she is employed for over sixteen hours per week). An exception to our general rule is the case of the low-skilled woman with four children. In our simulations, such a woman would have had some entitlement to Family Credit under the previous system, and so it has been assumed that she would be the recipient of any WFTC to which her family is entitled.
We have included some discussion of the effects of altering this assumption.

Since WFTC includes an allowance for a percentage of childcare costs (up to a ceiling), we have had to make some assumptions about these. Our assumptions about the use of purchased childcare are based on the stylised facts of current British experience. We assumed that women who were employed part-time used purchased childcare only if the youngest child was under school age and that the care was used for five hours a week more than their hours of employment. Mothers of pre-schoolers who were employed full-time were also assumed to use childcare for five hours per week more than their hours of employment. Other mothers employed full-time were assumed to use purchased childcare until the youngest child was twelve, in this case for 15 hours a week. There is some evidence (Duncan and Giles 1996) that the hourly price paid for childcare is greater where more than 20 hours per week are purchased. Presumably this reflects higher quality requirements where the children were entrusted to care for longer periods of time. We have thus used a higher price for care where it is used for a full-time working week. The hourly prices used were respectively the median (£1.40) and 70th percentile (£2) estimated from a 1994 survey (Finlayson et al. 1996). These were then inflated to 1999 levels using the average earnings index to proxy the price of childcare.[90] These are probably rather conservative estimates of childcare costs. The introduction of WFTC is itself likely to have an impact on the market for childcare. It is likely that the average price paid for childcare will rise, and this is likely to reflect both an increase in the price of purchased childcare of any given quality and an increase in the average quality of purchased childcare. We have only estimated childcare costs for their impact on WFTC entitlement. We have not in general calculated actual expenditures nor deducted them from net income. This would be a separate exercise requiring more study of the childcare market.

*Table A2: Working Families' Tax Credit –
lifetime totals paid in standard cases (£'000s)*

Family type	Two children	Four children	Four children
WFTC paid to		Man	Woman
Skill level			
Low	9.18		36.78
Mid		12.46	

Note: For method used to assign payment to man or woman, see text.

The lifetime totals of WFTC paid in the standard cases (e.g. no divorce, teenage motherhood or unemployment) are summarised in Table A.2. The low-skilled couple with four children is the one most affected by the assumption about who gets the WFTC. We calculate that this couple is entitled to about £37,000 WFTC. If this sum were paid to the husband rather than the wife, the wife's net income cost of her four children would go up to £335,000, while the husband's income would increase by a total of £51,000 as a result of having the children. The total cost to the couple would be unaffected (we take no account of WFTC payments

---

[90] We use the earnings index rather than a general price index because labour is the main element in the cost of childcare.

on labour supply). The other couples who would be entitled to WFTC are the low-skilled couple with one or two children (with lifetime totals of about £2,500 and £9,000 respectively) and the mid-skilled with 4 children (about £12,500).

Pensions and divorce

Legislation recently enacted (Welfare Reform and Pensions Act 1999) provides for pension sharing in cases of divorce: it will enable a couple to treat pension assets like other assets and divide them up on a "clean break" basis. The exact details of how this will be implemented are not yet known (they are due to be laid down in DSS regulations). However, it is intended that final salary pensions will be evaluated on the same basis as is currently used for assessing transfer values – the cash equivalent transfer value (CETV). We have used this method and have adopted a parallel approach for valuing SERPS[91]. The new legislation gives couples a mechanism by which they may share their pensions after divorce, but does not require them to do so. The pension valuation will be just one element influencing the divorce settlement. The actual outcome will no doubt depend, as at present, on the bargaining power of the parties, the competence of their legal advisers and the sagacity of the judiciary. In our simulations, we have, however, assumed that divorcing couples do share their pensions. Specifically, we have assumed that they split the value of their earnings-related pension rights equally, and that the value transferred is used to purchase pension (rather than being traded-off against other assets)[92]. Note that we are abstracting from any transactions costs involved: whether of having the pensions valued, or (much more importantly) of transferring pension rights.[93] In line with our assumptions of a static world, we assume a zero real interest rate.

Child support

We assume that child support payments are actually made by divorced men (or other non co-residential fathers) in accordance with the rules set out in the July 1999 White Paper (DSS 1999b). Divorcing fathers are assumed to remarry almost immediately, and to father two children in their second marriage – one

---

[91] We do not take into account the value of survivor's benefits or death-in-service benefits.

[92] The text describes the situation in England and Wales. In Scotland, things are different. The Family Law (Scotland) Act 1985 explicitly required that the value of occupational pension rights accrued during a marriage be taken into account in assessing resources to be divided at divorce, but made no provision for the sharing of state benefits. Furthermore, it provided no mechanism for liquefying the pension assets. Scots law places less reliance on the judiciary than English law, it recognizes the concept of matrimonial property and has an expectation that matrimonial property will be divided equally on divorce. In the case of pensions, the matrimonial property includes only pension rights accumulated during the marriage.

[93] See, for example, Blake and Orszag (1998).

born the year after the divorce and the second two years after that. These
assumptions affect the amount of child support payable.

National Insurance Contributions

NI Contributions are included in our model. They are paid only by people
under National Insurance pension age, and only on the slice of earnings
between a lower and an upper limit.

Child and maternity benefit

Child Benefit is paid (usually, and always in our hypothetical families) to
mothers of dependent children. Children from low-skilled families are treated as
dependent until they are 16. Others are assumed to stay on at school to the age
of 18 (and attract Child Benefit). There is no explicit modelling of maternity
benefits. The remuneration of those on maternity leave is treated as earnings.

Income Support

We have included Income Support – in the present context it is potentially
payable to lone mothers, retired people, and the long-term unemployed.

National Insurance pension age

We assume a common pension age of 65 for men and women, as will obtain
for people born since 1955. *The National Insurance Basic Pension* is paid at this
age – entitlement depends on a person's contribution history (or their spouse's).
A person who is not employed, but is responsible for the care of a dependant
child, will be entitled to "home responsibility protection" and will be granted
credits towards the accumulation of the Basic Pension for up to 22 such years.[94]

Earnings-linked pensions

We model both the state earnings-related pension scheme (SERPS) and
private final salary schemes. Most of those who are contracted out of SERPS
are in final salary pension schemes. Contributions to Final Salary schemes
are deductible from taxable income. We have assigned each person a default
pension type. For men the default is a final salary scheme, except that
low-skilled men are assumed to be in SERPS. By default, women are assumed
to be in SERPS except for the highly skilled who are assumed to be in a final

---

[94] We freeze participation rates between 60–64 because we are in unknown territory, having not
yet observed a regime with a retirement age of 65 for women.

salary scheme.[95] Those who are contracted out of SERPS pay a lower rate of National Insurance Contributions. SERPS benefits are related to (lifetime) earnings between the NI floor and ceiling. In the following we count the contributions payable in respect of SERPS as pension contributions rather than as taxes, and SERPS benefits as pensions rather than state benefits.

The original design of SERPS provided that payments were based on Best Twenty Years of earnings, and thus offered considerable protection for those who had periods out of paid work. The revised scheme allowed for the possibility of excluding years covered by home responsibility credits from the denominator in calculating the average on which SERPS is based. Our simulations incorporate this feature of the scheme.[96] It is arguable that our assumptions about pension schemes are backward- rather than forward-looking. Defined contribution schemes are beginning to make inroads in private pension provision at the expense of final salary schemes. The government has reviewed its upper-tier pension arrangements, and SERPS is likely to be phased out in favour of the new State Second Pension and stakeholder pensions. In undertaking our simulation exercises, however, we did not want to make too many variations from the existing system, particularly since the new system will take many years to come into full effect, and many details have yet to be finalised, particularly the transitional arrangements for people switching regime mid-career.

Widowhood

We assume that, under both SERPS and final salary, scheme a survivor's benefit of one-half of the primary beneficiary's annual pension is paid to a surviving spouse. On our assumptions, the survivor is always female. We have not attempted to take on board transitional arrangements concerning the phasing in of SERPS. The survivor's benefit is not included in the calculation of pension splitting on divorce.

---

[95] There is some evidence to suggest that around a half of mid-skilled women currently do have some Second Pension coverage (see ONS 1998a). The number who are in such schemes for their whole working lives may be much smaller. We discuss the effect of our assumption that mid-skilled women are in SERPS further in Chapter 6.

[96] See Tonge and Self (1999), p. 21 and p.33. The provision was intended to apply to people reaching state pension age after 5 April 1999, when more than 20 years of working life were included in the SERPS calculation for the first time. Implementation of this aspect of SERPS required secondary legislation, but the necessary regulations have not been laid. Instead, the Government has proposed that the new State Second Pension would (a) treat contributors who earn less than £9,000 p.a. as if they earned £9,000 and (b) grant credits to those caring for pre-school children (DSS, 1998). These aspects of the new scheme would benefit those who, in our simulations, benefit from the HRP aspect of SERPS. As we have not attempted to model the new State Second Pension and as it was apparently the prospect of this legislative change which accounted for the non-introduction of the HRP provisions into SERPS, we assumed for the purposes of our timewarp that the old plan had been implemented.

APPENDIX III
ECONOMETRIC EQUATIONS IN THE SIMULATION MODEL

APPENDIX III
ECONOMETRIC EQUATIONS IN THE SIMULATION MODEL

In this appendix we describe the econometric equations underlying the model used to simulate the lifetime participation profiles and earnings discussed extensively in this report.

The data used to estimate the labour market equations in the model come from the British Household Panel Survey (BHPS) carried out under the auspices of ISER at the University of Essex. The details of the survey can be found in Taylor et al. (1996).

The wage and participation data used for our estimation are drawn from the 4th Wave of the survey, the bulk of the fieldwork for which was carried out in the autumn of 1994[97]. At Wave 2, the survey questionnaire contained a section with questions on employment and partnership history. The employment experience data used here were derived from these records, updated by data from the next two waves. The sample is therefore selected from men and women who were full respondents in the second, third and fourth waves of the survey, and who were aged at least 16 at Wave 2. Men aged 65 or over and women aged 60 or over at Wave 4 (1994/1995) were excluded. We excluded the self-employed and those in full-time education or who had long-term sicknesses or disabilities. We also excluded people with missing values on the variables of interest. Most of the missing values are due to inadequate non-labour income (or spouse's income) data, necessary to estimate the participation equation. The earnings and hours measures used are for "usual" payments and hours and include "usual" overtime payments and hours. We excluded a few observations with implausibly low wages or implausibly long hours. We excluded observations which had a usual hourly wage of under £1 per hour (5 observations for women and 2 for men) and those which reported usual hours in excess of 84 per week (3 cases for women and 7 cases for men).

The samples analysed here consisted of 1,570 men for the men's wage equation, and 2,221 women, of whom 598 were not employed, 596 were employed part-time and 1,027 were employed full-time.

---

[97] The timescale for this project did not permit re-estimation on more recent data.

The estimates of the equations used in the simulations are given in the tables following. These are men's wages (Table A2), women's wages (Table A3) and women's participation (Table A4).

Wage equations are based on standard human capital specifications, with educational attainment measured by dummy variables rather than years of schooling. For men, the effects of (actual) employment experience on wages were modelled by two quartics – one for those with only school-level education, and another for those with post-school education[98]. The specification used here is a variant of that employed in Davies and Peronaci (1997). For women, separate equations are fitted for earnings in part-time and full-time employment. We follow the BHPS convention that full-time employment means working for at least 30 hours per week (normal hours plus paid overtime hours), except that we have used a lower cut-off of 25 hours in the case of teachers. The women's wage equations include a sample selection correction term. This was estimated from a reduced form multinomial logit participation equation (not shown), which included all the explanatory variables in the wage equation, plus partnership status, non-labour income of the woman, her partner's net income, and variables for the number and ages of children.

Apart from the sample selection correction, the full-time earnings equation for women has a similar specification to that fitted to men. For women's part-time earnings, a linear term in experience was found sufficient. Experience in part-time work was not found to be significant in explaining women's wages. This contrasts with estimates from the 1980 Women and Employment Survey (Ermisch and Wright 1992 and 1993) which underlay our earlier estimates of forgone earnings. Time out of employment arises from different sources for men and women. For men, it primarily reflects unemployment, whereas for women it mainly reflects time spent in domestic work (principally childcare). The median length of time out of employment for men in the wage regression sample is about four months, whereas for women it is about four years. The current estimates of the effect of time out of employment on women's wages are very similar to that estimated by Ermisch and Wright (1992 and 1993) on the 1980 Women and Employment Survey data and used in our previous work.[99] In the equations used here, a year out of employment produces a reduction in the full-time wage of about 1.35%, as compared to an estimated 1.15% on the 1980 data. For men, a year out of employment is estimated to reduce the wage by 4%. The estimated reduction in the part-time wage for

[98] Marital status is not included as a determinant of men's wages – we interpret the empirical evidence on the male "marriage premium" as reflecting primarily a selection effect (Davies and Peronaci, 1997).

[99] Our previous simulations of men's wages were based on the analysis of the Women and Employment Survey data by Wright and Ermisch (1991).

women is much smaller than the reduction in their full-time wage – about 0.03% in 1994 and about 0.045% in 1980. A much fuller discussion of the wage equations can be found in Davies, Peronaci and Joshi (1998).

Women's participation is modelled by a multinomial logit where the outcomes are "not employed", "employed part-time" and "employed full-time". The specification allows for considerable detail in the way that the number of children and their ages (especially the age of the youngest child) affect participation and, in that respect, follows earlier work quite closely (Joshi 1990, Joshi, Davies and Land, 1996 and references therein). The effect of earning power on participation is captured by the wage in full-time work predicted by the equation discussed above. In the earlier simulation modelling, based around the equations estimated from the WES, the measure of earning power employed did not vary over the lifecycle. The present specification does not impose the hypothesis of income-pooling within the family, but allows a woman's own non-labour income and her partner's net income to affect her participation differently. Davies, Peronaci and Joshi (1997) give a fuller account of our participation modelling.

The hours of full-time employment were fixed at means drawn from the BHPS regression sample, classified by job type. For men these were 47 hours for low-skilled, 44 for mid-skilled, and 41 for highly-skilled. For women the corresponding figures were: 38, 38 39, while hours of part-time employment depended on the relative probabilities of part-time and full-time employment.

Table A3: Male wages

Male Wages

Dependent variable: log of male hourly wage

	Coeffiicent	t
Employment experience		
If low or medium skill level		
Linear	1.232	6.243
Quadratic	-6.003	-3.592
Cubic	1.299	2.483
Quartic	-0.104	-1.912
If high skill level		
Linear	1.912	7.336
Quadratic	-12.528	-5.621
Cubic	3.462	4.781
Quartic	-0.34	-4.314
Time out of employment	-0.408	-5.922
Education level (dummies)		
Degree	0.727	6.054
other higher/further education	0.363	2.969
A levels	0.39	9.391
O levels	0.287	7.444
CSE	0.236	4.135
Other	0.091	1.435
London (dummy)	0.162	4.657
Constant	0.753	10.018
N	1570	
F (16, 1553)	64.17	
R-squared	0.398	
Standard error	0.41	

Notes:
Omitted categories: no educational qualifications, living outside London
Powers of years of experience are measured as follows:
linear: years x 10-1   quadratic: years 2x 10-3
cubic: years 3 x 10-4   quartic: years 4 x 10-5
Similarly for years out of employment

Table A4: Female wages

Female Wages

Dependent variable: log of female hourly wage

	PART-TIME Coefficient	t	FULL-TIME Coefficient	t
Employment experience				
If low or medium skill level				
Linear	0.135	3.797	1.185	4.981
Quadratic			-6.196	-2.526
Cubic			1.422	1.518
Quartic			-0.13	-1.109
If high skill level				
Linear	0.111	2.009	1.767	6.443
Quadratic			-11.629	-4.056
Cubic			3.422	3.089
Quartic			-0.369	-2.69
Time out of employment	-0.031	-0.934	-0.135	-4.32
Education level (dummies)				
Degree	0.78	8.401	0.68	5.9
other higher/further education	0.381	4.862	0.294	2.545
A levels	0.251	3.581	0.338	6.695
O levels	0.177	3.698	0.23	5.456
CSE	0.066	1.065	0.151	2.89
Other	0.421	2.248	0.192	1.421
London (dummy)	0.216	3.398	0.223	6.264
Lambda	-0.12	-3.041	0.039	1.221
Constant	1.244	20.266	0.752	9.119
N		596		1027
F (17, 1009)		15.11		51.23
R-squared		0.222		0.463
Standard error of regression		0.41		0.367

Notes:
Omitted categories: no educational qualifications, living outside London
Lambda is a sample-selectivity correction term, derived from a reduced-form multinomial logit participation function which includes age and family composition variables
Powers of years of experience are measured as follows:

linear: years x 10-1   quadratic: years 2x 10-3
cubic: years 3 x 10-4   quartic: years 4 x 10-5
Similarly for years out of employment

Table A5: Multinomial logit female participation estimates

Multinomial logit female participation estimates

	PART-TIME Coefficient	z	FULL-TIME Coefficient	z
Partnered (D)	1.098	4.762	0.303	1.288
Square of age -45, if partnered*	-0.351	-1.926	-1.023	-5.16
Square of age -45, not partnered*	0.127	0.518	-0.888	-3.139
Presence of child under 16(D)	-1.737	-5.477	-3.107	-9.192
Presence of dependent child 16-18(D)	-0.964	-0.951	-1.897	-1.858
Age of youngest child+				
if under 5	0.245	3.356	0.003	0.036
if 5 , but under 11	0.12	2.171	0.343	5.167
if 11, but under 16	0.061	0.621	0.124	1.164
if 16–18	-2.873	-1.807	-2.389	-1.666
Number of other pre-school children	0.123	0.471	-1.449	-3.164
Number of grownup children**	-0.023	-0.359	-0.228	-3.224
Log of full-time wage (imputed)	1.343	6.395	3.764	15.713
Has mortgage(D)	0.595	4.08	0.769	4.974
Partner unemployed(D)	-1.411	-4.213	-1.023	-2.773
Partner not working, other reason	-1.434	-5.332	-1.044	-3.805
Woman's non-labour inome, if unpartnered++	-0.03	-1.11	-0.161	-4.954
Woman's non-labour income, if partnered++	-0.152	-4.324	-0.254	-5.85
Partner's net income++	-0.005	-1.111	-0.017	-2.96
London(D)	-0.522	-2.266	-0.95	-4.025
constant	-2.119	-6.261	-3.646	-9.984
N		2221		
chi2(38)		1306.81		
Log Likelihood		-1707.41		
Pseudo R2		0.2768		

Notes:
(D) indicates dummy variable
* measured as square of (Years-45)/10
+ linear spline function – coefficients shown are marginal effects
** whether or not coresident
++ pounds per week/10

Bibliography

Allen, I., Bourke Dowling, S. (1999), *Teenage mothers: decisions and outcomes*, London: Policy Studies Institute.

Arnot et al. (1998) *Recent Research on Gender and Educational Attainment.* London: The Stationery Office.

Armitage, B., and Babb, P. (1996),"Population Review: (4) Trends in fertility", *Population Trends*, no.84, Summer 1996, London: HMSO, pp. 7–13.

Arulampalam, W. and A. Booth (1997) *Labour Market Flexibility and Skills Acquisition: Is There a Trade-Off?* Institute for Labour Research Discussion Paper 97/13 Colchester: University of Essex.

Banks, J. and S. Tanner (1999) *Household Saving in the UK*. London: Institute for Fiscal Studies.

Banks, J., A. Dilnot and H. Low (1994) *The Distribution of Wealth in the UK*. London: Institute for Fiscal Studies.

Becker, G. (1991) *A Treatise on the Family* Enlarged edition, Cambridge, Mass.: Harvard University Press. The quote on page 22 is from a paper published in 1985 Journal of Labour Economics and incorporated in the 1991 edition of the Treatise.

Benefit Agency (1999), *A Guide to Benefits: a concise guide to benefits and pension*, MG1 from April 1999, London: Department for Social Security.

Benefits Agency (1999), *Social Security Benefits Rates*, GL 23, London: Department for Social Security.

Blackaby, D., D. Clark, G. Lester and P. Murphy (1997) "The distribution of male and female earnings, 1973-91: Evidence for Britain" *Oxford Economic Papers* 49: 256–272.

Blackwell, L. (1998), *Occupational Sex Segregation and Part-time work in Modern Britain*, Ph.D thesis City University.

Blake, D. and Orszag, M. (1997), "Portability and Preservation of Pension Rights", in *Report of the Director General's Inquiry into Pensions*, Vol. 3, Appendix E, OFT191a, London: Office of Fair Trading.

Blau, F. and L. Kahn (1992) 'The gender earnings gap: Learning from international comparisons' *American Economic Association Papers and Proceedings* 82 (2): 533–538.

Böheim, R. and J. Ermisch (1999) *Breaking up – Financial surprises and partnership dissolution.* ISER Working paper 99–9, Colchester, Essex: ISER.

Booth, A. C. Garcia-Serrano and S. Jenkins (1996) *New men and new women: Is there convergence in patterns of labour market transition?* Institute for Labour Research Discussion Paper 96/01. Colchester, Essex: University of Essex.

Booth, A., M. Francesconi and J. Frank (1998) *Glass Ceilings or Sticky Floors?* Institute for Labour Research Discussion Paper 98/23. Colchester, Essex: University of Essex.

Botting, B., and Cooper, J. (1993),"Analysing fertility and infant mortality by mother's social class as defined by occupation –Part II", *Population Trends*, no.74, Winter 1993, London: HMSO, pp. 29–33.

Brannen, J., P. Moss, C. Owen and C. Wale (1997) *Mothers, Fathers and the Labour Market in Britain 1984–1994* DfEE Research Report no. 10.

Bruegel, I. (forthcoming, 2000) "The Full Monty: Men into women's work?" In M. Noon and E. Ogbonna *Equality and Employment* London: Macmillan.

Bynner, J., Joshi, H. and Tsatsas, M. (1999) *Obstacles and opportunities: Report to the Smith Institute* September, unpublished.

Callender, C. and H. Metcalf (1997) *Women and Training* DfEE Research Report RR35.

Callender, C, Millward, N., Lissenburgh, S., and Forth, J. (1997) *Maternity Rights and Benefits in Britain.* Social Security Research Report 67., London: The Stationery Office.

Campbell, N (1999), "Older workers and the labour market." In J Hills (ed.) *Persistent Poverty and Lifetime Inequality: The Evidence*" CASE report 5. London: LSE.

Carey, S., S. Low and J. Hansbro (1997) *Adult Literacy in Britain.* London: The Stationery Office.

Davies, H. and H. Joshi (1994a), "The earnings forgone by Europe's mothers", in Ekert-Jaffe, O., (ed.), *Standards of living and families: observations and analysis*, J.Libbey Eurotex and INED, Paris.

Davies, H. and H. Joshi (1994b), Sex, Sharing and the Distribution of Income, *Journal of Social Policy* 23(3): 301–340.

Davies, H., and Joshi, H. (1994) "Gender and Income Inequality in the UK 1968-1990: The Feminization of Earning or of Poverty?" *Journal of Royal Statistical Society, Series A*, 1998, 1, pp. 33–61.

Davies, H., H. Joshi, M. Killingsworth, M., and R. Peronaci (1999), *How do couples spend their time? An investigation of the hours of market and domestic work time reported to the British Household Panel Study.* Birkbeck College Discussion Paper in Economics 4/99.

Davies, H, R. Peronaci R and H. Joshi (1997) *Female Labour Force Participation in Britain, 1980 v 1994,* Typescript, Birkbeck College.

Davies, H., Peronaci, R., and H. Joshi (1998), *The Gender Wage Gap and Partnership*, Birkbeck College Discussion Paper in Economics, 6/98.

Davies, H., and R. Peronaci (1997) *Male Wages and Living Arrangements: Recent Evidence for Britain.* Birkbeck College Discussion Paper in Economics, 5/97.

Davies, H.B., Joshi H., and R Peronaci (1998a), *Dual and zero earner couples in Britain: longitudinal evidence on polarization and persistence*, Birkbeck College Discussion Paper in Economics 8/98.

Department for Social Security (DSS) (1999a) Unpublished analysis of the 1996/7 Family Resources Survey – Women's Individual Income Series.

Department for Social Security (DSS) (1999b), *A New Contract for Welfare: Children's Rights and Parents' Responsabilities*, CM4349, London: The Stationery Office, July 1999.

Department for Social Security (DSS) (1999c) *Households Below Average Income 1994/5–1997/8.* London: Government Statistical Services.

Department for Social Security (DSS) (1999d) Unpublished analysis of the Households Below Average Income series.

Department for Social Security (DSS) (1999e) Unpublished analysis of the Pensioner's Income series.

Dex, S. (ed.) (1999) *Families and the Labour Market: Trends, Pressures and Policies.* London: Family Policy Studies Centre.

Dex, S. (1984), *Women's Work Histories: Analysis of the Women and Employment Survey,* Research Paper 46, Department of Employment, London.

Dex, S., H. Joshi, and S. Macran (1996 b). "A widening gulf among Britain's mothers", *Oxford Review of Economic Policy* 12(1): 65–75.

Dex, S., H. Joshi, A. McCulloch, and S. Macran (1998) "Women's employment transitions around childbearing", *Oxford Bulletin of Economics and Statistics*, 60, no 1.

Dex, S. and A. McCulloch (1995). *Flexible Employment in Britain: A Statistical Analysis*, Discussion Series No.15. Manchester: Equal Opportunities Commission

Disney et al. (1998) *Public Pay in Britain in the 1990s*. London: Institute for Fiscal Studies.

Disney, R, E. Grundy and P. Johnson (1997) *The Dynamics of Retirement: Analyses of the Retirement Surveys* London: The Stationery Office.

Duncan, A. and C. Giles (1996). "Should we subsidise pre-school childcare, and if so, how?", *Fiscal Studies*, 17(3): 39–61.

Endean, R. (1999) 'Work, low pay and poverty evidence from the BHPS and LLMDB' in J. Hills (ed.) *Persistent Poverty and Lifetime Inequality: The Evidence*. CASE report 5. London: LSE.

Equal Opportunities Commission (1999a) *Pay and Income* EOC Research brief. Manchester: EOC.

Equal Opportunities Commission (1999b) *How Pay is Allocated: The Attitudes of Line Managers* EOC Research brief. Manchester: EOC.

Ermisch, J., H. Joshi and R. Wright, (1992). "Women's wages in Great Britain" In S.L. Willborn, (ed), *Women's Wages: Stability and Change in Six Industrial Countries*, Greenwich, CT: JAI Press.

Ermisch, J.F. and Wright, R.E. (1992), "Differential Returns to Human Capital in Full-time and Part-time Employment", in Folbre, N. et al (ed.) *Women's Work in the World Economy*, London: Macmillan, pp. 195–212.

Ermisch, J.F. and Wright, R.E. (1993), "Wage offers and full-time and part-time employment by British women", *Journal of Human Resources*, 28, pp. 111–133.

Eurostat (1999) *Statistics in Focus, Population and Social Conditions* 6(99).

Evandrou, M. (1995) "Employment and care, paid and unpaid work: The socio-economic position of informal carers in Britain" In J. Phillips (ed.) *Working Carers: International Perspectives on Working and Caring for Older People*. Aldershot: Avebury.

Evandrou, M. and J. Falkingham (forthcoming, 2000) "Looking back to look forward: Lessons from four birth cohorts for ageing in the 21st Century" *Population Trends* (forthcoming No. 99).

Ferri, E (ed.) (1993) *Life at 33: The Fifth Follow-up of the National Child Development Study*. London: National Children's Bureau.

Finlayson, L. R, Ford R and Marsh A (1996), "Paying more for childcare", *Labour Market Trends,* July 1996, pp. 296–303

Finlayson, L. and J. Nazroo (1998) *Gender Inequalities in Nursing Careers* London: Policy Studies Institute.

Ford, R. (1996), *Childcare in the Balance: how lone parents make decisions about work*, London: Policy Studies Institute.

Ford, R., Marsh, A., Finlayson, L. (1998), *What happens to lone parents*, Department of Social Security, Research Report No.77.

Goodman, A. P. Johnson and S. Webb (1997) *Inequality in The UK* Oxford: Oxford University Press.

Gosling, A., P. Johnson, J. McCrae and G. Paull (1997) *The Dynamics of Low Pay and Unemployment in early 1990s Britain* Institute for Fiscal Studies: London.

Gosling, A., S. Machin and C. Meghir (1994) 'What has happened to men's wages since the mid-1960s?' *Fiscal Studies* 4: 63–87.

Gregg, P. S. Harkness and S. Machin (1999) "Poor kids: trends in child poverty in Britain 1968–96" *Fiscal Studies* 20(2): 163–87.

Gregg, P. and J. Wadsworth (1996), "More work in fewer households" In J. Hills (ed.) *New Inequalities: The changing distribution of income and wealth in the United Kingdom,* Cambridge, CUP, pp. 181–207.

Hakim, C. (1996) *Key Issues in Women's Work: Female Heterogeneity and the Polarisation of Women's Employment.* London: Athlone.

Harkness, S. (1996) 'The gender earnings gap: Evidence from the UK' *Fiscal Studies* 17 (2): 1–36.

Harkness, S. and S. Machin (1999) *Graduate Earnings in Britain, 1974–95* Department for Education and Employment, Research Report No. 95.

Harkness, S., S. Machin and J. Waldfogel (1996) " Women's pay and family incomes in Britain, 1979–91", in Hills, J (ed) *New Inequalities: The changing distribution of income and wealth in the United Kingdom,* Cambridge, CUP, pp. 158–180.

Haskey, J. (1997) "Children who experience divorce in their family", *Population Trends,* No.87, Spring 1997, London: HMSO, pp.5–10.

Haskey, J. (1998a) "One parent families and their dependent children in Great Britain", *Population Trends,* No.91, Spring 1998, London: HMSO.

Haskey, J. (1998b) "Birth cohort analyses of dependent children and lone mothers living in one-parent families", *Population Trends*, No.92, Summer 1998 London: HMSO, pp. 15–22.

Haskey, J. (1999a) "Divorce and remarriage in England and Wales", *Population Trends*, No. 95, Spring 1999, London: HMSO, pp. 18–25.

Haskey, J. (1999b) "Cohabitational and marital histories of adults in Great Britain" *Population Trends*, No. 96, Summer 1999, London: HMSO, pp13–24

Haskey, J. (1999c), "Having a birth outside marriage: the proportions of lone mothers and cohabiting mothers who subsequent marry", *Population Trends*, No. 97, Autumn 1999, London: HMSO, pp. 6–18.

Hattersley, L (1999), "Trends in Life Expectancy by social class – an update", *Health Statistics Quarterly*, (2), pp. 16–24.

HM Treasury (HMT) (1999) *Supporting Children Through the Tax and Benefit System. The Modernisation of Britain's Tax and Benefit System Number 5.* London: HM Treasury or via http://www.hm-treasury.gov.uk.

Hills, J. (1995) *Joseph Rowntree Foundation Inquiry into Income and Wealth Volume 2: The Evidence.* York: Joseph Rowntree Foundation.

Hills, J. (1998). Does income mobility mean that we do not need to worry about poverty? In *Exclusion, Employment and Opportunity* CASE Paper no. 4. London: STICERD, LSE.

Hills, J. (ed.) (1999) *Persistent Poverty and Lifetime Inequality: The Evidence.* CASEreport 5. LSE: London.

Holtermann et al. 1999

Humphries, J. and J. Rubery (eds.) (1995) *The Economics of Equal Opportunities* Manchester: EOC.

Hunter, L., and S., Rimmer (1995), "an exploration of the UK and Australian experiences", in Humphries, J., and Rubery, J., (eds.), *The Economics of Equal Opportunities*, Manchester: the Equal Opportunities Commission.

Jacobs, S. (1995) 'Changing patterns of sex-segregated occupations throughout the lifecourse' *European Sociological Review* 11 (2); 157–71.

Jacobs, S. (1997) 'Employment changes over childbirth: A retrospective view' *Sociology* 31(3): 577–90.

Jacobs, S. (1999) 'Trends in women's career patterns and in gender occupational mobility in Britain' *Gender, Work and Organisation* 6 (1); 32–46.

Jarvis, S and Jenkins, S. (1998) "How much income mobility is there in Britain?" *The Economic Journal* 108: 428–44.

Jarvis, S. and Jenkins, S. (1999) "Marital Splits and Income Change: Evidence from the British Household Panel Survey" *Population Studies* 53; 237–54.

Jenkins, S. (1998) "The incomes of UK women: limited progress towards equality with men", in Jenkins, S.P., Kapteyn, A., and van Praag, B.M.S., *The distribution of Welfare and Household Production: International Perspectives*, Cambridge: Cambridge University Press.

Jenkins, S. and N. O'Leary (1996) "Household income plus household production: The distribution of extended income in the UK", *Review of Income and Wealth* 42(4): 401–19.

Jenkins, S. and N. O'Leary (1997) "Gender differentials in domestic work, market work and total work time: UK time budget survey evidence for 1974/5 and 1987", *Scottish Journal of Political Economy* 44(2): 153–64.

Joshi, H. (1989) "The changing form of women's economic dependency" In Joshi, H. (ed.) *The Changing Population of Britain*. Oxford: Basil Blackwell.

Joshi, H. (1990), "The Opportunity Cost of Childbearing: an approach to estimation using British data", *Population Studies*, 44: 41–60.

Joshi, H., A. Dale, C. Ward and H. Davies (1995) *Dependence and Independence in the finances of women aged 33*. London: Family Policy Studies Centre

Joshi, H and H. Davies (1992) "Daycare in Europe and Mothers' Forgone Earnings", *International Labour Review* 131, 6 (561–579).

Joshi, H, H. Davies and H. Land (1996) *The Tale of Mrs Typical*. London: Family Policy Studies Centre.

Joshi, H., H. Davies and R. Peronaci (1999) *The Distribution of the Costs of Children*, Paper presented at AEA meeting, New York, January.

Joshi, H, S, Dex and S. Macran (1996) "Employment after childbearing and women's subsequent labour force participation: Evidence for the 1958 birth cohort." *Journal of Population Economics* 9: 325–48.

Joshi, H. and P. Hinde (1993) 'Employment after childbearing in post-war Britain: cohort study evidence on contrasts within and across generations' *European Sociological Review.* 9 (3); 203–28.

Joshi, H. and P. Paci (1997a), 'Life in the Labour Market', in Bynner and Ferri (eds) *Twenty-something in the Nineteen Nineties, Getting On, Getting By and Getting Nowhere*, Dartmouth Press.(31-52).

Joshi, H. and P. Paci (1998) *Unequal Pay for Women and Men: Evidence from the British Birth Cohort Studies*. Cambridge, Mass. and London: The MIT Press.

Joshi, H., P. Paci and J. Waldfogel (1999a) 'The wages of motherhood: better or worse?' *Cambridge Journal of Economics*, vol.23, no.5, pp. 543–564.

Joshi, H, Cooksey, E, Wiggins, R D, and McCulloch, Verropoulou, G., Clarke, L, (1999b) "Diverse Family Living Situations and Child Development: a multi-level analysis comparing longitudinal evidence from Britain and the United States", *International Journal of Law, Policy and the Family*, Vol.13, pp.292–314.

Kempeneers, M. and Lelievre, E. (1991), *Employment and Family within the Twelve*. (Eurobarometer 34), Brussels: Commission of the European Communities.

Kiernan, K. (1999) "Cohabitation in Western Europe" *Population Trends* No. 96, Summer 1999, London: HMSO, pp25-32

King, S. and Murray, K. (1996) *Family and Working Lives Survey – preliminary results*. Labour Market Trends, March 115–118.

Liesering, L. and R. Walker (eds.) (1998) *The Dynamics of Modern Society* Bristol: The Policy Press.

Lundberg, Shelley and Pollak, R. (1996) Bargaining and Distribution in Marriage, *Journal of Economic Perspectives*, vol 10, 4, pp 139–158.

Lundberg, Shelley, Pollak, R. and T. Wales (1997) Do Husbands and Wives Pool Their Resources? *Journal of Human Resources*, 32,3, pp 463–480.

Macran, S., H. Joshi and S. Dex (1996) 'Employment after childbearing: A survival analysis' *Work, Employment and Society* 10(2) 273–296.

McCrudden, C. (1991), "Between legality and reality: The implementation of equal pay for equal work in Britain", in Willbron, S.L., (ed.), *Women's wages: Stability and Change in Six Industrial Countries*, Greenwich, CT: JAI Press.

McKnight, A. (1998) *Low Wage Mobility in a Working Life Perspective* Unpublished paper, Institute for Employment Research: Warwick.

McKnight, A., P. Elias and R. Wilson (1998) *Low-Pay and the National Insurance System: A Statistical Picture*. Manchester: Equal Opportunities Commission.

McRae, S. (1991) 'Occupational change over childbirth: Some evidence from a national survey'. 25(4); 589–605.

McRae, S. (1993) 'Returning to work after childbirth: opportunities and inequalities' *European Sociological Review* 9(2); 125–37.

Manning, A. (1996), "The Equal Pay Act as an experiment to test theories of the labour market", *Economica*, 663: 191-212.

Marsh, A. (1999) Unpublished tabulations from the DSS/PSI Lone Parent Cohort study, 1991-1998.

Martin, J and Roberts, C (1984), *Women and Employment: a Lifetime Perspective*. London, HMSO.

Middleton, S., K. Ashworth and I. Braithwaite (1999) *Small Fortunes: Spending on Children, Childhood Poverty and Parental Sacrifice*. York: Joseph Rowntree Foundation.

Miller, P.W. (1987) The wage effect of the occupational segregation of women. *Economic Journal*, 97:885-896.

Millward, S and N. Woodland (1995) "Gender segregation and male/female wage differences" In J. Humphries and J. Rubery (eds.) *The Economics of Equal Opportunities* Manchester: Equal Opportunities Commission.

Murgatroyd, L. and H. Neuberger (1997) A household satellite account for the UK *Economic Trends* 527: 63–71.

Office for National Statistics (1997) *Labour Market Trends* Vol. 105, No. 2 London: The Stationery Office

Office for National Statistics (1998a) British Labour Market Projections, 1998–2011.

Office for National Statistics (1998b) *Social Focus on Women and Men*, London, The Stationery Office

Office for National Statistics (1998c), *Living in Britain: Results from the 1996 General Household Survey*, London, The Stationery Office.

Office for National Statistics (1999) *Population Trends* Summer, No. 96.

Office of Population Censuses and Surveys (OPCS) (1997) *Births Statistics 1997 Great Britain*. London: The Stationery Office.

Organisation for Economic Co-operation and Development (OECD) (1998) *The Future of Female Dominated Occupations* Paris: OECD.

Paci, P., H. Joshi, and G. Makepeace (1995) "Pay gaps facing men and women born in 1958: differences in the labour market" In J. Humphries and J. Rubery, (eds.) *The Economics of Equal Opportunities* Manchester: Equal Opportunities Commission.

Pearce, D., Giambattista, C., and Laihonen, A., (1999), "Changes in fertility and family sizes in Europe", *Population Trends*, No. 95, Spring 1999, London: HMSO pp. 33–40.

Penn, H. and S. McQuail (1997) *Childcare as a Gendered Occupation* DfEE Research Report RR23.

Rowlingson, K. C. Whyley and T. Warren (1999) *Wealth in Britain: A Lifecycle Perspective*. London: Policy Studies Institute.

Rowntree, B. (1901. *Poverty: A Study in Town Life*. London: Macmillan.

Rubery, J. (1997) 'Wages and the labour market' *British Journal of Industrial Relations* 35(3): 337–366.

Rubery, J. and C. Fagan (1993) "Occupational segregation of women and men in the European Community", *Social Europe*, Supplement 3/93.

Rubery, J and C. Fagan (1994) *Wage Determination and Sex Segregation in Employment in the European Community*. Brussels: Commission of the European Communities.

Shouls, S, M. Whitehead, B. Burström, and F. Diderichsen (1999) "The health and socio-economic circumstances of British lone mothers over the last two decades" *Population Trends* No.95, Spring 1999: 41–46.

Shropshire, J. and S. Middleton (1999) *Small expectations: Learning to be poor?* York: Joseph Rowntree Foundation.

Sly, F., T. Thair and A. Risdon (1999) "Trends in the labour market participation of ethnic groups" *Labour Market Trends* December 1999 Vol. 107, No. 12.: 631-639.

The Social Exclusion Unit (1999a) *Bridging the Gap: New Opportunities for 16–18 Year Olds not in Education, Employment or Training* Cm 4405 London: The Stationery Office.

The Social Exclusion Unit (1999b) *Teenage Pregnancy* Cm 4342 London: The Stationery Office.

Sutherland, H. (1997). 'Women, men and the redistribution of income.' *Fiscal Studies* **18**(1): 1–22.

Taylor, M F (ed.) with J Brice, N. Buck and E. Prentice (1996) British Household Panel Survey User Manual. *Colchester: University of Essex.*

Thair, T. and A. Risdon (1999) 'Women in the labour market: Results from the spring 1998 LFS' *Labour Market Trends* March 1999: 103-114.

Tonge, K and Self, R. (1999) *Tolley's Social Security and State Benefits Handbook*. April 1999 re-issue. Croydon, Tolley.

Webb, S. (1993) "Women's incomes: Past, present and prospects" *Fiscal Studies* 14: 14–36.

Women's Unit (1999) *Women's Individual Incomes 1996/97*. London: Government Statistical Services.

Wright, R. and J. Ermisch (1991) "Gender Discrimination in the British Labour Market: a reassessment", *Economic Journal*, 101, no. 406, pp. 508-552.

Zabalza, A., and Z. Tzannatos (1986), *Women and Equal Pay: the Effects of Legislation on Female Employment and Wages in Britain*,. Cambridge, Cambridge University Press.

Zabalza, A and J. L. Arrufat (1985), The extent of sex discrimination in Great Britain. In Zabalza, A., and Z.,Tzannatos, *Women and Equal Pay: the Effects of Legislation on Female Employment and Wages in Britain*, pp 70–96

The Women's Unit
Cabinet Office
2nd Floor
10 Great George Street
London SW1P 3AE
Telephone 020 7273 8800
Fax 020 7273 8813
www.womens-unit.gov.uk
E-mail womens-unit@gtnet.gov.uk

Copies of full report are available from:

The Stationery Office
(Mail, telephone and fax orders only)
P.O. Box 29
Norwich NR3 1GN
General Enquiries *Lo-call* 0845 758 5463
Fax orders 0870 600 5533
Telephone orders 0800 600 5522
E-mail orders book.orders@theso.co.uk
www.tsonline.co.uk

Printed in the United Kingdom for The Stationery Office
TJ000578, C15, 2/00, 5673